The
Draft Horse
Primer

The Draft Horse Primer

A Guide to the Care and Use
of Work Horses and Mules

Maurice Telleen

Rodale Press
Emmaus, PA

2   4   6   8   10   9   7   5   3

Printed on recycled paper

Library of Congress Cataloging in Publication Data

Main entry under title:

The Draft horse primer.

Includes index.
1. Draft horses.   2. Mules.   I. Telleen, Maurice.   II. Title.
SF311.D7   636.1'5   77–898
ISBN 0–87857–161–2

Dedication

This book is dedicated to the memory of my parents, farmers born and bred, secure in the knowledge that their vocation of farming was the most fundamental vocation on earth—the one upon which all others depend; knowing that each day's tasks, however menial, were worth doing as well as you could or as well as time and circumstance allowed; confident of their competence but aware of their limitations as farmers and stockmen; and filled with both respect and awe for the sacredness of life and the forces of nature which shaped every working day of their lives.

Their attitudes toward the animal and plant life in their charge, the health of the soil upon which both depended, the community upon which they depended—and which could depend on them—were deeply rooted in the concepts of *animal husbandry*, *soil stewardship*, and the *brotherhood of man* rather than in status, exploitation, and wealth.

This is not to suggest that they were unusually gifted, prominent, brilliant, altruistic, or saintly people, for they were none of these things. Rather, attitudes such as theirs were commonplace but a generation ago, and since they were my parents they were sometimes all, or none, of these things to me, as they were to my brothers and sister. This book has been prepared in the hope that it may contribute something to a regeneration in our times of those attitudes and some of the skills attendant to them, which I believe are essential to our survival on this planet.

As for the draft horse, the topic of this book, I'm sure my Dad had no idea of how the affection he felt and showed toward his work horses and the lingering doubts he expressed about the wisdom of the total mechanization of agriculture with its subsequent impact on community and national life would literally shape and direct my life. As I work my own horses I have often felt a special closeness and kinship with him, though he has now been gone for over fifteen years. May I always use them with the same respect for both their limitations and mine, and treat them with the same brand of firm kindness and common sense that he did.

Contents

Preface

The great rebirth in the interest of draft horses has come at a time when many young people (and some not so young) find it difficult to learn the essentials of heavy horsemanship from Dad, uncles, or neighbors. Because of this we have had an increasing demand for "literature," over and above the trade news offered in the *Draft Horse Journal*.

This book has been assembled with this need in mind. It is made up largely of material from booklets published by our land grant schools during the twenties and thirties when they had an active interest in heavy horses as a major source of agricultural power. Virtually all of these booklets are now out of print. Rather than reprinting them piecemeal, I have taken what I consider the most useful material out of several and put it together for you in this volume. There is also some material reprinted from previous issues of *Draft Horse Journal*, some that has been written specifically for this book, and some that I had written for *Western Horseman* and *Organic Gardening and Farming* over the years, and reprint with their permission.

I hope this will answer some of the questions the many new draft horse owners in this country have. I have no illusions about this being "the complete draft horse text" or the "final authority" on draft horses. It is certainly neither. It is offered merely as the best help to a beginner that I can give via the printed page. The best instruction will still be found in the company of your own horses *and* a competent horseman. And I cannot urge you too strongly to seek out the counsel of the good old teamsters in your own community.

Maurice Telleen

HORSES

When I was a boy here,
traveling the fields for pleasure,
the farms were worked with teams.
As late as then a teamster
was thought an accomplished man,
his art an essential discipline.
A boy learned it by delight
as he learned to use
his body, following the example
of men. The reins of a team
were put into my hands
when I thought the work was play.
And in the corrective gaze
of men now dead I learned
to flesh my will in power
great enough to kill me
should I let it turn.
I learned the other tongue
by which men spoke to beasts
—all its terms and tones.
And by the time I learned,
new ways had changed the time.

The tractors came. The horses
stood in the fields, keepsakes,
grew old, and died. Or were sold
as dogmeat. Our minds received
the revolution of engines, our will
stretched toward the numb endurance
of metal. And that old speech
by which we magnified
our flesh in other flesh
fell dead in our mouths.
The songs of the world died
in our ears as we went within
the uproar of the long syllable
of the motors. Our intent entered
the world as combustion.
Like our travels, our workdays
burned upon the world,

lifting its inwards up
in fire. Veiled in that power
our minds gave up the endless
cycle of growth and decay
and took the unreturning way,
the breathless distance of iron.

But that work, empowered by burning
the world's body, showed us
finally the world's limits
and our own. We had then
the life of a candle, no longer
the ever-returning song
among the grassblades and the leaves.

Did I never forget?
Or did I, after years,
remember? To hear that song
again, though brokenly
in the distances of memory,
is coming home. I came to
a farm, some of it unreachable
by machines, as some of the world
will always be. And so
I came to a team, a pair
of mares—sorrels, with white
tails and manes, beautiful!—
to keep my sloping fields.
Going behind them, the reins
tight over their backs as they stepped
their long strides, revived
again on my tongue the cries
of dead men in the living
fields. Now every move
answers what is still.
This work of love rhymes
living and dead. A dance
is what this plodding is.
A song, whatever is said.

by Wendell Berry

reprinted with permission from
Larkspur Press, Monterey, Kentucky

Chapter 1

The Return of
the Draft Horse*

To those of us actively involved in the draft horse and mule trade, the "return" of the draft animal to some degree of public favor and esteem has become an accomplished fact in recent years. Yet, we realize that to the great majority of our countrymen, this has been an unnoticed phenomenon; that the draft (or work) horse remains something that grandpa had and that has, for all practical purposes, vanished from the public eye.

We are now entering the fourth decade since the power structure of American agriculture (since renamed agribusiness) decreed that the draft horse and mule had become useless artifacts of history. In that respect, the horse has been in some excellent company, such as crop rotation, small owner-operated farms, diversified livestock and crop programs, home gardening, the use of natural fertilizers (manure), and thrift. In brief, the decline hit most of the things that had lent stability to agriculture in good times and endurability in bad times ever since the days when Tom Jefferson had envisioned his race of farmer philosophers, which would serve as the balance wheel and strength of the republic. All of these things were discarded in haste following World War II. The work horse and mule were but two of many casualties.

*Parts of this chapter have appeared in *Organic Gardening and Farming* and *Western Horseman*. They are reprinted with permission.

The fact that today, some thirty years later, the demand for draft horses and mules far exceeds the available supply suggests that those judgments handed out so freely in the late forties were both wrong-headed and shortsighted.

In fact, our country was full of farmers in the forties who regarded them in just that light, but the overwhelming weight of official, social, and economic opinion took its toll and eventually most of them discarded their last teams, quit farming, or died off. Thousands of farmers who abandoned the horse at that time did so with nothing more articulate than "a feeling in their bones" that this was wrong, just as they adopted the blanket use of chemicals for weed and pest control with a similar feeling. They had few champions to confirm their beliefs in public or in print, so ultimately they were intimidated into accepting the unbelievably vain concept that the "conquest" of physical nature was an accomplished fact and that we had entered a new era in terms of our relationship with our earth.

Fig. 1-1. The winning six-horse hitch of Belgians at a recent National Dairy Cattle Congress in Waterloo, Iowa. Fairs and expositions, as they lost their rural flavor and the rural audience declined, turned increasingly to draft horse hitches to attract crowds.
(Courtesy of Harold Cline)

In this sort of social and economic climate the draft horse and mule stocks of this country dwindled to the point where they were invisible to most people by 1960. But three basic groups were responsible for keeping a nucleus of draft breeding stock alive through those times. Most obvious were the purebred breeders who kept and propagated heavy horses for show purposes and the big hitches. For the most part, this group was, and is, made up of prosperous agribusinessmen who kept the horse, not because they believed in him as a source of power, but simply because they liked him, enjoyed showing him, and in many cases were carrying on a family tradition of horse breeding.

The second group, considerably larger numerically, were the Amish who retained the horse as their only source of motive power and as an integral part of their way of life, both economic and cultural.

The third group, and the one of which we are dangerously short (thirty years does take its toll) are non-Amish farmers who kept horses, frequently in combination with tractor power, out of a reasoned belief that they were the most economical source of power, a keystone in maintaining soil fertility, and fundamental to the economic independence and continuity of the small family farm.

Many of the farmers in this latter category are either wholly or predominantly organic. This is probably best explained by the fact that horse farming does not lend itself to: 1. one crop agriculture (you must have pasture and hayland for the work stock, so you almost always find other types of livestock and crop rotation being practiced on such farms); 2. huge acreage (you simply haven't the time to work it); and 3. farming distant patches of ground. You don't take four horses and a disk ten miles down the road. You farm, in effect, within sight and easy walking distance of your home. For whatever reason, there does seem to be a natural marriage of thought between organic agriculture and work horses—a source of power that reproduces itself, with good care is self-repairing, consumes home-grown fuel, and contributes to the fertility of the soil. Horse farming and organic farming are very comfortable with one another.

Without belaboring the economic and ecological ramifications of horsepower, I would like to quote one of those

"reluctant converts" to mechanization. The following state-
ment appeared in the *Suffolk Bulletin* of 1946. The writer, a
New Jersey farmer, was in the forefront of Suffolk horse
breeders at that time, and wrote in response to an article in
Farm Journal, wherein True Morse of Doane's Agricultural
Services had advised farmer readers to "Sell that last team."
Part of this response follows:

As I gave up the use of the horse with greatest
reluctance, I have examined my reasons for doing so very
carefully and feel I can give all the answers as to why they
cannot be used with some authority. But there are still
serious questions in my mind.

Consider, first, the investment in power machinery as
compared to horse-drawn machinery. Last winter, when
offering to sell some of my useless equipment, I went
back through the records to determine what I had paid
for some of it. It now costs about as much for a single tire
for a tractor as it cost for a sulky corn cultivator about
eight years ago. One could then equip an entire farm for
what a tractor and cultivator now cost. Can farming support such an investment?

Consider the size of farm needed to utilize the larger
power units such as the field harvester, the pick-up baler
and the combine. I find one of each adequate for the
operation of my large unit. Custom work has proven un-
satisfactory in most cases. Can the American farmer work
out a plan for joint neighbor ownership of this equipment
or does this spell the end of the family-sized farm?

Consider the cost of upkeep. Mr. Morse gives figures
for the cost of keeping a team, the income from the extra
cows, and cost of operating a tractor. Will the income
from the cow stay where it is now? Can we overlook the
fact that the cost of keeping a team is largely money paid
back to oneself for hay, oats, and labor, while the cost of
operating a tractor is cash out of pocket for gas, oil,
repairs, and replacement?

Consider also the broad economic aspects of the problem. Should the day come when the farmer is again faced

with ruinous surpluses, will these not be much greater than they were when the acres that went to feeding horses will grow crops to sell? And what of our dwindling natural resources of petroleum? Will we eventually raise crops that are sold to be processed into fuel, to be repurchased by us to burn in our tractors, where we now have available a hay-burner of our own?

Under present conditions, I cannot afford to work horses. But the change from horse to tractor farming is a profound change. As a result the farmer will lose a measure of his independence; his fate will be more closely linked to the strength and effectiveness of organized labor; the family-sized farm may be the next aspect of rural life to be found obsolete and uneconomical.

Most of the concerns voiced by this farmer in 1946 have become the realities of the seventies. Agriculture was full of such reluctant converts, few as articulate as he, but all sharing the common fate of having their doubts and their thoughtfulness dismissed as useless nostalgia by the movers and shakers of the brave new world following World War II.

So much for background on the decline of the work horse. Now for a look at his recent resurgence.

About 1960 the draft horse market began to strengthen, ever so slightly at first, but with great acceleration in recent years. The reasons are manifold. First, our work stock inventory had gotten so low that those wishing to use them simply had to ante up a little more, a case of supply and demand. The wretched prices commanded by a good young work stock in the fifties had brought breeding to an almost complete standstill. Second, enough time had elapsed from the immediate post-war period when farm youngsters were ashamed of fathers who hung onto a horse so that the stigma attached to using horses was past, at least in part. Third, it became sort of fashionable in some quarters to have a team around. Fourth, the show and parade fad took hold a bit more. Many fairs which had dropped draft horse classifications in their rush to appear "modern" in the post-war period discovered that things had become so modern that they were almost useless in their traditional roles as agricultural institutions. Consequently, fairs turned more and more to entertainment and to attractions such as the big horse hitches. At his best the draft horse is a spectacular beast, and much more exciting to the urban crowds our fairs found themselves playing to than a calf or lamb, however good and useful they might be. The same can be said of parades. A team of horses was no big deal to the youngsters of the country when True Morse was urging everyone to send them to the kill, but they *are* to the sons and daughters of that generation. So, rather suddenly, there was an abundance of places to show off, and it stimulated the market. Fifth, any rising market attracts buyers, just by being a rising market. Farmers who hadn't owned a horse for a decade suddenly found themselves back in business. Lastly, and most important in the long pull, people began to raise serious questions about the dogmas of agribusiness. The result has been a rediscovery of the horse in his traditional role as servant, partner, and preserver on the land—in short, as a *work* horse.

Fig. 1-2.   English brewers have run time and cost studies on their horses versus trucks, and the horse has won hands down, on short hauls. This pair of Percherons was photographed in Sunderland, England, in 1970.
(Courtesy of Harold Cline)

Perhaps many will shrug this off as simply too preposterous to receive serious consideration in our highly mechanized age. But before dismissing this as "impossible nostalgia," let's examine the advantages that the work horse offers. Not with any thought that this country will ever again see twenty million working horses and mules on its farms and streets; but that there are thousands of working situations where horses can, do, and will perform useful work economically.

First, horses utilize farm-grown feeds for their fuel, thereby reducing cash outlay for operating expenses. Recently the cost of petroleum has risen sharply, and the consensus seems to be that we are in for more of the same. Of course, grain prices are high too, but the grain can be home-grown with the expense being the cost of production. With adequate pasture and good roughage, the out-of-pocket cost of maintaining a working team or two is not great. The use of horses also promotes good conserving methods of farming by demanding that a part of the land be used for grasses and legumes; this leads in turn to other livestock programs. You rarely find a draft horseman who does not raise either cattle or sheep on grass along with his horses.

Second, horses return most of the fertility from their feed to the land in the form of manure, from nine to fifteen tons annually per animal. This is both ecologically and economically significant today. Not only has the cost of commercial fertilizer skyrocketed, but serious doubts about the wisdom of its prolonged, intensive use are raised. Manure has again become fashionable, and the manure from those old drafters is some of nature's best, adding humus and tilth to your ground. The exhaust from a tractor has never been known to benefit your ground—or your lungs.

Third, mares will do their share of the work and produce colts as their own replacements and for sale. Well-bred draft colts, right off the mare in fall (or spring, if you fancy fall colts) have been very profitable in recent years. (They are another cash crop.) The mare, if handled properly, doesn't miss much time in harness because of her foal. As for the mare herself, when she heads off to St. Peter's pasture, she has left a legacy of young horses in your barn. Power-bred, born and raised at home on home-grown feeds. No need to go to town and borrow fifteen thousand dollars at 9 percent for a new power plant; Old Nell took care of that with those young horses now doing her job—not to mention the ones you sold.

Fourth, the question of raising your own replacements versus that loan for the new tractor leads quite logically into a consideration of depreciation. With proper care, work horses will live and perform their share of work in the harness until they are fifteen or twenty years of age, thus having a low rate of depreciation. For much of that time—the first part of their life cycle—they appreciate rather than depreciate. And throughout most of that long and useful life, nature furnishes most of the repairs.

Fig. 1-3. The single horse cultivating nursery stock in Minnesota.

Fifth, horses provide flexible power. Consider the moderate-sized horse farm where the five or six horses are used on a two-bottom plow in the spring. Plowing done, split them up, three or four for the disk and harrow, and two for the planter and seeder wagon. Corn plowing, split them up again, maybe with a pair of two-rows or a two-row for dad and a single-row for the boy (it beats having him lie in the house watching television even if he doesn't get over a lot of acres). And so on, throughout the year. The ones that aren't working are loafing out in the pasture—not consuming a lot of grain, as some would have you think. Contrast this with typical scenes on many of today's farms, where tractors twice, three, and five times as powerful as the job calls for are in use.

Sixth, horses are dependable power. They can work in mud and snow that would make insurmountable problems for mechanized equipment and on slopes that are dangerous with a tractor. They have a reserve of power to call on when the going gets tough—that extra bit of strength and determination can pull you out of a hole. This factor also allows you to work your land when those with heavy equipment are simply dry-docked.

The economics of horse power has simply been an abandoned study. I think it deserves serious consideration. There is forever a lot of talk about the "family farm." I don't know exactly what that means, but it conjures up a vision of moderate-sized, diversified, self-supporting units to me— quite contrary to the trend of modern agriculture. These are stable units that are to a considerable degree self-sufficient, and to some extent partially immune to many of the prices now putting farmers through the fire. This is the type of farm that lasts, that supports its own community, decade after

Fig. 1-4. Another example of one of the many specialized roles that the draft horse can fill is this draft horse being used to unroll telephone cable in the state of Washington.

(Courtesy of Ron Allen Photography)

decade, generation to generation. It has been fashionable in some quarters to hail the ever-declining farm population as proof of our wisdom, power, and efficiency. That too deserves serious study. How much of our urban unrest and the increased taxation to solve these man-made problems can be attributed to the almost forced exodus from the land? Inevitable? Phooey! Profitable—for someone? Yes! The social cost is always, and ultimately, measured in economic costs. The difference in this case is that agribusiness has been able to shift the burden of its social costs to another sector. And, I submit, those costs have been and are considerable.

You can't turn the clock back, so goes the story. Well, I'm not sure that draft horsemen *want* to turn the clock back. It isn't an either-or type of question. There are situations where our horses fit the bill, sometimes as the sole source of power, more often as part of a mixed power package. Nor does farming with horses mean that you abandon all the amenities of the seventies. It *does* mean that you pick and choose between the old and the new, that you adapt to your situation.

Well, you may ask, if it's such a good idea, why isn't it being done by more people?

The question is a reasonable one. It isn't being done because in most cases the horses, the tools, and the horsemen are not readily available. To understand *why* they aren't, we must go back to the rather unique nature of the competition between the horse and mule interests and the tractor companies during the 1920 to 1945 period.

The tractor companies were able to offer "financing" on their form of power. A farmer who either did not choose to raise his own colts, moved to a larger farm, or for any number of reasons needed more horsepower was thus confronted with the choice of buying a team from a neighbor for cash on the barrel head or purchasing a tractor on "easy terms." In the world of finance, the corporation (tractor dealer in this case) has a decided advantage over the cottage industry (colt raiser) and it was used to the hilt.

Other advantages that a corporation enjoys over a cottage industry were, in fact, carried several steps beyond the normal competitive situation where the draft horse and mule were concerned. I recall that in the late thirties and forties the local machinery dealers were among the biggest horse owners around. They would take horses in "on trade." If they could sell a few of the better teams off at a profit, that was done, but most of them went to the kill—thereby not merely defeating the opposition, but liquidating it. It was a case where one claimant to a market not only had the ability to "outsell" his competitor but also had within his grasp the means to quite literally destroy the opposition and its ability to replenish itself.

Add to this the fact that horse-drawn machinery came from the very same corporate sources as the tractor. The avowed purpose of these companies was to drive the horse into oblivion. Their interest in improving horse-drawn machinery cannot have been very great. It became their long range goal to eliminate it, not improve it. The manufacture of horse-drawn equipment was discontinued as soon as the demand (which equipment companies were working day and night to eliminate) dwindled to an uneconomic point. In fact, there has been little engineering or design input on horse-drawn machinery since the mid-thirties. Rubber tires, one of the greatest horse savers ever invented, are a case in point; they were never widely applied to horse-drawn machinery.

Even so, horse-drawn machinery (some of it was, and is, very good) had a built-in quality of lasting almost indefinitely, if given proper care and maintenance. The fact that it is operated at low field speeds adds to its longevity. About this time farm machinery took the same road as many other facets of American life and became a casualty of planned obsolescence. Simplicity of design and a long useful product life were no longer considered to be the cornerstones of good business. They did, in fact, interfere with producing greater sales volume and profits.

Accompanying and stimulating these changes was an advertising and propaganda effort to discredit the horse and mule that was devastating to the equine interests. The Horse and Mule Association of America did its best to present their story, but the contest between this organization of horse-minded farmers, harness manufacturers, and other small allied interests against the advertising expertise of corporate America was a very lopsided affair. The horse became the "beloved culprit" at best, the very reason for and symbol of drudgery and hard times at worst. The campaign had a telling effect on the rising generation of American farmers. By the late forties horsemanship was no longer something young farmers valued.

And it was about this time that the land-grant schools disposed of their draft stock, the farm papers no longer carried helpful articles, just occasional obituaries or nostalgia pieces, and the lending agencies that had once looked on good horses and mules as a part of a thrifty operation were no longer impressed, but actively discouraged their use.

Few commercial contests have ever resulted in a more complete victory. Most heavy horses ended up in dog food cans, and you can't manufacture more draft horses and mules—you must breed them. There were virtually no sources of new horse-drawn machinery. It was a case of "make do" or "convert," with no middle ground offered by either corporation or college. A farmer had to figure out and improvise his own middle ground. The skills of good draft horsemanship, once passed on to succeeding generations with great care and pride, were abandoned by the old and unlearned and scorned by the young.

I don't pretend to know what the future holds for the heavy horse. What I am certain of is that those who wish to farm a modest amount of ground with a minimum of cash outlay and do it with a source of power that is self-reproducing, consumes home-grown fuel, and contributes to the fertility of the soil, should consider the draft horse for a place in their future.

There are obstacles, of course. Horse machinery, a few years ago both cheap and plentiful, is now neither. Rust and the cutting torch of the junk men have taken a heavy toll. Good pieces now command respectable prices when you find them, but still far under the investment required for tractor farming. Hopefully, this trend is being reversed. An example is the firm of D. A. Hochstetler and Sons (Rt. 2, Box 162, Topeka, Indiana 46571), where they make new horse-drawn farm wagons and sulky plows. Last year they manufactured and sold 174 new horse-drawn plows—not a great number in this land of mass production, but a possible indication of things to come. We hope so.

Fig. 1-5.   One of the brand-new sulky plows being manufactured at the shop of D. A. Hochstetler and Sons, Topeka, Indiana.

Harness making lends itself to the cottage industry approach much more readily than the manufacture of plows, mowers, and other machinery. New harness is now available at many shops throughout the cornbelt states.

Along with good machinery, there's a dearth of experienced teamsters able to teach draft horse skills. Obviously a lot of the best practitioners of the art of horse farming are now in the cemeteries and quite out of reach. Treasure the ones that are left and willing to help you! If you will but look around, most rural communities still have some good old horsemen who will be happy to come out of retirement—not to do your farming for you, but to show you how.

None of these problems is insurmountable, and despite the obstacles involved in obtaining the prerequisite skills, equipment, and teams, farming with horses is being done. Thousands of acres are being farmed completely with horses in the many Amish communities across the country.

These communities also answer a question draft horsemen are often asked, "How will you get your work all done?" They get it done with more hands, more family involvement, fewer acres per unit, a simple life-style, and a sense of neighbor helping neighbor that is but a memory in most rural neighborhoods. Not only do they get it done, but with their modest sized farms, lighter weight machinery, and live horse-power, they frequently have their crops in and get them harvested *before* many of their mechanized neighbors, especially when either the spring or fall weather has proven extremely wet for extended periods of time.

They have improvised, adapting many new farm machines to horse and mule use. Symbolic of this improvisation is the "Amish Tractor," a two-wheeled cart, sometimes called a fore cart, used to pull machines built for tractor use.

But you aren't Amish and don't have Amish neighbors. Okay. That simply makes it more difficult, not impossible. And that, too, is being proven by many small (by 1977 standards) farmers across the land.

So let's take a look at the problems—and how you can solve them.

Before we get to the horse, let's make sure we have what it takes to use him. As previously stated, horse-drawn machinery is becoming difficult to find. My own feeling is that it is foolish to be a fanatic on authenticity; where a good piece of tractor equipment can be adapted without undue cost—do it. After all, you're running a farm, not a museum.

In either case, most everything you need will have to be obtained at farm sales, out of old sheds and groves, and just cruising the country. It is a time-consuming process. If you are well acquainted with an auctioneer that cries a lot of farm sales in your area, he can be an invaluable aid in spotting good horse equipment for you. In my own case, I haven't the time to attend a lot of farm sales but have an auctioneer friend buy a number of very useful items for me. He knows what I need and what I'll pay, and it has worked out very well. He and several other horse-minded auctioneers have performed a real service for the draft horse business by securing good usable items and buying them for resale.

In buying old machinery don't be overimpressed by a new paint job. Rather, make sure that bearings and boxings are tight, that the wear on the machine is not excessive (for instance, is the moldboard of an old horse-drawn plow worn down to soft steel and badly pitted; if so, it won't do a good job for you), that the frame has not been sprung, rewelded, etc. Rust has probably been harder on a lot of the horse-drawn equipment than wear, especially if it was manufactured in the late thirties and purchased just before its owner switched to tractor power.

By and large, I shy away from machinery that was manufactured for the slower speed of the horse, and then with the tongue sawed off used behind a tractor. The temptation to use this machinery at higher field speeds than it was intended for usually proved too great. I would rather buy a piece that was abandoned or a machine built for tractor use and convertible to horses, than a piece of horse equipment that has been used helter-skelter behind a high speed tractor. And I certainly prefer zerk fittings to the old grease cups.

Parts are a problem. That is the very reason you will find two Case mowers on our farm. One we use and the junker is for parts. Sickles are no problem for us; we just buy a seven foot tractor sickle and cut a foot off. Some of the old machines you will find on horse farms are not there to simply detract from the appearance of the place—they are a reservoir of spare parts, but it is nice if you have a place to hide them.

There is no gainsaying the fact that it is not as easy to trade help with neighbors (unless they, too, happen to be horse farmers) and that can be an aggravation. But it is not an insurmountable problem.

Finding horses can also be a problem because draft breeds aren't nearly as common as the pleasure breeds. Your best bet if you're looking for a good broke team is to find someone in your area who can sell you one. Go talk to him and ask questions. Watch him work with his horses and get some pointers on how to do it. Find out how to harness a team.

How do you find someone to sell you draft horses? If you've got Amish or Mennonite neighbors you're in luck because if your neighbors don't use drafters themselves chances are they know someone who does. If not, don't despair—many people who use horses on their farms go about their work quietly and don't broadcast the fact in their community. You can ferret them out by placing ads in local farm papers, asking around local feed mills or hardware stores, contacting farriers or blacksmiths, checking equipment dealers, and contacting people at the local farm museum or living historical farm. You should also check the ads in *Draft Horse Journal* (a modest plug here) and write letters to advertisers who live close to you.

Fig. 1-6. The recreation industry also beckons the draft horse to return to harness. These Percheron teams are used for hayrides in Michigan.

You can also buy drafters at auctions. The horse auction at Waverly, Iowa, is the biggest in the states, but there are other well-known regional auctions at which teams can be purchased.

If you decide to go out and get yourself a good broke team, try to take an experienced horseman with you, pick up pieces of usable horse machinery you can find at local farm sales, prepare to work a little harder physically than your mechanized neighbor, and go at it kind of easy, not all in one jump. Work a pair for a while on the spreader, corn planter, and seeder before you put four on the disk. You may just discover that horse farming is what fits you, your concept of what farming should be, and your place on this earth.

And if you do like the company of good horses, you will be richly rewarded by working with them. There is a sense of partnership between a teamster and his horses that is worth a great deal. To take them in and care for them after hitting a good lick in the field is a fulfillment. If it isn't—if it is a burden—then you best not have them.

A working team, at its best, is a part of the family and the very embodiment of the life of the farm. For me, and for many others, the quietness of working with well broke horses is a pleasure and satisfaction that covering more acres simply wouldn't yield. I'm often asked questions such as "How many acres did you plow or cultivate or disk, or whatever, today?" Once in awhile, it is a loaded question, and my answer in those cases, I'm sure, generally serves to convince the questioner that I am, after all, a bit feeble-minded. But I remain quite unconvinced that "faster" and "more" is always better.

Chapter 2

Conformation and Breeds of Draft Horses *

There are many factors to be considered in a decision to use horsepower on the farm, as I hope you're aware after reading the past chapter. For the general homesteader or small farmer probably one of the *least* important considerations initially is in choosing a particular breed. Let me state at the outset that there is no "best breed," although there are sound reasons for preferring any of the breeds, and not too much importance should be attached to extremely partisan statements in this regard. The five breeds have far more in common than otherwise and a person's choice of breeds depends on the conditions to be met, the characteristics required, and most of all, on personal preference.

What is really more important in choosing an animal is *conformation*. Draft horse conformation is simply the relationship of the physical structure of the beast to the job at hand. In other words, utility.

The late R. B. Ogilvie, former secretary of the Clydesdale Association, stated the important qualities of a draft horse very well when he said, "Utility in a draft horse means absolute soundness, a willingness to work, wearing qualities, and the ability to move large loads at a long, easy stride. Accessories to these desirable qualities in a drafter are oblique shoulders, short backs, deep ribs, long level quarters with

*I published parts of this chapter in *Western Horseman* in the October 1972 and October 1973 issues; they are reprinted here with permission.

heavily muscled thighs extending well down to the hocks, shanks of ample size and quality, pasterns properly set, and strong, shapely feet."

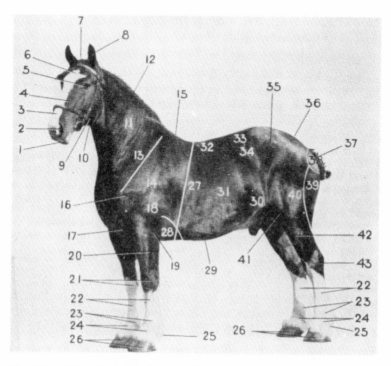

Fig. 2-1. The points of the horse: 1. Mouth; 2. Nostril; 3. Nose; 4. Face; 5. Eye; 6. Forehead; 7. Poll; 8. Ear; 9. Lower jaw; 10. Throatlatch; 11. Neck; 12. Crest; 13. Shoulder bed; 14. Shoulder; 15. Withers; 16. Point of shoulder; 17. Breast; 18. Arm; 19. Elbow; 20. Forearm; 21. Knees; 22. Cannons; 23. Fetlocks; 24. Pasterns; 25. Feather; 26. Feet; 27. Heart girth; 28. Foreflank; 29. Underline; 30. Hind flank; 31. Barrel; 32. Back; 33. Loin; 34. Coupling; 35. Hip; 36. Croup; 37. Tail; 38. Buttock; 39. Quarters; 40. Thigh; 41. Stifle; 42. Gaskin; 43. Hock.

Let us examine each part of the whole as outlined by Mr. Ogilvie.

The feet and legs constitute the working foundation of any horse and are thus of most importance. One may as well start his examination of a horse at the ground, for if he doesn't have it there it makes little difference what is topside. The foot of a draft horse must be of good size. If you doubt this, try working a small-footed horse in a soft, plowed field. He will expend much of his energy just pulling his feet out of the ground, and the heavier the horse, the worse this is. Tractor manufacturers would talk about traction or flotation of their machines in this respect, and the draft horse is, after all, an equine motor—and a very good one.

The hoof should be sloping, wide and deep at the heel with a good-sized frog (see diagram of the foot, Fig. 6-2, p. 199). A medium-sized foot with a deep heel and well developed frog are much to be preferred over an overly large, shelly foot with low heels and little frog development. A shallow heel is likely to result in lameness when the horse is worked on hard ground or roads. Narrow, contracted heels are also a serious fault and will interfere with free action. The horn of the foot should be of very dense texture to wear well, and the frog, in addition to being large, should yield to pressure from your thumbs. It is the horse's shock absorber, as it were.

The pastern should be moderately long and slope at about a 45° angle to insure elasticity of motion and lessen the impact on the foot as it strikes the ground. A short, stubby, straight pastern often goes with a short, stumbly stride and, quite possibly, with the development of sidebones since it does not take the impact out of the foot striking the ground as a good sloping pastern would. While it *is* possible to have too long and sloping a pastern, the contrary fault is much more commonplace.

Draft horsemen like a strong, deep, wide hock in a draft horse. Strength in the hock is indicated by the distance from the point of the hock to the lower inner bottom part of the hock. The proper set of hock, as viewed from the side, should be fairly straight with just enough set to insure that the horse can move with a bit of a bang, and when viewed from the rear, the hocks should incline slightly inwards. Horses that stand wide at the hocks will tend to spread their legs in heavy pullings rather than keeping them in a straight line, resulting in a loss of power.

The knees should be broad as viewed from the front, deep and well supported as viewed from the side. The knees should be directly set under each shoulder. Either "buck knees" or "calf knees" are objectionable. Calf knees (or back in the knees) are a pretty serious flaw in that they tend to interfere with a horse's pulling power (see Fig. 2-2).

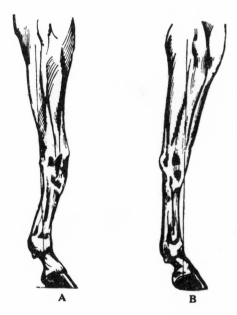

Fig. 2-2. Side views of the forelimbs A. Buck knees B. Calf knees

With well set feet and legs of adequate size, strong leg joints that are well defined, with dense bone of good, flat quality, one should get the type of action and wearing qualities called for by Mr. Ogilvie.

From the standpoint of action, draft horsemen desire a long, straight stride at the walk. The walk is the working gait of the draft horse and each foot should move straight forward and be lifted high enough to set squarely every time it hits the ground. The hocks should brush past one another, as closely as possible without touching. A horse that toes in or is pigeon-toed may paddle or wing when he moves. One that toes out may interfere, that is, strike the supporting front foot as it passes.

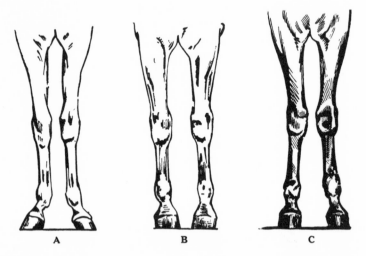

A   B   C

Fig. 2-3.   Front views of the forelimbs   A. Toe-wide, splay-footed, or toed-out   B. Toe-narrow, toed-in, or pigeon-toed   C. Knock-kneed

Other body characteristics that result in faulty action are extreme width of chest, which may cause the horse to roll, and too short a body, which may cause "forging" or striking the front supporting foot with the rear moving foot. It is a question of proportion in that both a short back and wide chest are desirable up to a point.

Points to stress in body conformation should, as in the case of underpinning, relate to the job at hand; namely, wearing harness.

The shoulder should, like the pastern, carry a reasonable slope, thus getting the horse's head up in the air, giving him style. A straight shoulder, like a straight, upright pastern, causes a short stride and excessive concussion, and the result is both sore shoulders and tendon trouble in the feet and legs. On the other hand, a shoulder that slopes too much is difficult to fit to a collar, but as with pasterns, the short, upright shoulder is the more common fault. The withers should be wide and well defined, offering a seat for the collar. A work horse does throw his weight into the collar; this is difficult on a short, bull-necked horse without well-defined withers. The chest should be deep and comparatively broad with ample heart girth, providing room for the horse's vital organs. We look for a strong, heavily muscled back which seems short. In this respect, the relationship of the back and shoulder is obvious; a horse with a good slope of shoulder will appear to have a shorter back. There is a relationship between length of back and length of neck; the right kind of shoulder integrates the two. A short, wide, heavily muscled loin, a roomy middle with well-sprung ribs, and a croup that is fairly level, long, broad, and well muscled are most desirable. A shallow-bodied horse is usually a poor feeder.

Most of the power of a horse, when pulling, is developed in the hind quarters. This carries forward to the shoulders, where the collar rests. The muscling over the loin and croup are, in a way, the power train. This, I'm sure, is what Mr. Ogilvie meant when he called for "oblique shoulders, short backs, deep ribs, long level quarters, with heavily muscled thighs extending well down to the hocks."

The typical draft horse head is comparatively lean, wide between the eyes, and proportionate in size to the body. The eye should be large and prominent. A broad, flat forehead and erect ears set relatively close together are preferred.

I believe all five breeds can subscribe substantially to the above qualities, though some will stress one aspect more than another. The Clydesdale, for instance, lays claim to superlative pasterns, hocks, and action; the Percheron to a quality and refinement of head and neck not unlike that of an Arabian horse, and a gay way of going; the Belgian to excellent muscling and tremendous power, coupled with style; the Suffolk to being an easy keeper, with a very fast walk, and great stamina and longevity; and the Shire to Clydesdale-like feather and action coupled with great bulk. So wear the shoe that fits you; there are good ones in all breeds, and lemons too.

Fig. 2-4. A recent champion Clydesdale mare of Scotland, illustrating the roan pattern that is fairly common in the breed. Note the long sloping pasterns and the quality of the legs and feather. This mare also shows the wee bit of set in the hind legs which, along with that pastern and feather, gives the breed the type of action that has made them big hitch favorites.

(Courtesy of A. Brown & Company)

Some new buyers who have no interest in showing but simply want an economical source of power may prefer what the trade calls "draft chunks" to a heavy drafter. Many chunks or light drafters are the result of a couple top crosses of draft stallions on light or general purpose mares. Draft chunks did most of the farm work in the early part of this century because city demand took most of the heavy draft geldings for the extremely heavy loads called for in commerce. The difference is mostly a question of size, the heavy drafter standing sixteen hands or better, the chunk or light draft horse being smaller. Otherwise the bill of particulars is about the same and whilst there is some difference in size *between* breeds, the truth of the matter is that the variations *within* breeds are great enough to provide you with either a heavy or light drafter in the breed of your choice.

Northern Europe is the historical nursery of all the breeds of heavy draft. Five breeds, three British, one French, and one from Belgium, make up the present draft horse community of North America. There are other breeds in Europe that are not established on this side of the Atlantic, so I'll deal only with the five that are active on our side of the water.

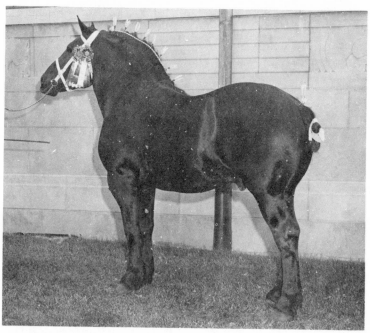

Fig. 2-5. Donald Laet, a recent Royal Winter Fair grand champion, with characteristics typical of the modern Percheron.

Most of the draft breeds were originally developed for warfare. The big chargers were bred to bear the enormous weight of warriors in armor. Protected by heavy, jointed metal skirts and headgear, ridden by cavaliers in cumbersome armor, the great horses of Europe (like the tanks of modern warfare) mowed down everything in their path. The advent of gunpowder and the resulting change in military tactics put an end to their usefulness as military chargers.

Having attained great size and strength and having emerged from this military usage as a distinct type, the heavy horse gradually found his way into more recent and familiar roles in agriculture and city drayage and thence to advertising and recreation in the form of horse pulls and hayrides.

This evolution, as it relates to the Percheron, is poetically described in a sketch of the late Mark Dunham, pioneer Percheron importer, in A. H. Sanders's book, *At the Sign of the Stock Yard Inn* (Chicago: Breeder's Gazette, 1915):

Under a gray old castle's frowning walls a drawbridge falls across the moat. The trumpets sound. A glittering cavalcade emerges. Pennons gay and guidons flutter in the breeze. Steel and silver-corselet, hilt and morion glisten in the morning sun, and noble chargers, mostly white and gray, prance proudly, bearing out into the medieval world brave belted knights and their retainers faring forth to meet what ere betides.

Generations pass: in the far distance the rhythmic beating of heavy hurrying hoofs! It is a highway builded by the kings of France. To the sound of the horn and the sharp note of the lash, the great diligence bearing the royal mails and laden deep with passengers and their gear comes into view. A rush, a roar of wheels, and the great freighted coach is gone.

Agriculture calls: down the long furrows see the shining plowshares deeply driven. The mellow earth awakens, and lo, the stored up riches of a fertile field await the seed. Long is the journey and repeated oft. From "early morn to dewy eve" the living shuttles travel, back and forth; but weight that wearies not is harnessed.

And yet again, last scene of all: a busy modern city street. Huge vans and trucks are rumbling ever on the granite blocks. Big grays and blacks march proudly to the music of a nation's commerce. Power, patience, dignity personified. Glory be to men who can produce such prodigies!

Having been thus introduced to the Percheron, we will consider that breed first. The cradle of this breed is one of the smallest provinces of old France, the district known as The Perche. The shape of the Perche is an ellipse about fifty-three by sixty-six miles, located some seventy miles southeast of Paris. It is a region of green hills and verdant valleys, well suited to stock raising and inhabited by thrifty small landholders. The Perche farmer has always been a producer of horses and does not often buy elsewhere, breeding new types of drafters to meet changing market demands. In this, the government has been helpful, providing excellent stallions—primarily through the government stud at Haras du Pin (a stud in this case is a collection of horses for breeding purposes). As in the past, the typical French breeder has only a few mares and either patronizes the government stud or one of several stallioners. Stallion owners generally have no mares, and the mare men no stallions. The stallioner usually

Fig. 2-6. Peggy's Pride, a many times grand champion Percheron mare at leading midwestern state fairs, owned by Mrs. R. L. Robinson, Richland, Michigan. The Percheron breed has always been blessed with stylish matrons such as this.
(Courtesy of Ed Schneckloth)

buys up some of the more promising stud colts sired by his own horses (or even by the government stallions at du Pin) and grows them out. In other words, he will have a paddock of yearlings, another of two-year olds, and when they are rising three-year olds and ready for service, he either sells them or puts them into his own battery of stallions.

The breed was first introduced to North America in 1839, but it was the 1880s, with the tremendous agricultural expansion that characterized the decade, that gave the Percheron its big boost. In 1884, more than 2,000 Percherons were brought to our shores. The depression of the nineties stopped all importations and scattered much of the early blood to the four winds, but the early 1900s were again halcyon days for the Percheron breed. For the first three decades of this century the Percheron was the leader of the field. According to the 1930 census two-thirds of the registered draft horses in America were Percherons—but there was a rapidly growing sorrel and roan cloud on the Percheron horizon, destined to challenge and eventually wrest the number one spot from the blacks and grays.

But we are getting ahead of ourselves. The Percheron has much to commend him. One theory claims that he is the only draft breed with an infusion of Arab blood. The story goes that French military officers brought Arab stallions home from their campaigns and that some of this blood found its way into the Percherons. Whatever the truth of that is, the Percheron is a big horse with a lot of animation, and many specimens of the breed do have lovely heads and necks that bespeak a possible ancient debt to the horses of the desert. One former Iowa breeder always referred to his favorites as "the horse that can haul a load of corn to town and trot all the way home." This combination of size with action and spirit with tractability has won the allegiance of many a horseman to the Percheron standard.

Today the breed is made up of about 50 percent black horses and 50 percent gray horses in this country. Chestnut, bay, and blue roan occur occasionally but have never been well-accepted Percheron colors. Presently there is some effort to breed sorrel or chestnut Percherons, but it is a very small minority within the breed which is generally regarded as a two-color breed. In France most of them are gray. The breed enjoys its share of favor from farmer, puller, and show hitch man alike. Ohio is the leading state in both registrations and transfers of ownership, followed by Wisconsin, Pennsylvania, and Indiana. The association puts out an annual publication. The address is: Percheron Horse Association of America, Rt. 1, Belmont, Ohio 43718.

In terms of present-day popularity the Percheron is second only to the Belgian—that sorrel and roan cloud of the twenties

Fig. 2-7. A 1970 champion of Belgium. Thick, massive, and roan, with an abundance of feather, he does not resemble his American cousins very much. The breed has gone very divergent ways in its homeland and over here.
(Courtesy of Harold Cline)

and thirties referred to earlier. Originally a slow starter in America, this Flemish breed, a bit thicker than the Percheron, also came from a great horse breeding country of limited size. The methods of horse production were and are very similar to those in France, i.e., colt production is almost entirely in the hands of small farmers, with the stallioner rarely raising foals but buying and developing promising young stud foals, much like his French counterpart.

There is currently a lot of talk in beef and sheep circles about this or that breed being a "sire breed." The Belgian has very much been a sire breed, being exported in abundance to all parts of Europe as well as North America.

The Belgians came on very strong in the twenties and thirties in the United States. Excellent feeders and shippers, they were very popular with horse buyers who shipped them by the carload to eastern cities from buying points in the Midwest, our traditional colt-producing section. It was also about this time that the sorrel with white mane and tail became the Cadillac of colors with American farmers, a position it retains to this day. It has, in fact, been so popular that the red roan— very common in the twenties and thirties—has become a fairly scarce commodity even within the Belgian ranks.

Belgian stallions crossed extremely well on Percheron mares, which were dominant numerically at that time. The chestnut or sorrel and roan colors had become very popular and was uncommon in the Percheron breed, which made up most of our mare stock. Most of the Belgian stallions were chestnuts or sorrels and roans, and farmers, always aware of market trends, were interested in trying to breed sorrels from the mares they had. Naturally, you also get bays, blacks, grays, and roans from this cross, but sorrel was the number one color in the market place with roan popular in the thirties, and this fact was not lost on stallioners in our country. When a horse of a given color will bring you more business than an equally good one of another color, you are quite likely to find a stallion of the preferred color in the stallion man's paddock. The keen demand for Belgian stallions, coupled with the reduced level of breeding during the twenties, put the Belgian breed solidly back into the importing business for a time in the thirties.

Since then, however, the breed has taken divergent ways here and in Belgium. In Europe the more massive, thick, "old-fashioned" type has prevailed and the roan and bay or bay-brown are the breed colors. The American Belgian has been bred to be more upheaded, upstanding, and hitchier than his European cousin. In brief, the American Belgian has been bred to look stylish on the big hitch wagons while his European ancestor has pretty well stuck to the plow.

Fig. 2-8. Major de Malmaison, an international champion Belgian stallion of the late 1920s. Note the difference in type. The farmer of that period demanded a thick, close to the ground horse.

However, the Belgian breed has been, and continues to be, very popular with farmers. It is now in a position comparable to the Percherons some thirty or forty years ago, recording more colts than all the other draft breeds combined. Belgians have always been dominant in the horse pulling sport (see Chapter 9), and take their share of honors in interbreed hitch competition as well.

Indiana, Ohio, and Iowa are the chief producers of Belgian horses. The address of the association which also puts out an annual publication is: Belgian Draft Horse Corporation of America, P.O. Box 335, Wabash, Indiana 46992.

The Clydesdale though ranking third in the number of horses in the states, may well be the best-known of our draft breeds amongst urban people due to the immense popularity of the big hitches, most notably Budweiser's. The Clyde, with his white face and white legs endowed with silky feather (the fine hair on the legs) and his superb action has always been a

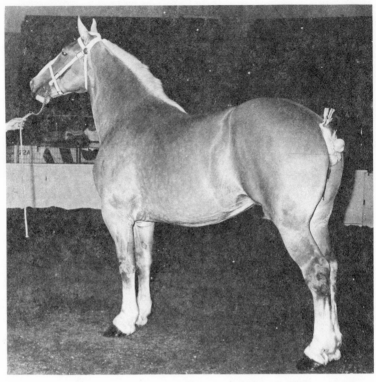

Fig. 2-9.   Contilda, bred and sold by Harold Clark, Millersburg, Indiana, to J. M. McKeehan, Greencastle, Indiana, for $16,500—the highest price ever recorded for a draft mare at public auction. She has been grand champion at most of the major shows in the Midwest. She is an excellent example of the "modern type" of Belgian.
(Courtesy of Ed Schneckloth)

great favorite for advertising purposes. In the show ring, he is a flashy horse.

As the name implies, this breed is a native of the valley of the Clyde River in Scotland where the lowland farmers of Lanarkshire developed their breed of heavy draft. As with all breeds of horses, the Clydesdale has seen shifting emphasis on breed types through the years, but, amidst all such variations, one cardinal feature has been retained—the breed's substantial underpinning. It is no accident that two anonymous Scotch horsemen are credited with the old adages "No foot-no horse" and "Tops may go, but bottoms never."

Fig. 2-10. Probably the best-known draft horses in North America are the famous Budweiser Eight-Horse Team, shown here pulling a City of St. Louis entry in a recent Rose Bowl Parade in Pasadena, California. The Anheuser-Busch Company maintains two such hitches, one headquartering out of St. Louis, Missouri, and the other out of Merrimack, New Hampshire. The company also maintains a large breeding farm near St. Louis, the primary purpose of which is to provide replacement geldings for the hitches.

(Courtesy of J. Allen Hawkins)

The dominant color in the Clydesdale is bay, with quite a few browns and blacks and a few chestnuts. The white markings are more prominent than in other draft breeds, frequently resulting in the white extending well up into the stifle, belly, and chest. This also results in quite a few roans. A roan is a mixture of white and colored hairs. As you get the white markings more pronounced on the extremities, i.e., the legs and face, you are more likely to get it sprinkled throughout the hair coat.

Like the Percheron, the Clyde enjoys a reputation for ample gaiety with an even disposition. The Clyde has also inspired his share of poetry—as the following example illustrates:

THE CLYDESDALE

Thudding hoof and flowing hair,
Style and action sweet and fair,
Bone and sinew well defined,

> Movement close both fore and hind,
> Noble eye and handsome head,
> Bold, intelligent, well-bred,
> Lovely neck and shoulder laid,
> See how shapely he is made,
> Muscle strong and frame well knit,
> Strength personified and fit,
> Thus the Clydesdale—see him go,
> To the field, the stud, the show,
> Proper back and ribs well sprung,
> Sound of limb, and sound of lung,
> Powerful loin, and quarter wide,
> Grace and majesty allied,
> Basic power—living force—
> Equine king—The Clydesdale Horse.

Anonymous

Michigan and Wisconsin are the leading states for Clydesdales. The office of the Clydesdale Breeders Association of the United States is located at Rt. 1, Box 131, Pecatonica, Illinois 61063.

There are two lesser-known breeds of British origin with us—the Shire and the Suffolk. Both endured some very lean days in the fifties and both associations virtually ceased to function for a few years. With the draft horse revival of the sixties, plus several recent importations from England, both are now very much back in the picture.

The Shire is, in many respects, a cousin of the Clyde. Developed in the low-lying Fen country of England he was bred along somewhat more massive lines with such an abundance of feather that it retarded his acceptance in America. This is no longer true; the feather is now considerably finer and silkier. Many of the early Shires found their life's work on the narrow streets and crowded docks of Liverpool and London where they were expected to pull immense loads and speed was no great consideration. Thus it was that early livestock texts almost always described the Shire as the biggest of the breeds and charged him with some degree of coarseness and sluggishness.

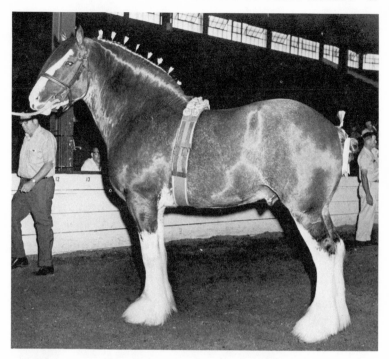

Fig. 2-11. Bardrill Glenord, five times grand champion at the Royal Agricultural Winter Fair of Canada for Anheuser-Busch, Inc., St. Louis, Missouri. He is the only Clydesdale to ever do so and is a prime example of the present-day Clydesdale type. His color markings—bright bay with white extending up to and a little beyond the knees and hocks and a full stripe in the face—are considered to be about ideal.

(Courtesy of Harold Cline)

Neither charge is valid today. He is neither coarse nor sluggish, but a very bold moving and hitchy kind of horse that almost completely dominates the hitch competition in his native country. Nor would I call the Shire the biggest breed at this time. I would say there is no "biggest breed"—all draft breeds have their share of "big uns" and "little ones."

Upwards to fifty head of Shires have been imported into the United States in recent years. Most of the Shire activity centers in Idaho, Washington, and Maryland. Black is the dominant color of the breed in America at this time. In England, bay and black predominate, with a fair sprinkling of grays.

Fig. 2-12. Grange Wood William, a recent champion at the Shire Horse Show in Peterborough, England. This horse is typical of the modern Shire.

Fig. 2-13. The champion Suffolk mare at the Royal Norfolk Show in 1974, an excellent example of the breed.

The other British breed, staging a more modest comeback, is the Suffolk. This is the only breed of the five popular in America developed initially and deliberately for farm work, rather than as a spin-off from warfare, diligence work (big stagecoaches for mail and people in France before the advent of railroads), or city drayage. They are truly agricultural horses and the only draft breed that is limited to one color. Suffolks are all chestnuts, or sorrels if you prefer. Their markings are similar to black Percherons, i.e., very little white. Their conformation is similar to Belgians of twenty-five years ago.

The breed was developed in Norwich and Suffolk counties of England where the soil is heavy. Unlike the other two British breeds, Suffolks have little or no feather. Due to their rather rotund appearance they were originally called Suffolk Punches. The breed never emphasized size or action, as did the other British breeds, but rather durability and longevity. They are said to be very fast walkers, but without extremely high action and with a great willingness to work. Like the Belgians, they are very easy keepers, staying in good flesh on a modest quantity of feed. The Suffolk is, as a breed, very true to its ancient and honorable heritage as a "farmers' horse."

Spread very thinly across the United States, the principal area of Suffolk activity is in Pennsylvania. The office of the American Shire Horse Association is located at 14410 High Bridge Road, Monroe, Washington 98272. The American Suffolk Horse Association is located at 672 Polk Boulevard, Des Moines, Iowa 50312.

The chunk, a small draft horse of any of the major breeds or combinations thereof, has been briefly mentioned. Depending on your personal preferences, size of operation, and pocketbook, a team of chunks of undetermined origin may be your best bet.

The heavy drafter of good conformation will bring (when selling) or cost (when buying) the most money. But there are other considerations. Feed requirements are pretty much in proportion to size and weight. Wayne Dinsmore, in *Our Equine Friends* (Chicago: Horse and Mule Association of America, Inc., 1944), states that it costs 20 percent more to feed, raise, and maintain an 1800-pound horse than a 1500-pound animal. If they are equal in type—both built along true draft horse lines—this can amount to a considerable saving in fuel costs for the person primarily interested in working them. The other factor is the work you have in mind; the horse should be matched to the work load.

These considerations can also apply to draft-type ponies, such as the old-fashioned Shetland and some of the European breeds, where the work and terrain is of such a nature that an even smaller animal is required.

For still others, the mule, a sterile hybrid resulting from the mating of a jack donkey and a draft mare, may be the best bet. The resulting offspring resembles the sire in the shape of his head (Roman nose), the size of the ears, set of eyes, and the shape of the leg bones with the smaller contracted foot of the jack. The barrel of the mule is, for the most part, fashioned after the dam, as is the texture (in contrast to shape) of the foot and bone. The height and weight of the male are more dependent upon the dam than the sire.

Why would one want a mule since he is a sterile hybrid, and since jack and jennet stock is unsuitable for work? There are real and substantial differences between horses and mules, with the mule having some obvious advantages. The mule has smaller feet than a horse, which can be an advantage for certain kinds of work, such as cultivation. He is tougher than a horse. By that I mean he can endure more hardship than a horse and will stay in better condition under adverse conditions and hard labor. He is more careful than a horse—i.e., not as likely to blemish himself—and his sale price does not suffer as much when he is blemished. He is, by and large, longer lived, and in extreme old age the mule is generally more useful than a horse of the same age. A mule will not overeat (founder) and overheat like a horse. Thus, you might say that mules can put up with more mismanagement and just plain ignorance on the part of the teamster.

In the first part of this century, American breeders of jack stock developed a distinctive type of jack, known as the Mammoth Jack. The best specimens stand up to sixteen hands and

Fig. 2-14. J. Olen White, jack and jennet breeder from Amity, Missouri, presenting a young Mammoth Jack. With his coloration you can expect this fellow to sire many of the blonde mules currently so popular when mated to Belgian mares.

weigh up to 1200 pounds. When jacks of this type are used on good brood mares they produce the finest mules that America has been able to produce.

Broadly speaking, there were three classes of mules when horses and mules were more commonplace: the draft mule (resulting from a cross of the Mammoth Jack and a draft mare); the cotton mule (resulting from a medium-sized jack and utility farm mares or light horse mares); and mine mules (small, tough mules to work in the mines, obviously). Today you might describe these as the draft mule, the southern mule, and the mini-mule. For our purposes here I'll discuss the first two.

The draft mule is usually the mule one sees at shows and has a good Belgian or Percheron dam and a Mammoth Jack for a sire. They will stand from fifteen to sixteen hands as a rule and are the mules favored in the North. They are sometimes

Fig. 2-15.   Southern or cotton mules used to haul hunting dogs and hunters into the brush at the Forshee Plantation near Tallahassee, Florida.
(Courtesy of Florida Game & Fresh Water Fish Commission)

seen working in combination with horses and are just what the name implies—a mule of heavy draft.

The southern mule, or cotton mule, is the result of a mating between a jack and a mare weighing from 900 to 1200 pounds and standing in height from fourteen to sixteen hands. With the lightleg dam you get an animal that is extremely durable and steps lively, is lighter framed and more active. If improperly broken these mules are likely to be erratic and handy with their heels, but if handled properly they can do a tremendous amount of work on a minimum of feed. Mules of this smaller type were commonly used in the mountain sections for riding and pack mules as well as for inter-row cultivation of cotton. As a draft animal this mule can probably endure about as much hardship as any animal.

Missouri, Tennessee, and Kentucky have always been the primary mule-producing states. In most other regions of the country the availability of jacks is pretty slim, a factor which works against mule production. One of the hardest hit sectors of the horse and mule industry during the decline of work stock was the jack and jennet breeder, since for our conditions they do not make suitable work animals in themselves. This situation has changed with the rekindled interest in breeding, but the welfare of the jack and jennet business depends wholly on the mule breeding business. Their only real role is as parents.

There is an interesting difference between show hitches of horses and mules. Virtually all the big show hitches of draft horses are geldings. They are bigger, more massive, and less temperamental. Nursing foals or mares coming in heat during a show are not bonuses where presenting show hitches is concerned, and for this reason show people shy away from draft horse mares. However, you will find the molly (or mare) mule doing most of the hitching on a mule hitch. The horse mule when gelded tends to become more angular, a condition that feeding will not correct, and seems to lose more of his pizazz than does a gelded stallion. The molly, being sterile, does not present the problems that hitching draft mares can present. Thus, the female mules will usually outsell males.

Fig. 2-16. A Texas farmer using a team of mules for cultivation—always one of the favorite jobs for a mule with his smaller feet.

GENERAL APPEARANCE—18 points
    Height: Estimated hands_____ ; actual hands_____
    Weight: Estimated_____ ; actual_____ ; according to age and type.......... 4
    Form: Broad, deep, massive, well proportioned, low set.................................... 4
    Quality and substance: Abundance of clean, flat bone; broad, well-
        defined joints and tendons; refined head and ears; fine skin and hair;
        feather, if present, silky.. 6
    Temperament: Energetic, good disposition 4

HEAD AND NECK—7 points
    Head: Proportionate, medium size, clean cut; wide lower jaw........................ 1
    Forehead: Broad, full.. 1
    Eyes: Large, prominent, bright, clear.. 1
    Muzzle: Broad, fine; large nostrils; trim, even lips................................ 1
    Ears: Of medium size, well set, carried alert..................................... 1
    Neck: Medium long, muscular; good crest; clean throatlatch 2

FOREHAND—26 points
    Shoulders: Sloping, muscular, blending into smooth withers 3
    Arms: Short, muscular, elbow in 1
    Forearms: Wide, muscular 2
    Knees: Straight, wide, deep, well supported 2
    Cannons: Short, wide, lean, flat; large, well-defined tendons.................... 2
    Fetlocks: Wide, straight, tendons well back, well supported 1
    Pasterns: Of medium length, oblique (about 45^0), clean, strong................ 3
    Feet: Large, round, set straight; dense, smooth horn; slope of wall
        parallel to pastern; wide heels; concave sole; strong bars; prominent,
        elastic frog.. 8
    Leg position: In front, a perpendicular line from point of shoulder
        should divide the leg and foot into lateral halves; from the side, a
        similar line from the bony prominence on shoulder blade should pass
        through the center of elbow, knee, and pastern joints, and meet the
        ground back of foot.. 4

BODY—9 points
    Chest: Deep, wide, large girth.. 2
    Ribs: Long, well sprung, close, strongly coupled 2
    Back: Short, broad, heavily muscled.. 2
    Loin: Short, wide, heavily muscled... 2
    Flanks: Deep, full; long, low underline.. 1

HIND QUARTERS—30 points
    Hips: Wide, smooth, level, well muscled.. 2
    Croup: Long, wide, muscular, not markedly drooping 2
    Tail: Set high, well carried... 1
    Quarters and thighs: Deep, thick, muscular, strongly joined to gaskins 3
    Stifles: Muscular, well set.. 1
    Gaskins (lower thighs): Wide, heavily muscled................................... 2
    Hocks: Wide, deep, prominent point, clean cut, straight, well supported.......... 6
    Cannons: Similar to front except a trifle longer and wider...................... 2
    Fetlocks: Wide, straight, tendons well back, well supported 1
    Pasterns: Similar to front but less sloping (about 50^0)....................... 2
    Feet: Similar to front but not quite so large or so round....................... 4
    Leg position: From rear, a perpendicular line from point of buttock
        should divide the leg and foot into lateral halves; from the side, this
        same line should touch the point of hock and run parallel to the
        cannon. A similar line from the hip joint should meet the ground
        midway between the heel and toe.. 4

ACTION—10 points
    Walk: Straight, long stride, springy and balanced................................. 6
    Trot: Straight, long stride; free and regular 4
    Total.. 100

Fig. 2-17. Score card for the draft horse from the 1930s

AGE—Estimated

HEIGHT—Estimated

WEIGHT—1 year, 1,000 lb.; 2 years, 1,400 lb.; 3 years, 1,600 lb.;
4 years, 1,700 lb.; 5 years, 1,800 lb. 4

FORM—68 points

Head and neck—7 points

Head: Medium size, straight face line, clean-cut features,
wide angle in lower jaw; muzzle broad, nostrils large, lips
thin, even; eyes prominent, large, full, bright, clear; fore-
head broad; ears medium size, set close, carried alertly 5

Neck: Medium long, muscular, medium crest, clean throat 2

Forequarters—19 points

Shoulders: Sloping, muscular, well laid in 4

Arms: Short, muscular; forearms muscular, wide 2

Knees: Wide, deep, straight, clean, strongly supported 2

Cannons: Short, wide, flat tendons well defined and set back 2

Fetlocks: Wide, straight, strong, clean 2

Pasterns: Long, sloping (45°), strong, clean 3

Feet: Large, deep; heels wide, hoofs dense; smooth and free
from cracks 4

Body—14 points

Withers: Well defined, level with hips 1

Chest: Deep, wide, full, large heart girth 3

Ribs: Long, well sprung, close 3

Back: Short, broad, strong, muscular 3

Loin (or coupling): Wide, short, heavily muscled 3

Underline: Relatively long, flank low and full 1

Hindquarters—28 points

Hips: Smooth, wide, level 2

Croup: Long, level, wide, heavily muscled 2

Tail: Attached high, well carried 1

Thighs: Muscular, deep, wide between the stifles 2

Quarters: Deep, heavily muscled 2

Gaskins: Wide, heavily muscled 2

Hocks: Large, wide, deep, straight, clean, caps turned in
slightly 8

Cannons: Short, wide, flat tendons well defined and set back 2

Fetlocks: Wide, straight, strong, clean 2

Pasterns: Fairly long, sloping (50°), strong, clean 2

Feet: Large, deep, heels wide, hoofs dense, smooth, free from
cracks 3

SUBSTANCE—Large bones and joints 4

QUALITY—Bones and joints clean; tendons well defined; skin and hair
fine; head and ears medium size 3

TEMPERAMENT—Energetic, good disposition 2

ACTION—10 points

Walk: Long, straight, snappy, springy, well-balanced stride 6

Trot: Long, straight, snappy, springy, moderately high, well-
balanced stride with good flection of knees and hocks 4

Fig. 2-18. Perfect score for the draft horse from the 1940s

Figs. 2-17 and 2-18. A Score Card of Excellence is usually associated with judging livestock. It is nothing more than an agreed-upon standard with various weights assigned to certain characteristics (or lack of them). In practice, these score cards are periodically updated as the desired breed type evolves or changes to meet changing economic requirements. For example, the score card for the lard type hog of several decades ago would be quite meaningless today. The same applies to beef cattle. Due to the long dormancy of the purebred draft horse trade and the fact that our colleges have not had draft horses for some time—and they are the chief source of things such as "score cards"—there has been no update on a draft horse card for years. These are two such score cards, one from the 1930s (Fig. 2-17), the other from the 1940s (Fig. 2-18). I'm sure any draft horseman would have no trouble picking an all-night quarrel with either one and on several points. But they do serve to illustrate some of the things talked about in the discussion of conformation and will perhaps give a little more meaning to a draft horse show the next time you attend one. The desired type for the show ring calls for a much taller, hitchier horse than was true when these were devised. For my part, I will certainly quarrel with any score card that assigns only two points out of one hundred to having an energetic, good disposition. That is worth a great deal more than two out of one hundred to me. And so it is with everyone, we all carry our own unofficial score cards around in our heads . . . and are governed by them.

Chapter 3

Buying
a Team

With the foregoing chapters in mind, let us assume that you have decided to buy a team. You probably have some breed preference in mind by now, along with a color prejudice. May I suggest that you leave most of those prejudices behind on the purchase of your first team and simply seek out a well-broke team of horses or mules of about the size you need that you can learn from and feel at ease with. You will find in driving your horses that having two that are gaited alike is much more important than having two that look like peas in a pod. Of course, if you can find two look-alikes that also work well together, so much the better—at least aesthetically. When possible, have a competent draft horse or mule friend with you, one with sense enough to leave his own prejudices behind, who can help you buy a team that will do for you— whether they suit him and his purposes or not.

Hopefully, you will also have some familiarity with horses through your attendance at draft horse shows and auctions, and have a basic knowledge of horses through observation and reading. During this time, you will note in observing experienced horsemen that they follow a pattern when inspecting a horse. It is not a random act. You too will find that it is easier to examine a horse if a logical order is followed. Following are segments of an Iowa State bulletin, called *Examining Horses for Soundness*, written by K. W. Stouder and first published in 1919, suggesting a procedure to use in examining horses for soundness and conformation. We think it makes a lot of sense and are happy to pass it on to you.

Examining the Horse

METHOD OF EXAMINATION

See the animal first in the stable. If at all possible, go there ahead of the owner or attendant to view the horse before he is disturbed in order to notice his attitude, that is, how he holds his head, how he uses his feet, etc.

Slight founder is most likely to be seen in the stable attitude rather than in action. If a "dummy," his head may be resting against the wall or senselessly pushing against the wall with the forehead. A "hoofer" stands with one heel on the coronet of the opposite foot; the marks on the upper forepart of the hoof may betray his trait.

Fig. 3-1.   "Pointing," an indication of lameness

If the animal is in a tie stall, note the bedding, especially near his front feet. Slight lameness which might otherwise go unnoticed will sometimes be indicated here by the "pointing" which has moved away the bedding. Notice the manner of tying. He may be a "weaver," "cribber," or "halter puller." See if the manger is lined with metal to prevent cribbing. Notice the presence of straps or marks of them to prevent cribbing. Notice the breathing while in the stall at rest. See if it is regular and uninterrupted. Make him stand over. Note willingness to obey and disposition and training. Note also any signs of stringhalt or spavin lameness.

PAY ATTENTION TO HIS ATTITUDE

A normal horse often stands at ease on his hind feet, but never rests the fore limbs in the stable unless diseased. Resting of hind legs should not be mistaken for lameness.

Now lead the horse from the stall and stop on arrival at the door. Here is a good place to conduct an examination for blindness. The top light often found over stable doors is a good light for conducting eye examinations. It is not often there is eye trouble which cannot be determined by examination of the front part of the eye. The pupil, or central dark portion, which admits light to the lens has the power to open and close according to the amount of light needed.

Notice quickly when bringing the animal from darkness to bright light to see if there is any tendency for the pupil to contract to accommodate the eye to the increase of light. Failure of the pupil to open and close in changing light conditions indicates impaired eyesight or blindness. Compare the two eyes for size. Repeated attacks of periodic ophthalmia, or moon blindness, often leave one eye smaller than the other. To compensate, the edge of the upper lid often makes a sharp break near its central lower border (familiar to those who have seen moon blindness in horses). Often the pupil may change in size and shape.

Covering of both eyes with the cupped hands for a few minutes, later quickly uncovering them, will reveal the adhesions of the iris, or the muscle which surrounds the pupil, to the lens or cornea, or front of the eyeball. These examinations for moon blindness are important as the disease is fairly com-

Fig. 3-2. Koncarhope, a noted Percheron stallion, on the move. He was an outstanding mover, showing his bottoms and moving straight as a die. A horse is an animal of movement. When examining a horse, have the horse moved away from you at the walk. His feet should be lifted with a snap, and the joints flexed so that the shoe (or bottom of the unshod foot) shows plainly and is carried forward in a straight line with the hocks close. Observe from the side to ascertain the length and freedom of stride—it takes a long stride to cover ground. Then have the horse brought back toward you at the walk. His feet should be lifted clear off the ground, brought straight forward, and meet the ground so that no dirt or dust is kicked forward by the impact. This means that the heel is meeting the ground ahead of the toe. If the toe strikes the ground first you have a stubby, stumbling gait. Repeat the process at a brisk trot. The trot will sometimes bring faults to light that the walk will not. For instance, if he has a tendency to go wide at the hocks, or interferes by going too close, this fault is more likely to show up at the trot. Extremely high-going action usually shortens the stride but looks spectacular.

mon. It is practically always sure to produce blindness eventually and yet at the time of sale there is often no indication of its presence without careful examination.

EXAMINE THE HORSE IN MOTION

Examine the horse in motion and if possible, try him on both hard and soft roads. Have him led properly with a free strap held about eighteen inches from the head. Allow no whip to excite him and thus cover slight lameness. Have him moved from you and towards you at a walk and a trot.

From the side note length of stride and evenness of gait, stumbling, forging and stringhalt. From the front and rear, by observing movement of hind and front limbs, note croup lameness. Look for paddling, the feet going wide or interfering or brushing where the foot of one leg strikes the cannon of the opposite limb.

In lameness of the fore limb, the head nods when weight is placed on the sound limb, while in lameness of the hind limb the croup drops with placing of weight on the sound limb. If equally lame in a pair of limbs, nodding may not be noticeable. A horse is said to be sore when the irregularity of gait is slight; lame when the irregularity is quite apparent and when he hobbles when he bears little or no weight on the diseased member.

A horse should turn easily in a circle, the diameter of which is equal to the length of his body. Turn him in a circle to detect soreness, stringhalt, or a slight or hidden hock lameness.

To be thorough, examine him when cool, warmed up and cooled off again. Splint lameness will usually get worse with exercise; spavin lameness becomes less noticeable as the exercise goes on. After exercise, bring him to a standstill on level ground, the feet being placed naturally by moving him backward and forward.

Watch the attendant. He may attempt to place the horse in a forced position or restrain him in some way. See if the horse will keep that position. This may reveal something which the attendant is endeavoring to conceal. Abnormal positions in the posture of the animal are sometimes used to mask defects. The free station of an animal is represented by a triangle, with one of three feet placed at each angle in support of the body; the fourth limb, generally a hind one if the animal is sound, is half bent and resting on the toe. A horse does not change position of front limbs unless greatly fatigued or lame. If lame or sore, the limbs are often moved up and down or backward and forward to relieve the tendon strain.

GENERAL EXAMINATION

Close attention tends to lessen dangers of overlooking any defect. When the horse is in proper position, make a general survey of him at four or five steps distance. Beginners are apt to lay hands on the subject too soon.

Commence at the head and estimate general size, conformation, type and adaptation to the service he is to be used in. Notice carriage and position of ears, position of limbs and any visible lesions on them, such as shoe boil, splint, windpuffs, ring bones or side bones, buck knees, bog and bone spavin, thorough pin, curbs, cocked ankles and any other conditions you want to investigate further.

Examine the four feet in regular order, tapping the sole with a solid object to see if he will stand shoeing and to observe cracks of wall and dropping of sole or contraction of heels. Passing upward from the foot for convenience, the parts to be examined are the pastern, the fetlock, cannon and knee in the fore limb. In the hind limbs, the parts are the same to the cannon. Above the cannon the hind knee is called the hock. Above the hock is the gaskin, then the stifle and then the hip.

Examine the trunk, and particularly note the flank to observe the respiration or breathing. In healthy animals the respirations are single, in emphysema, commonly called "heaves" there is a double lifting of the flank. Press the larynx (Adam's apple) to produce a cough.

Examine each part quickly but thoroughly.

WINDING THE ANIMAL

The process known as "winding" the horse should be thorough. Always try an animal in his own class. A saddler should be ridden, the light driver hitched, and the drafter made to pull. This is to determine adaptability and willingness as well as style, carriage and gait. When they are brought in, go the last fifty feet with them to detect any obscure breathing difficulties. Heaves and roaring are watched for at this time. Weak fetlocks or pitched ankles usually tremble after sharp exercise.

Exercise often starts a discharge from the nostrils if there is a collection of pus in the sinuses or cavities of the head. Examine the face for scars of trephining or opening the sinuses, twitch marks on nose and ears, and evidence of blisters. Observe any swellings or indentations indicating diseased teeth and feel the poll to determine if poll-evil has existed at any time. On the neck, scars of operations such as tracheotomy and seton marks may be observed.

EXAMINING THE FEET AND LIMBS

Now examine the fore limbs, beginning at the feet. The normal fore foot of a horse should be made up of good, dense horn of uniform color. The horny box known as the hoof is an appendage of the skin produced by an outgrowth of horny fibers from the coronary band, a heavy fold of skin at the top of the hoof, as well as the fleshy leaves which cover the wall of the coffin bone.

The hoof is studied in three parts: wall, sole, and frog. The wall should be a dense, hard horn of uniform color and density, have a circular outline at the lower extremity, with a slightly greater curve at the outer edge than in the inner, and a slope in front hoofs of about 45° at the toe, so that the top of the hoof is smaller than the bearing surface. The toe should be about twice as long as the heels and the wall at all points smooth, showing no ridges or bands. The slant of the hoof should continue in the slant of the pastern. In hind limbs, the foot is slightly straighter than in front, usually having an angle at the toe of about 50 to 55° with the ground. It is also somewhat narrower than the fore hoof.

Lift the foot and look at the bearing surface. This shows the bearing surface of the wall, which is nearly a circle open behind and bears most of the weight with the frog.

The sole should be arched enough so that it does not touch the ground or show "flat" or "dropped sole." Corns are to be looked for in the sole. The frog, a triangular elastic pad in the back part of the foot, should be full and elastic, have straight sides and help to bear weight. It should never be trimmed so thin that it will not bear weight. At each side of the frog are the bars which support the edge of the sole. These should be prominent, strong and not twisted or curved. Over all the hoof which is visible as the horse stands, the periople, a shining varnish, is spread by nature. It is to prevent undue drying and should not be rasped off under any conditions.

In examining the hoof, look in the wall for cracks at quarter and toe caused by faulty trimming and unbalanced weight bearing, or excessive dryness of horn. Rasping and rounding sharp edges and corners usually repairs this in time. The removal of weight bearing horn between the bottom of the hoof crack and the bottom of a perpendicular line dropped from the head of the hoof crack to the ground, or a perpendicular groove cut deeply with a rasp across the top of a toe or quarter crack often stops its further course. Look for rings on the wall which indicate unbalanced nutrition and at times indicate founder. Observe any calk wounds, and unusual length of toe or heel, which may add needless strain or shock in travel.

Checking for Unsoundness

Throughout your careful examination of the horse, you should be particularly aware of any unsoundness that could be a source of future problems for the animal—and, in turn, for you.

In 1939 Michigan State University put out a fine bulletin called *Guides for Horse Buyers*. It was written by R. S.

Hudson in response to an increasing number of requests for information from farmers and inexperienced men who wish to buy horses. So much uncertainty exists regarding age and soundness in horses that this publication is written and illustrated particularly to give assistance along those lines. It is a very good bulletin, unfortunately out of print. Since history seems to have repeated itself and there is again a demand for this information, the following several pages are reprinted from that bulletin.

INFLUENCE OF CARE AND FEEDING UPON VALUE

The buyer must remember that the well-fed, properly groomed horse always shows to advantage. If a horse has received excellent care for a considerable period but is still thin and rundown in condition, he may be either a very poor feeder and hard keeper, infested with parasites, suffering from a chronic disease, or has bad teeth. If no cause is obvious for the unthrifty appearance, it is advisable not to purchase the animal. On the other hand, many thin and poorly-cared-for individuals will respond quickly to good care and feeding and may become better animals than pampered highly fitted horses.

TEMPERAMENT AND VICES

The disposition of a horse must always be considered in determining his value. The ideal draft horse should be well-trained, quiet and docile, yet always alert and willing to do his work. Horsemen believe a wide, full forehead, well-carried ear and large prominent eye indicate a good disposition. The buyer should always ask that the horse be tried at the different types of work which he will expect the horse to perform.

Many of the common vices and habits may be detected by a careful examination of the horse and his stall.

Cribbing and Wind Sucking—This condition is indicated by freshly chewed mangers or feed boxes. The incisor teeth of the confirmed cribber are sometimes worn fairly short.

Halter Pulling—Halter pullers usually wear a very heavy halter or are tied with a heavy rope or chain around the neck.

Kicking—A kicker may be detected by examining the stall partitions for hoof or shoe marks. Heavy chains or bags of straw are sometimes suspended from the ceiling in an attempt to discourage this habit. Capped hocks or scarred hind legs indicate that the horse may be a kicker.

LAMENESS

Lameness is any irregularity in gait which results from moving with pain or difficulty because of some defect. Severe lameness may make a horse worthless; any lameness lowers his value.

Severe lameness may often be detected by examining the horse in the standing position. If the lameness is severe enough, he will refuse to place any weight whatsoever on the affected limb. "Pointing," or placing the limb in an unnatural position indicates that pain exists in that limb.

Most lameness may be detected at the walk, although the symptoms are usually accentuated at the trot. Since the individual is forced to carry most or all of his weight on the sound limb there is always a sinking or "nodding" of the hip or head as the sound limb strikes the ground. When the lameness is in the left fore leg, for example, the head will "nod" as the right foot is planted on the ground but will jerk up as the left or lame leg touches the ground. Lameness in the rear limbs may be detected in the same manner by observing the motion of the hips. The hip opposite the lame leg always drops as the sound foot hits the ground. Always observe the horse carefully from in front, from behind, and from the side.

Lameness in both front legs is indicated by stiff stilted action and short stride, which often gives the impression of stiffness in the shoulders. The head is carried higher than usual without "nodding." The hind feet are lifted high while the front feet scarcely leave the ground as the horse moves. When at rest, the weight of the body is constantly shifted from one foot to the other and the hind feet may be cramped under the body in an attempt to relieve the pain in the front feet. Such symptoms are characteristic of navicular disease.

Symptoms of lameness in both hind limbs are short stride, awkward gait, and lowered head. The front feet are raised higher than usual as the horse walks. It is very difficult or impossible to back a horse that is lame in both hind legs. When at rest the horse is very uneasy and constantly shifts his weight from one leg to another.

A swinging leg lameness is a symptom of pain resulting from advancing the limb. This type of lameness usually results from inflammation occurring above the knee or hock. A supporting leg lameness is characterized by pain when weight is put on the limb.

Shoulder lameness occurs occasionally but is less frequent than most horsemen believe. As the affected limb is advanced, pain is produced, resulting in a short stride and dragging of the toe of that limb.

The exact location of the lameness is usually more difficult to determine. Many common unsoundnesses of the limbs may be observed by carefully comparing the general outline of the opposite legs. Swellings or bony growths can usually be detected in this manner. Inflammatory areas can usually be detected by pressing the region firmly with the fingers. Many cases require the services of a veterinarian for a correct diagnosis.

Unscrupulous dealers often resort to many methods of relieving symptoms of lameness. If the lameness is slight, the sound foot is sometimes made equally lame by cutting the hoof to the sensitive portion in order to make the gait appear normal. Drugs are sometimes injected to deaden the nerves of the foot in order to relieve the pain which causes the animal to limp. Holding the rein close to the head when leading may prevent "nodding."

COMMON UNSOUNDNESSES

The horse buyer must be familiar with common unsoundnesses in order to evaluate a horse properly. The following discussions give a definition, description, and the usual causes of the most common unsoundnesses.

The subject of transmissible unsoundnesses is widely debated. Probably no disease is actually inherited, but the fact that individuals may inherit a predisposition to unsoundnesses through faulty conformation cannot be questioned. This predisposition to contract bone diseases is particularly marked; hence, breeding stock should be absolutely free from bone spavin, ringbone, sidebone, and similar diseases.

Defective Eyes   The eyes should always be examined very closely with a flashlight in a darkened stall, or by standing the horse in an open doorway. Cataracts and cloudiness of the cornea usually are easily detected. Other defects are not so easily observed, but the general expression of the head, with unnatural carriage of the ears, may indicate poor eyesight. The horse that is partially blind usually shies at objects, keeps his ears constantly moving, and stumbles frequently.

A pale blue or cloudy, watery eye is characteristic of periodic ophthalmia or "moon blindness." Since the eye may appear quite normal after recovery from the first few attacks, an examination of the interior of the eye by a veterinarian is necessary to determine if the horse is suffering from this disease. Repeated attacks of periodic ophthalmia usually produce permanent blindness in one or both eyes.

Poll-evil   Poll-evil is a fistula of the poll. It is similar to fistula of the withers except for location. Poll-evil usually follows a severe bruise of the poll or constant irritation produced by a tightly fitting halter or bridle. This condition must always be :egarded as serious. Many cases of poll-evil can be cured; the treatment, however, in most cases must be continued for many weeks under the direction of a veterinarian. Permanent scars are sometimes left as a result of the disease, and the horse may become "touchy" about the head and ears, making it difficult to halter or bridle him.

Fistula of the Withers   Fistula of the withers (see Fig. 3-3) usually follows a sore on the neck caused by a collar that does not fit properly. The fistula first appears as a large, hot, painful, fluctuating swelling upon the withers, which finally ruptures, permitting pus to escape. Some fistulas heal, leaving a large, fibrous tumor, but most of them continue to discharge pus indefinitely and show no tendency to heal. A large percentage of these cases may be successfully treated and cured by a veterinarian. The treatment, however, often has to be continued for many weeks. In cases where a surgical operation is necessary, permanent scars may be left.

Sweeney   Sweeney is an atrophy or decrease in size of a single muscle or a group of muscles. The term is commonly applied to the extreme atrophy of the shoulder muscle. It is usually caused by a blow, ill-fitting collar or severe strain. Sweeney of the hip may follow difficulty in foaling or an attack of azoturia. Some cases of sweeney recover after a few months' rest. Blisters and subcutaneous irritants applied under the direction of a veterinarian may hasten recovery.

Fig. 3-3.   Fistula of the withers

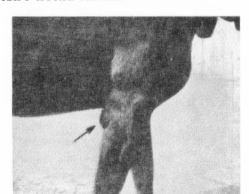

Fig. 3-4.   Shoe boil

Shoe Boil or Capped Elbow   Capped elbow or shoe boil is
a swelling at the point of the elbow (see Fig. 3-4). This condition is usually caused by constant irritation of the heel or shoe
upon the point of the elbow when the horse lies with the front
leg flexed underneath the body. Recovery usually follows
proper treatment.

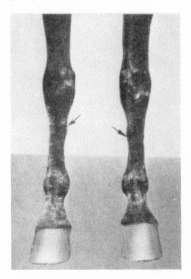

Fig. 3-5.   Splints   **Fig. 3-6.**   Wind-galls

Splint   A splint (see Fig. 3-5) is a bony enlargement usually found on the inside of the upper part of the front cannon bone of young horses. It may occasionally occur on the outside of the front cannon bone but is rarely seen on the rear cannon. Splints usually follow kicks, over-exertion or concussions produced by working on hard surfaces. The bony growth may result from irritation between the large cannon bone and small splint bone. Splints are very common blemishes of draft horses. Aside from the slight lameness which rarely occurs during the first stages of formation, splints are of little importance since horse dealers and judges ignore them almost entirely.

Wind-gall, Road-gall, Wind-puff, or Road-puff   Wind-galls (see Fig. 3-6) are small, puffy swellings which usually occur on each side of the tendons just above the fetlock or knee. Wind-galls are much more common in the young, light-legged breeds of horses than in draft horses. They are formed by an excessive secretion of synovia which distends the sheaths surrounding the tendons. Severe strain, over-exertion or infectious disease may be predisposing factors. Wind-galls are not often considered serious since they usually disappear and cause no lameness unless pathological changes occur within them.

Ringbone   Ringbone (see Fig. 3-7) is a bony growth on either or both of the bones of the pastern which may involve the joints, a result of sprains induced by violent exercise, or severe blows. The ringbone may appear as a hard bony swelling on any part of the pastern. It may be so small that it escapes notice or as large as a walnut or even larger. The outlines of right and left pasterns should always be compared in cases of doubt. Small ringbones may be felt by carefully passing the hand over the pastern. Lameness usually develops gradually but may appear suddenly after severe strain, and is most evident when the horse is required to step from side to side. The lameness produced may not be proportionate to the size of the growth, since a small ringbone may sometimes

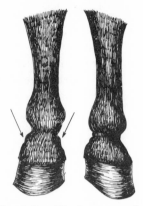

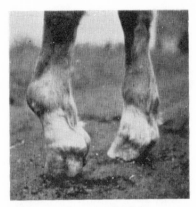

Fig. 3-7. Ringbone on the bones of the pastern

Fig. 3-8. Contracted tendons, cocked ankle, or knuckling

produce a more serious lameness than a larger one. The location of the swelling is of most importance. Ringbone at the front or rear of the pastern usually produces severe lameness because it interferes with the free movement of tendons. Ringbone on either side of the pastern is usually less serious. Severe chronic lameness always results if the joints become involved. There is no treatment known which will remove the bony enlargement, but firing or blistering may cause the bones of the diseased joints to grow together, thus relieving the pain. Nerving is occasionally performed as a last resort. The horse must be rested from four to six weeks after treatment.

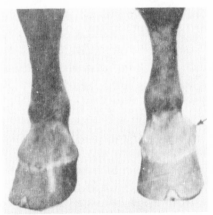

Fig. 3-9. Sidebone

Fig. 3-10. Quittor

Contracted Tendons, Cocked Ankle, or Knuckling   Contracted tendons, cocked ankle, or knuckling (see Fig. 3-8) is a partial dislocation of the fetlock or pastern joint produced by the shortening of the tendons at the back part of the cannon. The tendons may contract as a result of over-exertion, founder, or a local inflammation of the tendons. Knuckling must always be regarded as very serious, although some cases may be cured by expert veterinary surgery. Colts usually have a better chance for recovery than mature horses.

Sidebone   Sidebone (see Fig. 3-9) is an ossification of the lateral cartilage of the foot. The lateral cartilages extend upward above the margin of the hoof so that they may easily be felt under the skin. These cartilages are normally firm and elastic but yield to the pressure of the fingers. Depositions of mineral salts in these cartilages change them to bone so that they become very hard and unyielding to pressure, producing the condition known as sidebone. Sidebones usually occur on the front feet as a result of concussion or injury. They are common in draft horses more than two years old and vary greatly in size and severity. If lameness occurs, it is usually intermittent in character and rarely severe. Although sidebones are considered serious in show and breeding stock, they rarely produce lameness. Sidebones cannot be removed. "Nerving" is sometimes performed if the lameness is severe and persistent. Treatment should be followed by complete rest.

Quittor   Quittor (see Fig. 3-10) is a decay of the lateral cartilage of the foot characterized by a discharge of pus through a fistulous tract extending from the cartilage to the coronet or hoof head. Quittor produces severe lameness and shows no tendency to heal. Quittor is more common in the front feet but may sometimes occur in the hind feet. The degree of severity of this unsoundness is dependent upon the structures of the foot which are involved, although all cases must be considered serious. Many cases may be cured by an operation, but several months of rest are required for complete healing.

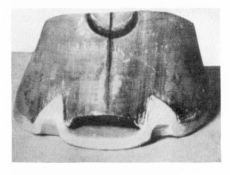

Fig. 3-11. Hoof showing sand-crack and the method of treatment

Fig. 3-12. Foundered hoof

Quarter-crack or Sand-crack   Quarter-crack or sand-crack (see Fig. 3-11) is a vertical split in the wall of the hoof which results from a dry or brittle hoof or improper shoeing. Proper treatment may hasten recovery, but lameness sometimes remains severe until the new hoof has formed. About twelve months are required for the growth of a new toe, while the heels grow in less than half that time.

Navicular Disease   Navicular disease is an inflammation of the small navicular bone and bursa inside the hoof just behind the coffin bone and small pastern bone of the front foot. The symptoms of this condition are "pointing" when at rest (see Fig. 3-1) and a short, stubby, painful stride which may give the impression that the horse is lame in the shoulders. Navicular disease is incurable. In selected cases, veterinarians sometimes perform a nerving operation that will relieve the lameness and increase the usefulness of the horse for a time.

Founder or Laminitis   Founder or laminitis (see Fig. 3-12) is an inflammation of the sensitive leaves which attach the hoof to the fleshy portion of the foot. It is usually the result of over-feeding, infectious disease, allowing the animal to drink too much cold water when overheated, long shipment or standing in a stall for long periods because of some other lameness. Founder may also follow foaling, as a result of infection and inflammation of the uterus. The chief symptoms are extreme pain in the feet and a high fever. All the feet may be affected, but the front feet are more susceptible. If laminitis is properly treated as soon as it occurs, most cases will completely recover in a few days. If the disease is neglected, however, it will often become chronic, resulting in a dropping of the hoof soles and a turning-up of the toe walls (chronic deformities of the hoof that are incurable). Call a competent veterinarian immediately. Early treatment is important since the course of the disease during the first three days determines whether it will develop into a chronic condition. The affected feet should be soaked in the coldest water obtainable. Use ice if available. If the condition seems to have been brought on by over-eating, prompt purgation is important.

If the disease develops into chronic laminitis, the animal will probably need special shoes for the rest of its life. Bar shoes are generally used for this purpose. These should be made without toe calks, having a rolling toe, and be fitted with quarter calks. They should be designed to apply as much frog pressure as possible.

Thrush   Thrush is a disease caused by decomposition of stable manure and other filth that is allowed to collect in the cleft of the horn frog, between the frog and the bars. Old, severe cases of thrush occasionally produce lameness, but most cases respond to cleanliness and proper treatment. (See Chapter 6 for further discussion.)

Scratches or Grease Heel   Scratches or grease heel is an inflammation of the posterior surfaces of the fetlocks characterized by extensive scab formations. Heavy, highly fitted show horses seem most susceptible to this condition. Most cases respond to treatment.

Stifled   A horse is said to be stifled when the patella of the stifle joint is displaced (see Fig. 3-13). If the patella is displaced toward the outside of the leg the condition is serious and usually incurable. If the displacement is in an upward direction, the reaction to a sudden fright that causes the horse to jump may throw the patella back to its normal position. However, this condition is likely to recur quite frequently.

Stringhalt   Stringhalt is a nervous disorder characterized by a sudden, involuntary flexion of one or both hocks in which the foot is jerked up much higher than normal. The symptoms are usually noticed as the horse is backing from his stall, turning on the affected leg, or when suddenly frightened. The exact cause is unknown, although many horsemen consider the disease hereditary. Stringhalt may be so mild that the jerking is noticed only occasionally or so severe that the leg is jerked upward at each step. Some cases may be cured by surgery.

Thoroughpin   Thoroughpin (see Fig. 3-14) is a soft puffy swelling which occurs on each side of the gaskin just above the hock in the region known as the "hollow." Pressure exerted on one side decreases the swelling on that side but increases the swelling on the opposite side. Lameness does not usually occur, but the condition greatly decreases the sale value of a horse and renders him worthless as a show animal. Most thoroughpins are incurable.

Bog Spavin   Bog spavin (see Fig. 3-15) is a large, soft, fluctuating swelling which usually occurs on the front and inside of the hock. This condition is fairly common in heavy highly fitted horses with soft, meaty hocks. It results from an excess secretion of joint fluids which produces a distention of the joint capsule. A bog spavin is very easily seen and is much larger than a blood spavin. Although a bog spavin does not usually cause lameness, its presence indicates a lack of wearing qualities and is the object of very unfavorable comment among judges and horsemen. Treatment is usually unsuccessful.

Blood Spavin   Blood spavin is a swelling over the front and inside of the hock caused by the dilation of the large vein which crosses that region. Since lameness never occurs, this condition may be regarded as a blemish of very little significance.

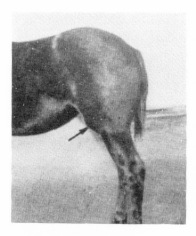

Fig. 3-13.   Stifled

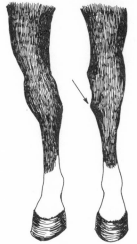

Fig. 3-14.   Thoroughpin

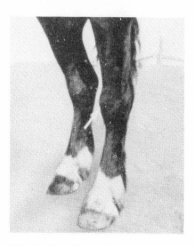

Fig. 3-15.   Bog spavin

Fig. 3-16.   Bone spavin

Bone Spavin or Jack   Bone spavin (see Fig. 3-16) is a bony growth which may occur on any of the bones which form the hock, although it is usually found on the inside and lower portions. It is caused by an inflammation of the periosteum such as may be produced by strain or over-exertion. Since a predis-position to the disease may be hereditary, affected animals should not be used for breeding purposes. The spavin usually may be seen by one standing directly behind or in front and a little to one side of the horse. In cases of doubt, lift the foot upward and forward in order to bend the hock as much as possible. After holding for two or three minutes, release the leg and start the horse at a brisk trot. A characteristic lame-ness will sometimes be noticed if the individual is affected. Bone spavin is one of the most serious unsoundnesses of the draft horse. The lameness persists until the diseased bones of the hock grow together, preventing movement. Firing tends to make the bones unite and will often relieve lameness if only the flat bones of the hock are affected. If the spavin is exten-sive, the entire hock may become stiff, rendering the horse worthless.

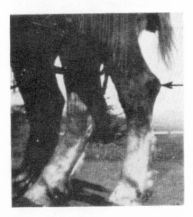
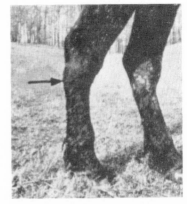

Fig. 3-17. Capped hock   **Fig. 3-18.** Curb

Capped Hock   Capped hock (see Fig. 3-17) is a firm swell-ing which occurs on the point of the hock. This blemish may be as large as an apple or so small that it escapes notice. Capped hock usually results from constant irritation, such as might be produced by rubbing or kicking the walls of the sta-ble; hence it may be indicative of the horse's disposition. Since lameness rarely occurs, the condition is not considered serious.

Curb   Curb (see Fig. 3-18) is a hard, firm swelling on the back surface of the rear cannon, about a hand's breadth below the point of the hock. A large curb is easily seen by observing the hock and cannon directly from the side. A smaller one may be felt by passing the fingers over the region. Crooked or sickle hocks are most subject to this unsoundness since this faulty conformation throws a greater strain on the hock. A curb usually follows strain or over-exertion but may result from a kick or blow. The initial lameness disappears after the formation of the curb, but the condition must still be considered an unsoundness because an affected hock is thought to be less likely to endure severe strain. Horsemen and judges look upon a curb with a great deal of criticism, although some horses are useful for light farm work for many years after they develop this unsoundness for which there is no cure.

White Horse Tumors, Black Pigment Tumors, or Melanomas   White horse tumors, black pigment tumors, or melanomas are common in old white horses but may occur in a horse of any color. They are usually found in the naturally black areas of the skin, especially around the anus. The tumor may remain small and harmless or become malignant and spread throughout the internal organs producing death. There is no effective treatment.

Hernia or Rupture   A hernia (see Fig. 3-19) is the protrusion of any internal organ through the wall of the containing cavity. The term commonly means the passage of intestine or omentum through an opening in the abdominal muscles. This type of hernia is usually caused by severe blows, kicks, or over-exertion. Death will occur if the hernial opening swells around the loop of intestine so that the circulation and passage of the intestinal contents is stopped. Umbilical, scrotal, and inguinal hernias are fairly common in young foals but sometimes disappear with age. Scrotal and inguinal hernias are often fatal in stallions if they become strangulated. Mares suffering from any type of hernia should never be used for breeding purposes. Many hernias may be cured by surgery. The operation, however, is usually a major one in which there is always an element of danger.

Thick Wind and Roaring   All horses should be given fast exercise immediately before examining their wind. "Thick wind" is difficult respiration due to any obstruction of the respiratory tract. The respiratory sound is usually made both on inspiration and expiration. "Thick wind" may be cured if it

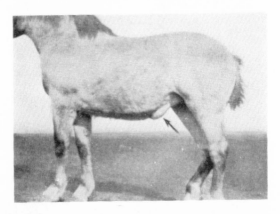

Fig. 3-19.   Umbilical hernia

is possible to remove the obstruction in the respiratory tract. "Roaring" is a whistling sound made only on inspiration of air. It is caused by a paralysis of the nerve which passes to the muscles of the larnyx. As a result, the laryngeal muscles atrophy and allow the vocal cords to relax and vibrate as air is inhaled. A large percentage of "roarers" are cured or improved by the roaring operation.

Heaves, Asthma, or Broken Wind   Heaves, asthma, or broken wind is an incurable disease of the lungs characterized by difficult expiration, characteristic movement of the abdomen and flanks, and a peculiar cough which is often accompanied by the expulsion of gas from the bowels. The disease is common in horses more than seven years of age. Improperly cured hay and strenuous work are believed to be predisposing factors. Contrary to popular opinion, the onset of the disease is usually gradual although the symptoms may appear suddenly after very strenuous work or over-heating, hence the term "broken wind" is often used. It is possible for unscrupulous dealers to "fix" heavey horses temporarily so that the symptoms are not apparent. However, the symptoms will usually reappear if the horse is given all the water he will drink and trotted briskly. Heaves is incurable although a veterinarian may prescribe drugs which will restore the usefulness of the horse for a time.

Determining the Age of the Horse

Probably the most reliable way for the experienced buyer to determine the age of a horse or mule is by examining the teeth. This method of establishing the age of animals is ancient, but still fairly reliable, and relies on both a knowledge of when certain teeth erupt in the mouth of a horse and a careful consideration of the wear of other teeth. The following article is reprinted from USDA Farmer's Bulletin 1721.

The ordinary observer can readily learn to tell the age of horses or mules with considerable accuracy until the animals have passed their eighth year. Beyond this time even those who are experienced may find it difficult to determine the exact age.

The mature male horse has forty teeth. Twenty-four of these are molars or grinders, twelve are incisors or front teeth, and four are tushes or pointed teeth. The two central incisors are known as centrals or nippers; the next two, one on each side of the nippers, are called intermediates or middles, and the last, or outer pair, the corners. The tushes are located between the incisors and the molars. They are not usually present in the mare, and accordingly she may be considered to have a total of thirty-six teeth, rather than forty, as in the male.

The young animal, whether male or female, has twenty-four temporary teeth, commonly called milk teeth, as they are much whiter than the permanent teeth. These milk teeth consist of twelve incisors and twelve molars. The latter are the three back teeth on each side of both the upper and lower jaw. The milk teeth are shed and replaced by permanent teeth at fairly definite periods, which serve as an index in determining the age of young colts.

Fig. 3-20. Temporary incisors to ten days of age: First or central upper and lower temporary incisors appear.

Fig. 3-21. Temporary incisors at four to six weeks of age: Second or intermediate upper and lower temporary incisors appear.

The temporary central incisors or nippers may be present at birth (see Fig. 3-20); otherwise they appear before the colt is ten days old. There are two in each jaw.

At the age of from four to six weeks the two temporary intermediates, upper and lower, appear (see Fig. 3-21). These teeth immediately adjoin the nippers.

When the colt is from six to ten months old the corner or outer incisors, two above and two below, are cut (see Fig. 3-22). This gives the young animals a full set of temporary front teeth.

By the time the colt has reached the age of one year the crowns of the central incisors show wear (see Fig. 3-23). In another six months the intermediates or middles are worn (see Fig. 3-24), and at two years all the teeth are worn (see Fig. 3-25). During the following six months there are no changes which will distinguish the exact age. At about two and one half years, however, the shedding of the milk teeth begins and at three years the temporary central nippers, two above and two below, are replaced by the permanent central incisors.

Fig. 3-22. Temporary incisors at six to ten months: Third or corner upper and lower temporary incisors appear.

Fig. 3-23. Temporary incisors at one year: Crowns of central temporary incisors show wear.

Fig. 3-24. Temporary incisors at 1½ years: Intermediate temporary incisors show wear.

Fig. 3-25. Temporary incisors at two years: All show wear.

Fig. 3-26. Incisors at four years: Permanent incisors replace temporary centrals and intermediates; temporary corner incisors remain.

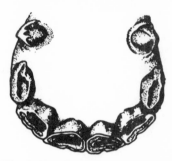

Fig. 3-27. Incisors at five years: All permanent; cups in all incisors.

Fig. 3-28. Incisors at six years: Cups worn out of lower central incisors.

Fig. 3-29. Incisors at seven years: Cups worn out of lower intermediate incisors.

At four years of age the four permanent intermediates have taken the place of the four temporary middles (see Fig. 3-26). When the animal is about four and one half years old the shedding of the four corners begins, and at five years the permanent teeth which replace them are well up but not in contact (see Fig. 3-27).

In a six-year-old horse the corner incisors are on a level with the adjoining teeth, with a well-marked dental cavity or "cup" showing practically no wear. The nippers show wear over the entire surface; the "cup" though visible, shows indications of gradual disappearance and at this stage is without a hollow (see Fig. 3-28).

When the animal is seven years old, not only the nippers but also the middles show wear (see Fig. 3-29). Each upper corner tooth has an indentation caused by wear from the corresponding lower tooth, resulting in a downward triangular projection of the posterior edge. This projection is commonly termed "dovetail" (see Fig. 3-35).

In the eight-year-old horse all the incisors are worn, the cup has entirely disappeared from the nippers, but shows to a

Fig. 3-30. Incisors at eight years: Cups worn out of all lower incisors, and dental star (dark line in front of cup) appears on lower central and intermediate pairs.

Fig. 3-31. Incisors at nine years: Cups worn out of upper central incisors; dental star on upper central and intermediate pairs.

slight extent in the middles, and is still well marked in the corners. At this stage what is termed the "dental star" makes its appearance as a yellow transverse line just back of the front edge of the table, or flat surface, of the nippers and middles (see Fig. 3-30). The dark line in front of the cup is the dental star.

Between the ages of nine and thirteen years there is a gradual change in the contour of the tables and the incisors. In a nine-year-old animal the nippers take on a more or less rounded contour; the dental cavity or cup has disappeared from all but the corners; the dental star is found in both the nippers and the middles and the former is near the center of the table (see Fig. 3-31).

Fig. 3-32. Incisors at ten years: Cups worn out of upper intermediate incisors; dental star is present in all incisors.

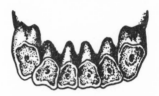

Fig. 3-33. Incisors at eleven or twelve years: Cups worn in all incisors (smooth mouthed); dental star approaches center of cups.

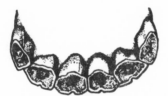

Fig. 3-34. Characteristic shape of lower incisors at eighteen years

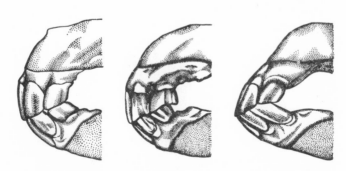

Fig. 3-35. Side view of five-, seven-, and twenty-year-old mouths. Note that as the horse advances in age, the teeth change from nearly perpendicular to slanting sharply toward the front.

At ten years the middles become rounded, and the dental star, now seen on all the incisors, is near the center of both the nippers and middles (see Fig. 3-32).

At eleven or twelve years the corners have a somewhat rounded form, and the dental star approaches the center of the table (see Fig. 3-33). As the horse reaches thirteen years of age all the lower incisors are unmistakably rounded, the dental star is found in the center of all the tables, and the enamel rings which formerly surrounded the cups have entirely disappeared.

In a horse about fourteen years of age the tables of the incisors begin to change from a rounded to a triangular contour. This change occurs in the nippers at fourteen years, in the middles at fifteen years, and in the corners at sixteen or seventeen years. During the following four years after the appearance of the triangle, there is a gradual approach of the tables to the form of a rectangle (see Fig. 3-34).

The teeth during this period are usually elongated and directed obliquely. The dental arch also becomes contracted and pointed and the under edges of the lower jaw are thin and sharp as compared with the appearance of a young horse (see Fig. 3-35 for comparison of five-, seven-, and twenty-year-old mouths). Should the horse live more than twenty years, these conditions become marked and are accompanied by excessive wear and loosening or loss of molars.

TAMPERED OR "BISHOPED" TEETH

Occasionally unscrupulous dealers drill or burn cups in the teeth of old horses in an attempt to make them sell as young horses. This condition may sometimes be recognized by noting the slanting position and triangular cross section of the teeth as well as by the absence of the enamel ring around the cup. A veterinarian should be asked to examine the teeth if the buyer has any reason to suspect they have been tampered with.

Learning to Determine Size

In trying to mate a horse it is important that you be able to determine size with some degree of precision. After being around horses and attending a few auctions you will, of course, be able to form a general idea just by looking. But you can still get fooled if you don't chin the horse in question.

On a wall measure height in hands from fourteen to eighteen hands, remembering that a hand is four inches. Thus, your bottom measurement will be fifty-six inches and your top one seventy-two inches with two- or four-inch increments in between. Then stand up to this standard squarely and measure with the flat of your hand toward your face until you determine how many hands you are at the top of your head, your eye level, mouth, etc.

Having thus learned your own dimensions in terms of hands, you can then readily estimate the height of horses or mules. Stand squarely beside the animal, and at the same level just opposite the withers; place your hand, held flat, palm down, on top of the withers and then draw it straight out toward you until it touches your face. Knowing the height in hands at various points on your face, you can make a very close judgement on the height of the animal, and know about how he will fit with the one at home, at least in that respect.

In my own case, my facial features are not too useful in measuring big horses since I stand but sixteen hands plus two inches to the top of my head. Nonetheless, by determining where that strikes a big horse below the point of the withers I can usually come close enough.

The best definition of where to measure a horse is one used by Dave Haxton, one of America's all-time great heavy horsemen. He says when a horse is eating grass his highest point is the point of the withers. Common sense. Of course, they are never eating grass when you measure them—usually the fellow on the lead strap has the head as high as he can get it, but nonetheless, it is a useful definition. A horse that is overly conditioned may fool you a bit with an inch of lard over the bone, but by using this method you won't bring one home that is three or four inches taller than his intended mate in your barn . . . unless it is a very cloudy day.

I think it might be a trifle more accurate to measure when they are eating from a bucket held for them. To reach the ground, some horses will spread their front legs, thus making them measure a little shorter than if you measured them while they are eating from a bucket.

Going to a Horse Sale

I hope your experiences at horse sales are pleasant ones and that your first purchase turns out to be a continuing pleasure for many years. Auctions are strange institutions. They are like colic in that they affect people differently. Some are intoxicated by them, others intimidated. Anyhow, if it has reached the stage of either intoxication or intimidation, the following suggestions might be helpful.

Do not let time be your enemy. Arrive in plenty of time to inspect the horses at *your pace* before the sale. If it is preceded by a show, watch them move when being shown; if it is a broke team you are looking for, watch them hitched. Observe the horses' ears, feet, and manners at all times, including in the stalls, and watch the way the handlers behave, too. Having done this, you will have a few horses in mind that will fit your bill of particulars. Acquaint yourself with the selling order and watch a bunch of the others go, getting a feel of the market as the sale progresses.

Visit with the owners of your prospects before the sale, and give *them* a close inspection. Ask them all the questions you would ask if you were looking at the horses in their barnlot at home. You won't have the opportunity to ask these questions when the horses are in the ring. Satisfy yourself on the horse by observation and questions before he ever gets that far.

Acquaint yourself with the vocabulary. Here are some common terms that you are likely to encounter:

Serviceably Sound—nothing wrong that will seriously interfere with the horses' ability to work.

Choice or Privilege—the *choice* of taking one of a team at bid price or the *privilege* of taking both at two times the money.

Two Times the Money—the bid is for one horse, but you are obliged to take them both at two times the money. (Sometimes during the course of bidding on a pair, choice or privilege, one of the bidders will indicate that his bid is for both, two times the money, and thus force his contenders to bid on both.)

Hard on the Heels—generally a polite way to say "sidebones."

Other Unsoundnesses—this was dealt with at length previously. At a reputable auction and from reputable consignors, unsoundness should be called.

Bruises—often happen in shipment. The usual term is that it doesn't "belong to him"—in other words, it will go away.

Green Broke—this can mean an awful lot of different things to a lot of people. If you are green, you better leave the green broke ones to someone else. In auctions where the hitch wagon is used prior to the sale you will have an opportunity to watch them go, and that is the best arrangement. In other situations it will pretty much be the seller's word, and that can be just as good—or shaky—as the seller himself. Generally if a horse is broke both single and double and will work on one side as well as on the other, this will be stated.

There has been a bit written about the "psychology of bidding." Some of it may be true. Some writers urge boldness to scare off the contenders. Others, timidity, for reasons that now escape me. The point is, bold or timid, fast or slow, it will probably be a reflection of you generally and be about the same way you would play a hand of poker. There is no "right way" to bid, or, if it *is* right for you, it mightn't be for me.

It is important for the newcomer to have limits. After he has assessed the animals available, he should have a very clear idea of just what he will pay for a given team or animal. The best time to decide what something is worth is at your leisure; i.e., before the auction commences. So whatever your style of bidding, have your price tag firmly in mind, and quit when the bidding hits that point. If you have been right in your previous assessment, you will have no cause for regret about the ones you didn't get. If you are too low in your prior assessments you will never get any bought. This will not cost much, and you will probably have more time and money to attend more sales than the successful bidder. If this becomes a habit, you can be pretty sure that horses are worth more than you think they are and either raise your intended bid or become a pure spectator. Good luck.

Chapter 4

Machinery for the Horsepowered Farm

I've already briefly discussed some of the problems one encounters in obtaining horse-drawn equipment for use on the farm—and some of the ways the problems can be surmounted. Not much more can be said about *how* you can go about obtaining the equipment you'll need to begin working horses on your farm, especially if you're trying to buy old equipment. This requires ample amounts of ingenuity, legwork, time, and persistence—but it's worth it all when you finally come home with a two-row cultivator you've been after for months, in good shape and minus only a shovel or two.

One big headache that arises with older machinery is upkeep and repair. To help with that problem, I've consulted the best single source I know for repair and maintenance on horse-drawn machinery.

In the late 1930s the John Deere Company widely distributed a small hardback book called *The Operation, Care, and Repair of Farm Machinery*. John Deere then, as now, made some of the finest agricultural machines in the world. Their horse-drawn line was one of the best, and that book, published during the transition time, devoted considerable space to their horse-drawn machines. It was distributed freely by John Deere to tens of thousands of Future Farmers of America students, ag short course students, and farmers. The parts of it dealing with horse-drawn machinery are reprinted in the following section. Much of the horse machinery you will come home from sales with was manufactured during this period, and whether it carries the John Deere label, or was made by another manufacturer, this section will serve as a help in maintaining and operating it.

Plows

PLOW BOTTOMS

Importance of the Bottoms   A plow is no better than its bottoms. No matter how well the frame may be built, how strong its beams, how modern its design, the plow will be only as satisfactory as its bottoms. If the bottoms fail to scour and turn the soil properly, the seed bed will be uneven and lumpy, resulting in lower yields. If the bottoms turn an even furrow, cover trash well, and pulverize the furrow slice as desired, a uniform seed bed will result.

Costly delays at plowing time are often caused by plow bottoms that refuse to scour. The trouble may be in the way the bottoms are made. It may be in the adjustment of the hitch, it may be due to dull or improperly set shares, or to looseness or misalignment of the bottoms on the beams. The plowman must be constantly on the alert for signs of inefficiency in his plow bottoms.

Parts of the Bottom   The plow bottom consists of share, landside, moldboard, and frog (see Fig. 4-1). The share and landside act as a wedge in the soil, cutting the furrow loose from the subsoil much as a wedge splits a log. The curved surface of the upper part of the share and the properly curved moldboard act as a single curve to invert the furrow slice. In passing over this curved surface, the furrow is twisted and broken, and the soil is pulverized, mixed, and aerated.

The steel frog holds the bottom parts and beam together. The landside and moldboard are bolted solidly to the frog. Most riding plows and tractor plows of the moldboard type now have quick-detachable shares. To remove or replace the share, it is necessary to loosen but one nut. This quick-

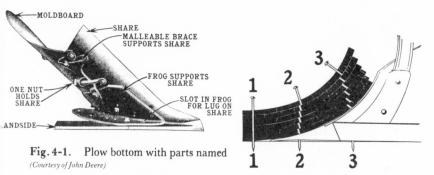

Fig. 4-1. Plow bottom with parts named
(Courtesy of John Deere)

Fig. 4-2. Principle of the pulverizing effect of the plow bottom under most soil conditions. The shearing effect produced by the curved surface is illustrated by pins 1, 2, and 3. Pin 1 is sheared into many parts when it reaches position of pin 3. Bending the pages at the corner of a book will illustrate this principle. The breaking effect produced by the curved surface is also illustrated.
(Courtesy of John Deere)

detachable feature saves time when shares are removed for sharpening.

Certain types of chilled-iron plows have a detachable chilled shin-piece that serves as a long-wearing cutting edge for the shin of the moldboard where the hardest wear occurs.

Types of Bottoms   Different types of soils require different shapes of bottoms to accomplish the results desired in plowing. The texture of the soil and the amount of moisture it contains determine whether it should be thoroughly pulverized or merely turned over, to be pulverized with other implements. A mellow loam soil and soils of similar texture should be plowed with a bottom that will pulverize well, while a sticky, wet clay soil should be plowed with a bottom that will break it as little as possible, leaving the pulverizing to be done with other machines.

The pulverizing effect of a plow depends upon the shape of its bottom (see Fig. 4-2). A bottom with a long, gradual curve in the moldboard turns the furrow slice gently and disturbs its composition but little. The other extreme is the short, abruptly curved moldboard that twists and shears the soil as it passes over, making a mellow, well-pulverized furrow.

Fig. 4-3.
Prairie breaker
(Courtesy of John Deere)

Fig. 4-4.
Stubble bottom
(Courtesy of John Deere)

Fig. 4-5.
General-purpose bottom
(Courtesy of John Deere)

Between these two extremes are many types of bottoms designed to meet many different soil conditions, but for general use bottoms may be classified as breaker, stubble, general-purpose, slat moldboard, and black-land. The breaker (see Fig. 4-3) is used in tough sod where complete turning of the furrow slice without materially disturbing its texture is desired. Stubble bottoms (see Fig. 4-4) are especially adapted to plowing in old ground where good pulverizing of the soil is desired. General-purpose bottoms (see Fig. 4-5) meet the demand for bottoms that will do good work in stubble, tame sod, old ground, and a variety of similar conditions. The general-purpose is designed to do satisfactory work in the varying conditions found on the average farm.

The slat moldboard bottom (see Fig. 4-6) is used in loose, sticky soils, and the black-land bottom (see Fig. 4-7) in gumbo and "buckshot" soils. In both types of soil, scouring is a serious problem.

The deep tillage bottom (see Fig. 4-8) is used in certain restricted territories where it is desirable to plow to unusually great depths—as deep as sixteen inches.

There are a number of variations of these general bottom shapes built to meet a wide variety of soil conditions but, in every case, the manufacturer provides the implement dealer with the types of bottoms suited to his territory.

Fig. 4-6.
Slat moldboard bottom
(Courtesy of John Deere)

Fig. 4-7.
Black-land bottom
(Courtesy of John Deere)

Fig. 4-8.
Deep tillage bottom
(Courtesy of John Deere)

Materials Used in Bottoms   Classified according to materials used in manufacture, there are two kinds of plow bottoms—steel and chilled cast-iron. Steel bottoms may be either solid steel or hardened soft-center steel. The latter bottoms are in more general use. In some sections, the soil conditions are such that a combination of chilled-iron shares and soft-center steel moldboards is used with excellent results. Both steel and chilled bottoms are used by some farmers who have varying soil conditions on their farms.

Soft-Center Steel Bottoms   A very highly polished fine-textured steel moldboard is necessary to good scouring in sticky, fine-grained soils. Soft-center steel has the necessary hardness and thickness for good scouring and long wear on the outer surfaces, and strength enough in the inner layer to withstand shocks and heavy loads in difficult soils. The outside layers are dense steel, very high in carbon and extremely hard. Between these two hard layers is a layer of soft, tough steel, the hard steel having been fused to it. In genuine soft-center steel, all three layers are uniformly thick. There is no out-cropping of soft spots, no thin places in the outer layers to wear through rapidly.

Solid Steel Bottoms   Solid steel bottoms are used in soils where scouring as a rule is not difficult. They are made of solid steel and are not tempered. They should not be used in sandy or gravelly soil, as they would tend to wear too rapidly. Solid steel shares are sometimes used with soft-center steel moldboards where soil conditions do not require the more costly soft-center steel shares for scouring.

Chilled-Iron Bottoms   Plow bottoms made of chilled iron are designed primarily for use in sandy or gravelly soil where the share and moldboard must withstand the scratching and hard wear of a soil of this type, and where the denser, finer-grained surface of soft-center steel is not necessary for scour-

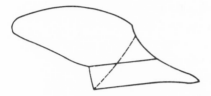

Fig. 4-9. Plow bottom showing area, below dotted line, which receives 75 percent of the draft when plowing, illustrating the necessity of keeping shares sharp for light draft of the plow.

(Courtesy of John Deere)

Fig. 4-10. Heavy lines show proper shape of sharp points for good penetration. Dotted lines show how worn points look before sharpening.

(Courtesy of John Deere)

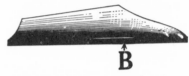

Fig. 4-11. Illustrating underpoint suction in landside of a plow share

(Courtesy of John Deere)

Fig. 4-12. Illustrating underpoint suction in throat of a plow share

(Courtesy of John Deere)

ing. The material used in these bottoms is extremely hard and long wearing due to a process called "chilling."

In casting chilled shares, a piece of metal called a "chill" is placed into a mold along the cutting edge and point where the finished share is to be chilled. When the hot metal comes into contact with the "chill," the sudden cooling leaves the grain of the metal at right angles to the surface. Thus, the dirt rubs the ends of the grain in the metal when passing over the share. A smooth and long-wearing surface results. Chilled shares may be sharpened by grinding but, because of their low cost, it is usually more satisfactory to replace worn shares with new ones.

Sharpening Plow Shares   The share is the most vital part of the bottom. It is the "business end"—the pioneer part in all of the work that a plow does. Draft, penetration, steady-running, and good work all depend upon the share (see Fig. 4-9, which shows the area of the plow bottom that is responsible for 75 percent of the draft when the plow is at work). This illustration clearly shows the importance of keeping the share in good cutting condition at all times (see also Fig. 4-10). A dull share may cause poor penetration and may greatly increase the draft of a plow. A sharp, correctly set share adds to the efficiency and good work of the plow bottom.

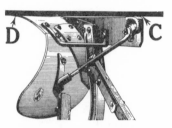

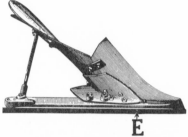

Fig. 4-13. Wing bearing point D is necessary to smooth running of walking plows.
(Courtesy of John Deere)

Fig. 4-14. Landside suction on a walking plow is distance between straight edge and landside at point E.
(Courtesy of John Deere)

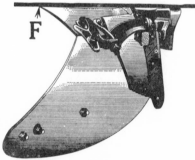

Fig. 4-15. Riding and tractor plows do not require wing bearing at F.
(Courtesy of John Deere)

Fig. 4-16. Landside suction for riding and tractor plows is less than required for walking plows.
(Courtesy of John Deere)

Many farmers have shop equipment for sharpening their plow shares, while the great majority depend upon local blacksmiths or mechanics for this service. In either case, it is well to know how shares should be sharpened.

When sharpening soft-center or solid steel shares, the point of the share should be heated to a low, cherry red (not too hot) and hammered on the top side until the point is sharp. Hammering should be done at a cherry red only. Working the share at a high heat destroys the quality of the steel. The entire cutting edge should be drawn from the underside until sharp. Only as much as can be hammered should be heated at one time. The body of the share should not be heated while sharpening, but should remain cool to prevent warping and disturbing of the fitted edges.

Should the share get out of shape or the fitted edges become warped during the sharpening process, the entire blade should be restored to proper shape before hardening. This can be done best at a black heat.

Soft-center steel shares should be hardened after sharpening. To do a thorough job of hardening, it is necessary to prepare the fire to heat the entire share uniformly to a cherry red. Care should be used in getting the heat uniform. The share is taken from the fire and dipped into a tub of clean, cold water with the cutting edge down. Care should be taken to keep the blade perpendicular during this process.

Solid steel shares should not be hardened.

Setting Shares for Suction   The plow bottom is led into the ground and held to its work by the underpoint suction of the share. Such suction is produced by turning the point of the share down slightly below the level of the underside of the share (see Fig. 4-11). The amount of suction necessary depends upon the type of plow and existing soil conditions. Stiff clay soils are harder to penetrate than light loam soils and require more suction in the share point.

Landside suction (see Fig. 4-14) in a plow share holds the bottom to its full-width cut. It is produced by turning the point of the share toward the unplowed ground. The land suction, as well as the down suction, should be measured when the share is new, so that the same amount of suck can be given the share when it is sharpened.

The importance of having the correct amount of suck in the share cannot be emphasized too strongly. Too little underpoint suction will cause the plow to "ride out" of the ground and cut a furrow of uneven depth. Too much will cause "bobbing" and heavy draft. In both cases, the plow is difficult to handle. If the landside suction is too great, the bottom tends to cut a wider furrow than can be handled properly, and the reverse is true when the landside suction is not sufficient.

The setting of walking plow shares and of riding and tractor plow shares is discussed separately, as the shares are different.

Directions for setting walking plow shares are as follows: Set the point of the share down so there is $1/16$- to $1/8$-inch suction, or clearance, under landside at point "A" (see Fig. 4-11). The clearance, or underpoint suction in the throat of the share should be $1/16$- to $1/8$-inch at point "B" (see Fig. 4-12). All twelve-, fourteen-, and sixteen-inch walking plow shares should have a wing bearing. The correct wing bearing (point "D"; see Fig. 4-13) is as follows: sixteen-inch plow, $1\frac{1}{2}$ inches; fourteen-inch plow, $1\frac{1}{4}$ inches; twelve-inch plow, $3/4$-inch. A straightedge placed at rear of the landside (point "C") and extending to wing of share should touch back of edge (point "D"; see Fig. 4-13). When sharpening the share, care must be taken not to turn the point to one side or the other. When fitted to the plow, there should be about $1/2$-inch clearance or landside suction at "E" (see Fig. 4-14).

For riding and tractor plows, set the point of the share down until there is $1/8$- to $3/16$-inch suction under the landside at point "A" (see Fig. 4-11). See that clearance in throat of share at "B" (see Fig. 4-12) is at least $1/8$ inch. Set edge of share at wing point, "F," without wing bearing (see Fig. 4-15). For landside, set should be about $3/16$-inch clearance at "H" (see Fig. 4-16).

Care of the Bottom   The plow bottom will give the best satisfaction when given the best care. If kept in good condition, it will give little scouring trouble. If permitted to rust, it may cause any amount of hard work and lost time.

One of the first rules a plowman should learn is to polish the bright surfaces of his plow bottoms and apply a light coating of oil whenever the plow is not in use. Strict observance of this rule will save many hours of difficulty in getting a rusted surface repolished. A heavy coating of a good hard oil should

Fig. 4-17. Proper adjustment of combination rolling coulter and jointer for ordinary plowing conditions
(Courtesy of John Deere)

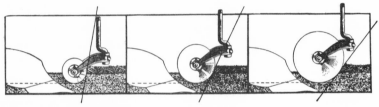

Fig. 4-18. Large rolling coulters mount trash more readily than small ones, thereby insuring a clean-cut furrow with less draft.
(Courtesy of John Deere)

be applied to the bottoms when storing the plow from season to season.

Plow manufacturers paint or varnish the surfaces of new plow bottoms to protect them from moisture from factory to user. This protective coating must be removed before the plow is taken into the field. This can be accomplished best by means of a paint and varnish remover which is obtainable at most paint stores. A can of concentrated lye dissolved in two or three quarts of water will serve the same purpose. The solution should be applied with a swab or a piece of gunnysack, the operator being careful not to get it on his hands. After the coating has been softened in this manner, it can be scraped off readily with a putty knife or similar instrument, care being taken not to scratch the polished surface.

If the new plow is not to be used immediately after the protective covering has been removed, the bottoms should be oiled, as the metal rusts readily if exposed to the air after treatment with the suggested strong solutions.

In case a plow bottom becomes badly rusted, working it in a coarse sandy or gravelly soil will aid in restoring a land polish.

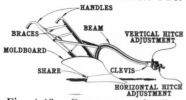

Fig. 4-19. Common type of walking plow with important parts
named

(Courtesy of John Deere)

Fig. 4-20. Walking middle-
breaker

(Courtesy of John Deere)

Rolling Coulter and Jointer   One of the most important
duties of the plow is to cover the stubble, stalks, or other trash
usually found on the surface of a field. Thorough covering of
such matter hurries its decomposition and makes cultivation
of future crops less difficult than when trash is left on top of
the seed bed to clog cultivating machines.

The rolling coulter and jointer attachments for moldboard
plows have proved to be big aids to clean plowing and good
covering. The rolling coulter cuts through the surface trash
and aids in securing a clean furrow wall, reducing the draft on
the cutting edge of the plow bottom. In reality, the jointer is a
miniature plow, the purpose of which is to cut a small furrow
off the main slice and throw it toward the furrow in such a
manner that all stubble and trash are buried in the bottom of
the furrow.

To get the best results with the combination rolling coulter
and jointer (see Fig. 4-17), the hub of the coulter should be
set about one inch back of the share point with the blade running just deep enough to cut the trash, about three to four
inches in ordinary conditions. The jointer should cut about
two inches deep. There should be about ⅛ inch space
between the jointer and the coulter blade.

The independent rolling coulter and jointer, which permit
a wider range of adjustment to meet field conditions, are gaining in popular use.

When the rolling coulter is used alone, it should be set
about ½ to ⅝ inch to the land. The hub of the coulter should
be about three inches behind the point of the share. In soil
that does not scour well, more pressure on the moldboard can
be secured by setting the coulter farther to land. If there is
considerable trash on the field, the coulter should be set just

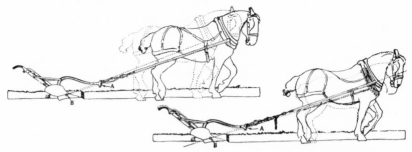

Fig. 4-21.   Horse drawn with heavy lines is hitched correctly. Dotted line shows same horse with hitch raised at A to accommodate short hitch. If both horses were hitched the same, an up-pull on beam would result. Too long tugs have an opposite effect. Raising or lowering clevis at point A corrects line of draft from hame to point B.

(Courtesy of John Deere)

Fig. 4-22.   Size of team has direct relation to point of hitch. The smaller horse in dotted outline requires a lower hitch at point A than the larger horse. Clevis must be lowered to maintain straight line from point B through point A to hame.

(Courtesy of John Deere)

deep enough to cut it—if set too deep, it pushes instead of cuts trash. The larger rolling coulters prove more effective in trashy conditions, as they mount trash more effectively than smaller coulters (see Fig. 4-18). When plowing sod, the coulter must be deep enough to cut the roots below the surface, usually about one inch shallower than the share is cutting.

Keeping the rolling coulter sharp and well oiled, and the jointer sharp and properly set will add greatly to the efficiency of their work.

WALKING PLOWS

Distribution and Use   On the great majority of farms, the walking plow has been supplanted by riding and tractor plows for general field work. However, in some sections, the walking plow is still depended upon to handle the bulk of the plowing. In certain cotton-raising districts in the South, and in small farm districts all over the United States, walking plows are used almost exclusively. Every farm, large or small, needs a walking plow for plowing gardens and small plots, but the general trend is to plows of larger capacity.

Steel and chilled cast-iron walking plows are built in a great variety of styles to meet a wide variety of soil conditions. The discussion of plow bottoms on a preceding page furnishes a picture of the requirements and the way they are met by plow manufacturers. Fig. 4-19 illustrates and names the parts of a general-purpose walking plow. Other types of walking plows are similarly constructed.

The hillside or swivel plow is a variation of the walking plow designed to turn all furrows one way, plowing back and forth.

Walking Middle-breaker   The middle-breaker (see Fig. 4-20) was developed to meet the request of the southern cotton grower for a double moldboard plow that would turn a furrow each way, burst out a ridge, or bed up a new row for planting, in one operation. The middle-breaker reduced production costs in these regions, and its principle has since been adapted to the lister and the listing plow.

Hitching Walking Plows   The proper adjustment of the hitch is the most important factor in the operation of a plow. The kind of work a walking plow will do, its draft, and its handling qualities depend to a great extent upon the correct relation between power and load.

By following a few simple rules, the most inexperienced can adjust his plow to run right. The most important rule to observe is this: the point of hitch should be on a straight line drawn from center of load to the center of power when plow is at work.

Fig. 4-21 shows the effect of long and short tugs on the work of a plow and the adjustments necessary to get correct working position of the hitch. Fig. 4-22 illustrates the changes necessary in the vertical or up-and-down hitch to accommodate horses of different sizes. The correct vertical hitch of walking plows is necessary to smooth running, correct depth, and the comfort of man and beast.

The horizontal adjustment of walking plow hitches is comparatively easy, provided the doubletree is about the right length and the share is properly set. If a right-hand plow is not taking enough land, the clevis may be moved one or two notches to the right; if taking too much land, an adjustment of one or two notches to the left will bring the desired results. A left-hand plow is adjusted in an exactly opposite manner.

RIDING PLOWS

Types and Distribution   The three general types of what are usually classed as riding plows are sulky plows, two-bottom gang, and three-bottom gang plows, each built in several different styles, to meet the requirements of a particular section of the country.

The sulky, or one-bottom riding plow, was the natural outgrowth of a desire for a plow more easily handled than the walking plow. The hard work of following and handling the walking plow in general field plowing tested the endurance of the most willing farmer. The sulky increased his working capacity and lightened his task.

Then came the two-bottom gang which doubled the number of acres one man could plow in a day, using one or two horses more than used on a sulky.

The three-bottom gang came into popularity in big-farm districts as a result of the success of the two-bottom gang in lowering production costs.

Styles of Riding Plows   For general usage, there may be considered four styles of riding plows, each style meeting a particular need. One of these styles has a frame, while three are frameless—that is, all parts attach directly to the beam.

The three-steel frame, or foot-lift, sulky is probably the most widely used style of the sulky plows. It is built much like the gang (see Fig. 4-24) except that it has only one bottom. Directions for its operation and care are the same as those given for the gang plow in later paragraphs.

The frameless, or low-lift, is extremely simple and easy to handle. Three levers provide quick and accurate adjustment for good plowing.

The two-way plow (see Fig. 4-23) is especially adapted to plowing hilly fields, irregular fields, and irrigated fields that must be kept level for proper regulation of water flow in the ditches. The operator starts at one side of the field and plows back and forth until the field is finished, thus eliminating dead furrows and back ridges. There are two complete bottoms, one left-hand and one right-hand. Pressure on a pedal causes the power lift to raise the working bottom when the end of the field is reached. By means of a lever, the idle bottom can be put to work for the return trip down the field.

While the operation of each style of sulky plow is somewhat different from the operation of gang plows, to avoid confusion, the details of operation and adjustment of all riding plows will be discussed collectively, using the two-bottom gang plow (see Fig. 4-24) as a basis.

Two- and Three-Bottom Gang Plows   The gang plows may be divided into frameless or low-lift, and frame or foot-lift styles. The frame styles are in more general use, although in certain limited sections the frameless styles are preferred.

The two-bottom frame or high-lift gang (see Fig. 4-24) is probably the most widely used style of two-bottom gang.

Care of Riding Plows   The importance of proper care for all types of plow bottoms has been emphasized in preceding paragraphs. The shares and coulters must be sharp and properly set, and the scouring surfaces of the entire bottom must be kept in good condition if the plow is to operate efficiently and satisfactorily.

Fig. 4-23. Two-way plow, popular for plowing irrigated, hilly, or irregularly shaped fields
(Courtesy of John Deere)

Fig. 4-24. Two-bottom foot-lift gang plow with important parts named
(Courtesy of John Deere)

Dust-proof and oil-tight boxings are provided on all wheels of riding plows. It is necessary that these boxings be kept generously greased with a good grade of hard oil to prevent excessive friction and wear. The regular oiling of rolling coulters will aid in their work and add years to their period of service. The liberal use of lubricants in the operation of plows as well as other farm machines will cut repair expenses and add to the life of the implements.

Adjustment and Operation of Riding Plows   When all parts of a riding plow are properly adjusted the combined weight of the plow, the driver, and the soil being turned is carried on the wheels. Heavy draft results when, because of wrong adjustments, all of the weight is not carried on the wheels, or wheels and rolling landside.

The first and most important point to remember is that shares must be sharp and properly set to do a good job of plowing. The entire bottom must be well polished for good scouring. Rolling coulters and jointers, if used, must be sharp and in correct position. The discussion of plow bottoms on preceding pages covers details of bottom and bottom-equipment adjustments.

Correct setting of the rear furrow wheel is necessary to uniform plowing and light draft. The wheel should run straight in the corner of the furrow on a level with the rear bottom. For proper penetration, there should be ½ inch space, or room enough to slip the fingers between heel of the landside and bottom of the furrow. If there is less than this amount of space, the share points are raised higher than the landside heel, interfering with quick and easy penetration and causing the plow to run shallower than desired in places, resulting in uneven plowing. If the clearance at heel of the landside is more than ½ inch, the share points run too deep and increase the draft of the plow. Moving up setscrew collar gives more space beneath landside heel. Moving it down has an opposite effect. There should also be ½ inch clearance or space enough to slip the fingers between the landside and furrow wall at heel of landside (see Fig. 4-25) causing the furrow wheel to

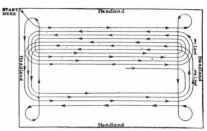

Fig. 4-25. Shows test for clearance between landside heel and furrow wall to determine if furrow wheel is carrying landside pressure. If there is not room for the fingers between straight edge and landside (X), adjust at F. Adjust at H on connection rod to set rear wheel to run straight.

(Courtesy of John Deere)

Fig. 4-26. Plan for laying out and plowing a field. First—Stake out headland, about twice the length of the outfit, clear around the field. This gives all room necessary for turning at ends. Second— Plow a furrow clear around the field, as staked out. These furrows may be thrown in or out. However, it is recommended to throw in, as this leaves the headland in better shape to finish. Then, too, the head furrows mark the point to raise and lower the plow. To begin the furrow, drop the plow when the first bottom reaches the dead furrow. This leaves square headlands. Third—Open land as shown in diagram; arrows show direction of travel. After land No. 1 has become too narrow to permit the sweeping turn, swing over and open up land No. 2, plowing alternate furrows in both lands until land No. 1 is finished. Then plow land No. 2 until it is too narrow for turning; open the third land, and so on. Fourth—After all lands are plowed, start in at one corner and plow around until the entire headland is plowed and field finished.

carry the landside pressure. Adjust bracket at "F" for correct setting.

The front furrow wheel should be set with a slight lead to the land. The lead should be just enough to hold the wheel in the corner of the furrow when the plow is in operation. The ratchet landing device is attached directly to the front furrow wheel axle. With this, the plow can be given more or less land for work on hillsides or to straighten crooked furrows.

When the furrows, turned by a gang plow, do not lie alike, it is usually due to the furrow slices not being the same width. This may be corrected by leveling the bottoms or adjusting the plow so both bottoms cut the same width furrows. The width of cut of the rear bottom is regulated by adjusting the rolling coulters. The same applies to the front bottom unless the plow is old and worn, in which case it is necessary to set the front furrow wheel in, thereby narrowing cut of the front bottom. This is done by moving the landing adjustment casting in on the frame (see Fig. 4-24),

The foot lift on a riding plow acts both as a lift and a lock. The plow is locked down when in plowing position by pushing forward on the upper lift pedal until the lock goes over center. In plowing stony land, the setscrew on the lock can be screwed down to set the strap anti-lock. When so set, the lifting spring should be loosened sufficiently to prevent bottoms lifting excepting when they strike an obstruction. The bottoms will then maintain their depth, but will come up automatically when the shares strike an obstruction.

The lifting spring, which aids in raising the bottoms, should be adjusted with enough tension to make the plow lift easily. If left too loose, the plow will lift heavily.

Overhauling Riding Plows   The plow should be overhauled and put in condition for the next season's work as soon as possible after finishing plowing. If new parts are needed before the plow can be used again, they should be ordered, attached, and the plow put in condition ready for the field, during slack seasons. The following instructions are designed to aid in a thorough inspection of riding plows:

First—Examine the wheel boxings. If they are badly worn, they should be renewed; if not, they should be slipped off the axle, and both axle and boxing washed clean with kerosene, and a fresh supply of grease applied. If the collar that holds the wheel to the axle is badly worn so as to allow excessive play of the wheel boxing on the axle, it should be replaced with a new one.

Second—Examine the shares. If they are not sharp, detach and have them sharpened and properly set. If they are worn excessively, get new shares that are made by the manufacturer of the plow.

Third—On the high-lift, foot-lift plows, suspended by one or two bails, examine the bail stops. These are located on the front frame bar and on the right frame bar. They should be so adjusted that when the plow is locked down in plowing position, the bails rest securely on the stops. The bail bearings should also be examined. If they are worn loose, take off the cap and file or grind it until it fits snugly with all bolts tight. This will help greatly in keeping the plow running steadily and quietly.

Fourth—Examine rolling coulters and hub bearings. Coulters should be sharp and well polished. If the hub bearings are badly worn, replace them with new ones.

Fifth—Check up the location of the rear axle collar (see Fig. 4-24). This collar should support rear end of the frame and transmit weight of rider to the rear wheel. If it has become loose, permitting it to slip on the axle, weight of plow and rider will be carried on the bottom of the plow landside instead of on the rear wheel.

Sixth—The rear axle frame bearing carries the weight of the rider and plow and transmits the side pressure created by the moldboards to the rear furrow wheel. If the bearing becomes badly worn, the landside of the rear bottom will carry this pressure, resulting in heavy draft and excessive wear on the landside. On some makes of plows, this bearing is provided with a take-up casting with bolts at both upper and lower ends. This makes the proper adjustments simple and easy.

Seventh—The front furrow wheel axle bearing should be reasonably snug, in order to keep the wheel running at the proper angle, and the front furrow to proper width.

Eighth—Look over the entire plow for loose nuts and worn bolts. A plow operates at great disadvantage when parts are loose, due to bolts not fitting bolt holes and nuts being loose.

Inspect all parts of the plow. See that the eveners and pole are in good condition. Lever dog boxes should be oiled so they will work freely. And, above all, keep the polished parts free from rust.

Opening a Land   To open a land with a riding plow, both the land wheel and front furrow wheel levers should be raised until the plow opens up to depth desired. On the next round, the landside lever is adjusted to permit bottoms to cut depth desired to plow, and the furrow wheel is set level with the bottoms. Once the correct setting has been made, the plow will run level and continue cutting at uniform depth. When plowing in "lands," the bottoms should be lifted out at each end while the plow is moving. The forward motion of the plow aids in lifting.

When plowing around a field, the plow is not lifted at the corners. The driver stops a short distance from the end, turns square, and does not permit his team to start ahead until completely turned.

Hitching Riding Plows   The satisfactory performance of a riding plow depends to a great extent upon correct hitching. If both horizontal and vertical hitch adjustments are correct, the plow will run smoother, pull lighter, and do a better job of plowing than when carelessly hitched.

Fig. 4-27 illustrates the correct up-and-down adjustment on the vertical clevis. The correct hitch at "A" is the place where "A" is in a true line between "B" and point of hitch at the hame. When plowing deep or using tall horses, hitch at "A" should be higher than when plowing shallow or using small horses. When hitching horses strung out, the hitch at "A" must be lower than when using four horses abreast.

The results of improper adjustment of the vertical hitch are easily noticed. If the hitch is too high at "A," there is a downpull on the front end of the plow and the rear end will tend to come up. If the hitch is too low at "A," the draft will tend to lift the front end of the plow. By changing the position of the clevis up or down one or two holes at "A," a trial will generally show which hole places the clevis in a true line of draft.

Hitches are adjustable horizontally for the purpose of accommodating the position of the horses and the various sizes and types of eveners. Consequently, the cross hitch is very long and has a large number of hitch positions.

The operator should aim to get the horizontal hitch as near as possible in direct line between the center of draft and the center of power when the plow is running straight and the horses are pulling straight ahead.

Fig. 4-28 shows how to determine the center of draft on any size plow. One-fourth of cut of one bottom measured to left of center of cut of the entire plow determines center of draft. This applies to one or any number of bottoms used.

"A" in Fig. 4-29 shows the approximate position of the evener and clevis for a four-horse strung out hitch. To accommodate horses, the hitch is to extreme right, tending to cause side draft and "running in" of plow.

"B" shows the correct gang plow hitch for best results—the five-horse strung out hitch. Line of draft is correct, the plow runs straight and steady, and the horses are not crowded in their positions.

"C" illustrates the four-horse abreast hitch. Note the necessity of hitching to extreme left to accommodate the furrow horse, resulting in side draft and "running out" of plow.

Fig. 4-27.   Illustrating the correct vertical hitch for riding plows. Straight line from center of draft, B, to center of power at hame, passes through point of hitch at A.

(Courtesy of John Deere)

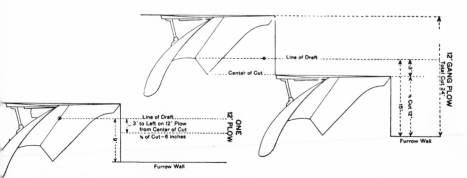

Fig. 4-28.   Finding the center of draft on any size plow is simple, if this illustration is followed. First, find total cut of plow. Half of total cut is center of cut. Measure to left of center of cut one quarter the width of cut of one bottom to get center of draft.

(Courtesy of John Deere)

Moving the hitch one or two holes to the left in "A" and to the right in "C" will lessen side draft to some extent. However, the five-horse strung out hitch shown in "B" should be used if conditions permit.

Lines and Traces   Comfort to horses when plowing depends a great deal upon the adjustment of lines and traces. The lines should be adjusted so the horses can not spread out too much, for when the horses are spread out, they will not be well under the control of the driver.

Long traces give the horses more room and tend to make the plow run steadier. Short traces do not lighten the draft and many add much discomfort to the horses.

If hip straps are used they should be adjusted so the loops hang free. If loops pull up the traces, they will change the line of draft, making the plow run unsteadily and cause weight to be carried on the horses' backs.

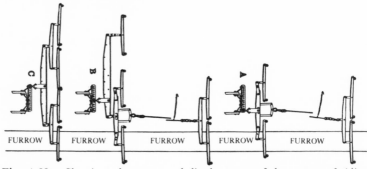

Fig. 4-29.   Showing advantages and disadvantages of three types of riding plow hitches
(Courtesy of John Deere)

Shovel Cultivators

Shovel cultivators are the most generally used type in the majority of farming communities. They are suited to practically all soils and produce most satisfactory results when used in average conditions.

Fig. 4-30 illustrates a popular style of two-row cultivator. It is a typical two-row for use with three or four horses. Levers

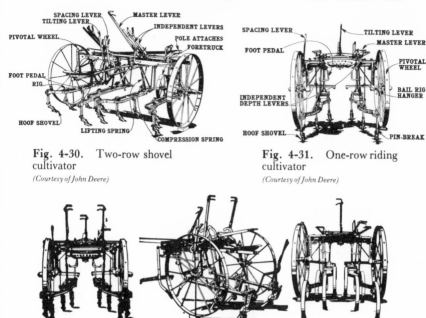

Fig. 4-30. Two-row shovel cultivator
(Courtesy of John Deere)

Fig. 4-31. One-row riding cultivator
(Courtesy of John Deere)

Fig. 4-32. Three types of cultivator rig equipment: Left, eight-shovel, I-beam rigs with spring-trip shanks; center, pipe beams with spring trips; right, spring-tooth rigs.
(Courtesy of John Deere)

are provided to make all field adjustments. The master lever raises all four rigs. Independent depth levers raise or lower each rig separately, permitting adjustment for good work in uneven ground. Spacing lever moves shovels closer to or farther from the rows, giving operator instant control of spacing while the cultivator is at work. The tilting lever levels rigs, causing front and rear shovels to run at same depth when going up or down hill or on uneven ground.

ONE-ROW CULTIVATORS

One-row cultivators are built in both walking and riding styles. Farmers in some sections, where farms are generally small, use the walking type of cultivator. Farmers in other sections much prefer the riding type.

The type of one-row cultivator illustrated in Fig. 4-31 is probably the most widely used shovel cultivator. It is shown with hoof shovels and pin-break rigs, equipment used quite generally. Other beam and shovel equipment that can be used on this and other styles of shovel cultivators is shown in Fig. 4-32.

These different combinations of equipment are necessary to meet the requirements of each section of the country and their use is governed by soil conditions and crops grown.

The lever adjustments on the one-row (see Fig. 4-31) are the same as on the two-row. The master lever, independent depth levers, tilting lever, and spread or spacing lever give the operator quick control for any setting required to meet field conditions.

The swinging rig type of cultivator (see Fig. 4-30) is adjusted for spacing at front end of the rigs. For cultivating closer to or farther from the row, loosen the arches and slide them in or out to width desired.

OPERATION AND ADJUSTMENT

When a cultivator is set properly for working in ordinary conditions, the shovels will penetrate well, run at the same depth without crowding toward or away from the row, and there will be no unnecessary draft. To set and maintain a cultivator in this desirable adjustment is comparatively easy, once the operator understands the causes of trouble and the adjustments provided on his cultivator for correcting them.

One of the most common adjustments that cultivator operators have to make is setting the shovels for proper penetration and uniform depth. The first requirement of an efficient shovel is that it be sharp, with the point properly shaped. A dull shovel will not penetrate easily; it does poor work and causes heavier draft. Fig. 4-33 shows a properly shaped shovel with a dotted line showing its shape when point is worn and dull. Frequent sharpening of shovels will insure a smooth-running, good-working cultivator.

Fig. 4-33. Cultivator shovel with dotted lines showing how point looks when shovel needs resharpening. Obviously, a shovel in this condition penetrates poorly and increases draft.

(Courtesy of John Deere)

Fig. 4-34. Correct and incorrect pitch of cultivator shovels: 1. Shovel properly adjusted; 2. Shovel set too flat, will not penetrate well; 3. Shovel set too straight, will not penetrate or run steadily.

(Courtesy of John Deere)

All shovels must run at the same depth for good work. If the front shovels run deeper than the rear ones, all shovels will stand straighter than they should, and will not penetrate easily. This condition is due to the front of rigs being lower than the rear. It can be corrected by raising the pole at hames or leveling the rigs with the tilting or leveling lever.

If the rear shovels run deeper than those in front, all shovels set too flat and will not penetrate as they should. This can be remedied with the tilting lever on some types of cultivators and with adjustment at the hames on types that do not have such a lever. These directions are based upon the supposition, of course, that all shovels are at uniform height on the shanks.

Pitch of Shovels   All cultivators are provided with an adjustment, either on the shovel shank or sleeve, whereby the pitch or angle of the shovel can be changed. This adjustment is correct for average soil conditions when the cultivator leaves the factory. However, it may become changed and it is well to know what the proper pitch is and how to get it when conditions demand.

If a shovel stands too straight, it will not penetrate readily; it will not run steadily. There will be a tendency to skip and jump, and it will require unusual pressure to keep the shovels at work. If set too flat, the underpart of the shovel will ride below the extreme point and the shovel will not penetrate unless forced into the ground.

The illustrations in Fig. 4-34 show the proper pitch of shovels for good work compared with shovels set too straight and too slanting.

In hilling row crops, it is necessary to turn the front shovels in by loosening the clamp attachment on the shank. This setting tends to pull the shovels away from the row. This tendency does not interfere with the work of a pivot axle cultivator, but with the swinging rig type, the operator finds difficulty in keeping the rigs running the proper distance from the row when a spread arch is not used. An opposite effect is produced when the front shovels are turned away from the row for first cultivation. In either case, the crowding tendency can be overcome and the rigs made to run straight by turning the rear shovel to an equal angle in the opposite direction. On parallel rig types of cultivators, turning the shovels in or out does not affect the operation of the cultivator.

The wheel tread is adjustable on most types of cultivators. This is an important feature in districts where several widths of rows must be cultivated with the same machines. The one-row cultivator, shown in Fig. 4-31, can be adjusted to several different row widths by removing a cotter key or loosening a setscrew and moving axles in or out an equal distance to the desired position. Other types of cultivators are adjusted in a similar manner.

Adjustment of Shields   Proper setting of the shields is important to good work during the first cultivation. There are three main types used—solid sheet iron, open rod wire, and rotating shield. The first, which is the most commonly used, is comparatively easy to set to allow the desired amount of dirt to roll up to the row without covering the plants. The rotating shield is often set too far back to be efficient. The greater part of the shield should be ahead on the front shovel, with its entire weight resting on the ground. For later cultivation, shields are removed, provided the crop has reached sufficient height.

Care of Cultivators   Like all other farm implements, the length of life and the satisfaction given by shovel cultivators depend upon the way they are handled and the care given them during operation and storage. A few minutes given to inspection and tightening of all parts, and thorough oiling at regular intervals while in the field will add to the service of a cultivator and save delays caused by breakage and wear. Shovels should be polished and coated with oil when standing overnight, and covered thoroughly with heavy grease when stored.

As stated previously, one of the most important factors in efficient cultivation is keeping the shovels sharp. A dull shovel is as inefficient as a dull knife. It is advisable to have the shovels sharpened and shaped by a good blacksmith during the storage season. If the points are too badly worn, new shovels or new points (on the slip-point type of shovel) should be obtained. If the shovels have become rusted and pitted between seasons, they should be polished before being taken into the field.

The slack season is the time to go over the cultivator thoroughly, ordering new parts wherever needed and tuning it up ready for the first day of the cultivating season.

Disk Cultivators

Under certain conditions, disk cultivators are used to better advantage than shovel cultivators. Their use is not general or widespread, being localized in many sections of the southern, eastern, and central states.

Disk cultivators are adapted to many different conditions. They are used in unusually weedy fields where shovel or surface cultivators would have a tendency to clog. In stony or rooty fields, and for hilling crops, the disk type of cultivator is favored.

Disk cultivators are operated in much the same manner as shovel cultivators. A master lever raises both rigs; independent levers for each rig control depth and give adjustment for varying field conditions. A crank at rear of the pole controls leveling of the rigs.

To change disks from out-throw to in-throw, the rigs are reversed, left to right. This is done by removing two cotter keys and tipping the gang so that the dog will clear the upright ratchet. The gangs are then transferred. The change from disk to shovel or spring-tooth rig equipment is made in the same manner.

Two ratchets with grip levers provide adjustment for angling and tilting the gangs to get desired results with any equipment.

Wheels, disks, and all other parts should be well oiled.

Disk Harrows

The function of the disk harrow is to pulverize and pack the soil, leaving a surface mulch and a compact subsurface. It is used to good advantage before plowing to break the surface and mix the trash with the topsoil, and after plowing to pulverize lumps and close air spaces in the turned furrows.

Types of Disk Harrows   Disk harrows are made in single-action and double-action types. Most of the double-action harrows (commonly called tandem disks) and some of the single-action harrows are designed for use with tractor only. Others may be used with either horses or tractor, by changing the hitch. Some types of single-action harrows can be converted into double-action harrows for use with horses or tractor by adding a rear section.

Requirements for Good Work   To do a good job of disking, the disk harrow, first of all, must penetrate well and evenly over its entire width. In the case of two-section machines, both sections must meet these requirements, the disks of the rear section cutting the ridges left by the front disks instead of trailing in their furrows.

Flexibility has much to do with even penetration and good work. When the gangs of each section work independently, one gang may pass over stones or stumps and conform to irregularities in the surface of the field without hindering the work of the other gangs.

Sun-Baked Stubble Land   Plowed, but Not Disked   Disked After Plowed, but Not Before.
                                                              Notice Air Spaces

Disked and Then Plowed.   Good Con-   Disked Before and After Plowed.   The
        tact with Subsoil   Ideal Seed Bed

Fig. 4-35. Drawings illustrating the value of disking both before and after plowing

(Courtesy of John Deere)

Operation and Adjustments   Penetration of a disk harrow is obtained by angling the disks, the angle necessary for good work depending upon the condition (or texture) of the soil and the amount of trash to be cut. On most disk harrows, provision is made for angling the disks for maximum penetration which is obtained at an angle of approximately 20°.

Front and rear gangs of the double-action harrow can be angled to the proper degree or straightened independently of each other.

The end gangs of the single-action harrow can be folded over when going through gateways, or to provide additional weight for better penetration in difficult conditions. In this way, a fifteen-foot harrow can be narrowed to 10½ feet, and a twenty-one-foot harrow to fourteen feet. The single-action harrow may be used for double-disking by lapping half the width of the machine each time across the field.

The scrapers are adjustable to suit soil conditions. Scrapers on both sections of the double-action tractor harrows shown can be oscillated by means of ropes, without leaving the trac-

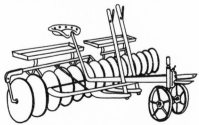

Fig. 4-36. A single-action disk harrow. Double-action disks are also known as tandem disks.

tor seat. Pressure on foot levers on the horse-drawn models oscillates scrapers.

Provision is made for locking scrapers at the edges of disks, or for locking them away from disks when not needed.

Good Care Lengthens Life   The efficiency and length of service of a disk harrow depend upon the care given it.

First in importance is thorough greasing of the bearings. Many of the modern disk harrows, especially the tractor types, are equipped with fittings for pressure lubrication, making it an easy matter to keep the bearings well oiled. Where hard oilers are used, cups should be kept full of a good grade of hard oil and should be turned down at regular intervals. The bearing bushings of hard maple are oil soaked before they are assembled, giving them long life. They are easily replaced when worn.

A good cutting edge on all disks is desirable, especially in hard ground and trashy conditions. Most disk blades are now made of tough steel, then heat-treated to hold a long-wearing edge.

During slack seasons, go over the entire disk harrow, tightening bolts, replacing worn parts, and getting the implement ready for the next season's work. Keep disks well greased with a good hard oil when harrow is not in use.

Harrows and Pulverizers (or Rollers)

Methods of finishing the seedbed vary according to soil conditions and established practices. Common to almost every horse farm is the spike tooth harrow, with the spring tooth harrow and pulverizer or land roller not so generally used.

SPIKE TOOTH HARROWS

Fig. 4-37 shows a popular style of spike tooth harrow. The operation and adjustment of a harrow of this type is simplicity

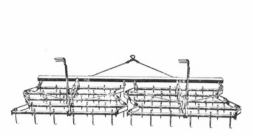

Fig. 4-37.
Spike tooth harrow with detail above showing how tooth is locked between bars

Fig. 4-38.
Soil pulverizer, land roller, or packer

itself, there being no field adjustment other than setting the slant of the teeth with the lever provided for each section. The set, or angle, you want to set the teeth will be governed entirely by field conditions.

Each tooth of this harrow is held between the two notched, semi-oval frame bars by a heavy bolt which creates a tension, thereby locking the tooth to position and preventing the nut from coming loose. When one side of the tooth becomes worn, the nut may be loosened and the tooth turned to present a new cutting edge. Teeth may also be removed for sharpening.

SPRING TOOTH HARROW

The spring tooth penetrates much deeper than the spike tooth and thus pulls considerably harder. It can be very useful in the eradication of weeds and grasses, but is not in as much use on horse farms as the spike tooth.

SOIL PULVERIZER

Some people call these machines land rollers or packers. They are good for finishing the seedbed. Like the spike harrow, they are simple and easy to operate. There are no adjustments and few parts that ever need replacing, with exception, possibly, of the oil-soaked wood boxings which are easily removed and replaced, providing you can find new ones (see Fig. 4-38).

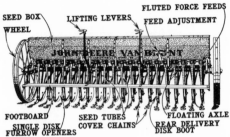

Fig. 4-39. Rear view of grain drill equipped with single-disk openers

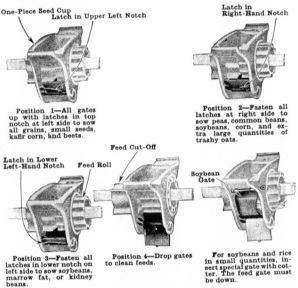

Fig. 4-40. Detail of the fluted feed showing different settings that can be made for planting seeds of various sizes. Quantity is controlled by shifting the feed roll and feed cut-off to permit more or less of the feed roll to turn within the seed cup. This is done with the feed shaft shifter.

Grain Drills and Planters

The necessity of planting all crops at the proper depth and distributing the seed uniformly is apparent. If seed is planted too deep or too shallow, too thick or too thin, if the planter skips hills or the grain drill leaves strips unplanted, the yield is bound to suffer.

GRAIN DRILLS

Like plows, grain drills are built in many different styles with a variety of equipment to meet conditions in every section of the country. In some sections, the single-disk furrow opener will work better than the double disk, while still other conditions may demand a hoe-type opener. In semi-arid regions, where every available bit of moisture must be conserved, the semi-deep furrow drill with its large disks solves the problem by placing the seed considerably deeper than the ordinary drill, thereby assuring contact with the moist soil found at greater depth. In territories where soil blowing is serious, the deep furrow drill with moldboards which throw the soil one way serves the purpose of deep planting and, at the same time, leaves the surface soil ridged to prevent or reduce soil drifting and seed blowing. The lister drill is still another variation of the grain drill, also useful in reducing soil blowing.

Of the various types of grain drills, the fluted feed (Fig. 4-40) is most general, though in some sections other styles are used almost exclusively. The fluted force-feed consists mainly of a feed roll, feed cut-off, seed cups, and an adjustable gate. The feed roll turns with the shaft, forcing the grain out over the feed gate which is adjustable for different sizes of seeds. The feed cut-off and the feed roll shift with the feed shaft, and their position determines the quantity of seed sown. The one-piece seed cups aid in maintaining accuracy because they do not become loose and get out of line.

Setting Fluted-Feed Drills for Quantity   The first adjustment in using any drill is to set it to sow the desired quantity per acre. This is done on fluted-feed drills by adjusting the feed shaft and the gates on the feeds to suit the size of seed and the quantity to be sown.

The setting of the adjustable gate force-feeds according to size of seed is described in Fig. 4-40. Before putting grain in the box, all gates should be let down as in No. 4, Fig. 4-40, and all grain and accumulations cleaned out. To insure uniform planting, the latches on all feeds must be kept in the same position while seeding.

The feed adjustment, or feed shaft shifter, moves the feed rolls and feed cut-offs to permit more or less grain to be forced out by the feed rolls. There are two of these shifters on drills having more than eight disks, one for each half of the drill. Both must be kept in the same position on the seed index plate, which is provided with a row of notches to hold shifters in position. These notches are numbered by the figures which are immediately above them. Figures above at left of notches indicate the amount of flax and alfalfa—in pounds—to be seeded per acre. Figures below notches indicate amount of oats, barley, wheat, and peas—in pounds—to be seeded per acre.

Double Run Feed Drills   The double run feed drill gets its name from its type of feed, illustration of which is shown in Fig. 4-41. The feed and the mechanism which drives it constitute the principal differences between this type of drill and the fluted-feed drill shown in Fig. 4-40.

Fig. 4-41 shows two views of the double run feed. It consists mainly of a feed wheel and a feed gate. The wheel is smaller on one side for use in planting small seeds. The large side is used for planting oats, barley, treated wheat, peas, beans, and other large seeds.

The adjustable gates, which are inside the seed cups, regulate the size of the feed openings, there being five different positions at which they can be set—three on the large side and two on the small side. These five gate adjustments provide five different quantity adjustments for each one of the five multiple gears, making a total of twenty-five different quantities in which seed may be planted without changing gears. By reversing the intermediate gear, twenty-five additional quantity adjustments are provided—fifty in all.

Calibrating Grain Drills   The operator should be sure to have his drill set properly before starting to sow. If there is doubt in his mind as to the accuracy of his machine, he may make the calibration test which follows:

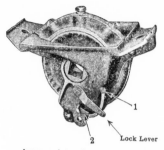

2 Lock Lever

Arrows point to lock lever on small side of feed, used for regulating inside quantity feed gate, and to the positions at which it may be set. Numerals indicate the two positions, No. 1 being for large quantities, and No. 2 for small quantities.

Showing adjustable gate inside the seed cup for regulating size of the feed opening to handle different quantities of seed. Gate is set on position 2.

Figure 71—Detail view of double-run feed, showing large and small sides.

Fig. 4-41. Detail view of double run feed, showing large and small sides

To check the accuracy of a grain drill, jack it up in working position, fill the box with grain, place a canvas in position to catch the grain, and set the gates and feed shifters properly. Find the total width of strip planted each time across the field. Divide 43,560—the number of square feet in an acre— by the width of strip planted and you have the length of a strip necessary to make one acre. Then find the number of times the drill wheel must turn in going this distance by dividing the number of feet by the circumference of the wheel.

Tie a cloth to a spoke of the wheel and count the revolutions as you turn the wheel, turning at about the same speed it would travel at work. You need not sow a whole acre—one-fourth of an acre is sufficient for the test.

When the correct number of revolutions has been made, weigh or measure the grain on the canvas and check it with the adjustment on the feed-shifter scale. If the drill is planting more or less than it should, the difference can be taken care of by adjusting the feed shifters.

Field Operation   To do a good job of sowing, the drill must be run steadily and evenly. Swinging of poles or unsteady driving causes bunching of seed and results in reduction of yields.

The depth of seeding over full width of the drill is controlled by the lifting levers and by a pressure spring on each

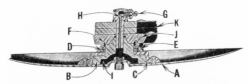

Fig. 4-42. Cross section of drill disk: A. Disk blade; B. Disk bearing; C. Bearing case; D. Felt washer; E. Hard-iron dust cap; F. Dust cap spring; G. Alemite fitting; H. Oil passage; I. Oil reservoir; J. Disk boot casting; K. Drawbar.

furrow opener. When pressure is applied to the furrow openers, it should be uniform. Uniform pressure can be gained only by having both lifting levers in the same notch and having the pressure on all springs the same. The pressure on each furrow opener is adjusted by raising or lowering the adjusting collar on the pressure rod.

The tilting levers on rear of poles provide easy adjustment for proper relation between penetration and depth of planting when using any type of furrow opener.

Disk scrapers should be adjusted as lightly as practical and disengaged entirely, when possible, to prevent wear.

The land measurer is provided to measure the number of acres covered by the drill. On some drills, the land measurer is driven from the main axle; on others, from the feed shaft. To set it when starting a new field, press top of measurer in to force the bottom gear out of contact with worm gear on feed shaft or axle. Turn bottom gear to right—about one-eighth of an acre—to disengage fraction gear from acre gear. Move the indicator to largest number on acre dial and turn bottom gear to left, with indicator on fraction dial in upward position.

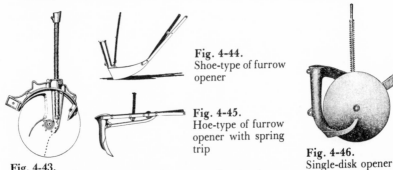

Fig. 4-44.
Shoe-type of furrow opener

Fig. 4-45.
Hoe-type of furrow opener with spring trip

Fig. 4-46.
Single-disk opener

Fig. 4-43.
Cutaway view of double-disk opener showing how seed is protected between disks until it reaches the open furrow

Care of Drills   The drill should be cleaned and put in condition for the next season's seeding before it is stored. All seed should be cleaned out, the disks or other opener surfaces cleaned and oiled, and the machine put under shelter. Good treatment prolongs the life of the drill. Most drills are equipped with fittings for pressure-gun lubrication. The disk bearings should be kept oiled thoroughly with oil or grease of proper viscosity as listed in the manufacturer's instruction book. Bear in mind that the disk bearings operate largely below the surface of the ground and, for that reason, it is highly important to keep the oil chamber well filled with oil of proper grade. See the cross section of disk and bearing, Fig. 4-42. Double-disk openers are oiled from the top of the boot.

Types of Openers   Fig. 4-43 shows a cutaway view of a double-disk furrow opener, illustrating how seed is protected in seed tube and between disks until it reaches the bottom of the furrow.

The shoe-type of furrow opener, shown in Fig. 4-44, works well in loose soils where the greater penetration of a disk opener is not required. Fig. 4-45 illustrates the hoe-type of opener which is especially adapted to seeding in rocky soils.

Fig. 4-46 shows a single-disk opener with pressure spring, scraper, and disk boot. The single-disk deep furrow opener is used with twelve-, fourteen-, or sixteen-inch spacing to make wide, deep trenches and ridge the soil to catch the moisture and prevent the soil from blowing. It is used most widely in winter-wheat sections.

The deep furrow opener with moldboard and seed deflector is shown in Fig. 4-47.

All of these types of furrow openers are interchangeable.

CORN PLANTERS

As with small grain, accuracy of planting has more to do with the yield of corn and other row crops than any other mechanical factor, and so, on to the corn planter. And, incidentally, the John Deere 999, was one of the very best horse planters ever made, and can still be picked up at farm sales in good condition, from time to time.

Drop and Seed Plates   The accuracy of a corn planter depends upon the accuracy of the drop and the selection of seed plates best suited to the size of seed to be planted—taking for granted, of course, that seed is of uniform size and that dirt has not clogged the seed passages.

There are two types of corn drops—the accumulative and the full hill. The accumulative drop is generally conceded to be more accurate because it takes one seed to each cell in the seed plate and then counts out the number of seeds to a hill as desired. A full hill drop planter takes all the seeds that make up the hill into one cell. It is claimed, and probably rightly so, that it is easier to get one seed in a cell each time than it is to get more than one, the same number each time. The accumulative drop is described in the following paragraphs.

Fig. 4-48 shows a cross section of a seed hopper bottom showing seed plate in position and sloping surface of the bottom. The weight of the seed causes it to move to the sides and enter the openings in seed plate. Fig. 4-49 shows top view of the hopper bottom.

The assembly of the hopper, seed plate, and bottom false plate is shown in Fig. 4-50. This also illustrates how seed plates are removed by tipping the hopper forward and releasing the spring latch that holds the bottom plate in place, without removing seed from hopper. Extra-wide seed is accommodated by reversing the false bottom plate as indicated in the drawing.

Seed plates are now available for seed of any size from kafir to lima beans, including a full range of plates for handling the various hybrid strains of corn. Fig. 4-51 illustrates the importance of selecting the right seed plates for corn by fitting the seed to be planted in the seed cells, as shown. If cells are too large, two kernels may pass into one cell, resulting in overcrowding the hill; if too small, less than the wanted number of kernels will be dropped.

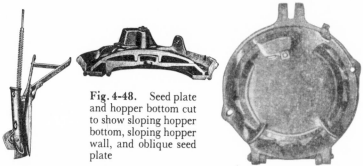

Fig. 4-48. Seed plate and hopper bottom cut to show sloping hopper bottom, sloping hopper wall, and oblique seed plate

Fig. 4-47. Furrow opener with moldboard and seed deflector as used on deep furrow drill

Fig. 4-49. Top view of corn hopper bottom showing seed plate in position

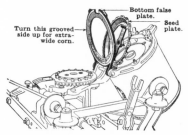

Turn this grooved side up for extra-wide corn.

Bottom false plate.

Seed plate.

Fig. 4-50. Assembly of the hopper, seed plate, and false plate showing how seed plates are removed by tipping hopper forward.

A   B   C

Fig. 4-51. Illustrating how to select proper seed plates for an accumulative drop. Corn must fit the cells of the plate like the kernel marked B. If kernels are too large as C, or too small as A, a plate having cells that will hold one kernel at a time should be selected.

Checking or Drilling   Practically all corn planters—horse-and tractor-drawn—can be used for both checking and drilling. The planters shown are easily adaptable for checking two, three, or four kernels per hill and for drilling seed in practically any spacing desired.

In drilling, seeds can be planted in any practical spacing desired. This wide range can be obtained by using plates having from two to twenty-four cells, setting the variable drop shifting lever on two, three, or four, or using the drive chain on the large, medium, or small drive sprockets. A scale, showing how to set machine for any drilling distance, is provided with each planter. If this scale is not available, a few minutes spent in experimenting with various settings will give the desired adjustment. The plates used for checking usually can be used for drilling, the operator using the shifting lever and sprocket adjustments to get desired spacing.

The information on drop, seed plates, and spacing, given above, applies generally to corn planters of both horse- and tractor-drawn types. Basic differences in construction in these two types of planters which require separate discussion will be considered in a following section on tractor planters.

Checking Horse-Drawn Planters   To test the accuracy of the drop and to determine if right seed plates are being used, jack up the planter, fill hoppers with seed, and turn the wheels. Trip check forks by hand and catch the seed, keeping accurate check on each dropping. Planter should not be turned faster than thirty-five revolutions per minute.

To find out if planter is giving a good cross-check, carefully dig up a row of at least eight hills crosswise, setting a stake in center of each hill. Due to the travel of wire, the hill of corn should be found about an inch behind the button. An adjustment is provided on planter which permits tilting front to place hills closer to or farther from button. Tilting front by lowering runner tips places hills farther back, while raising runner tips places hills closer to button.

To adjust width of planter, remove bolts that hold shanks to frame, remove bolt holding drive pinion on drive shaft, and adjust the shanks in or out to width of row desired. Be careful not to slip pinion off the shaft as the timing will be disturbed. Adjust wheels in line with the runners.

Field Operation   The object of checkrowing corn is to make cross cultivation possible. Cultivating crosswise of the rows is a difficult task if checking is not straight, and the straightness of crossrows depends more than anything else upon the handling of the check wire.

The check wire should be stretched reasonably tight when laid out and should be kept at that tension. The reel friction can be adjusted to hold wire to the desired tautness when un-winding, but uniform checking depends upon the judgment of the operator in pulling the wire to the same tension each time he moves the stakes.

Crooked crossrows may also be caused by running the front of the planter at an improper level, in which case every pair of rows will be out of check. This may be adjusted as explained in the preceding paragraph.

If only one side is out of check, it may be caused by valves not being adjusted correctly, frame of planter being bent, or by a weak rocker-shaft spring. A bent frame may also cause one row to be planted deeper than the other.

If the planter scatters seed between hills, the trouble may be due to kinks in the check wire, an obstruction in the valves, or too little tension on the rocker-shaft spring.

Caring for Corn Planters   To insure good work and ac-curate planting, corn planters must be well oiled and all parts must be firmly in position. Parts must be replaced when badly worn, or the efficiency of the planter will be impaired.

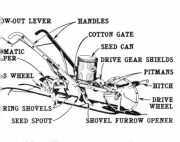

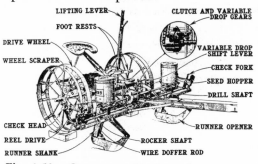

Fig. 4-52.   Two-row corn planter with important parts named

Fig. 4-53.   One-row combination cotton and corn planter with parts named

Oil holes in a new planter should be filled with kerosene to cut out the paint, after which a good grade of machine oil should be used liberally on all friction parts with the excep-tion of parts which are enclosed in housings and operate in a constant bath of oil inside the gear case. The gear case or housing in which these parts are enclosed should be filled to the level of the oil plug with clean, new oil of viscosity recommended by the manufacturer of your planter. Inspect the oil level occasionally and if low, add sufficient new oil to fill gear case to proper level. Before the planting season opens, remove drain plug from bottom of gear case, drain old oil, and flush out with kerosene. Refill housing to proper level with clean oil. Frequent oiling adds to the life of a planter except in extremely dusty conditions when it is better to use only kerosene on all working parts, excepting, of course, parts enclosed in housing.

COMBINATION COTTON AND CORN PLANTERS

The cotton grower requires a planter that will plant cotton, corn, and other row crops with equal accuracy. His multipurpose planter must be quickly and easily convertible from one type of planter to another.

Fig. 4-53 illustrates the type of mule- or horse-drawn planter most generally used where cotton is raised on ridges. This machine can be obtained with either runner or shovel opener. Fig. 4-54 shows a type of two-row planter available for both drilling and checking. One-row walking planters are also made for hill-dropping and drilling cotton and corn.

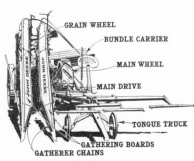

GRAIN WHEEL

BUNDLE CARRIER

MAIN WHEEL

MAIN DRIVE

TONGUE TRUCK

GATHERING BOARDS

GATHERER CHAINS

Fig. 4-54. Two-row combined cotton and corn planter

Fig. 4-55. Corn binder with tongue truck and power-driven bundle carrier

Corn Binders

On a good many small, horse-operated farms you will find the corn binder in use, both for corn and sorghum. It is not difficult to operate and adjust if the operator is familiar with the more common causes of trouble and knows how to correct them.

The corn binder is composed of three main units—the cutting, elevating, and binding units. Each has a definite and vital bearing upon the satisfactory operation of the binder. Each must be in perfect adjustment if the binder is to do its best work.

Cutting Unit Is Important   On the corn binder, the cutting parts are subjected to greater strain than any other part of the machine. This is due to the size of the stalks, their comparative hardness, and the fact that the load comes intermittently as the hills are reached. Even in the best of conditions, there is a much greater strain on the cutting unit of the corn binder than on the cutting parts of a grain binder.

To operate efficiently with the lightest draft under these severe conditions, the cutting parts of a corn binder must be sharp, properly aligned, and set to run smoothly.

Two stationary knives, one on either side in front of the sickle, aid in cutting the stalks as they approach the sickle. These knives must be kept sharp and set to a shear cut with the sickle. They can be removed and sharpened with very little difficulty. When replaced, the bevel edges should be down. Because of the fact that the side knives and the sickle are often forced to work in the dirt, frequent sharpening of both is necessary. Dull cutting parts increase the draft, add to the strain on the driving mechanism, and may cause clogging of the machine.

The sickle must run freely, yet fit snugly in the guides provided. If the sickle head becomes worn, the knife head guide is adjusted to take up the wear by loosening the two nuts and adjusting the guide in the slotted holes. When this adjustment is properly made, the sickle and side knives make a shear cut—one of the big essentials to light draft and good work in a corn binder.

The Elevating Unit   The elevating unit consists of six carrier chains, two chains on each of the upper gathering boards, and two chains on the lower part of the inner gatherer. The purpose of these chains is to elevate the corn in an upright position from the sickle to the binding unit. Their efficiency depends upon adjustment to the proper tension and position, which can best be determined by observation in the field.

Convenient tighteners are provided for each of the chains. They should be so adjusted that the chains run freely and are not too tight.

In addition to the adjustment for tightening the top chains, there is an adjustment provided for controlling the throat capacity or the distance between these chains (see Fig. 4-56). In cutting unusually tall corn on a windy day, it is often necessary to set the chains closer together to bring the tops back at the same speed as the butts. If it is desired to retard the tops, the throat capacity is increased by setting the chains farther apart. This is often necessary in cutting short corn.

Another aid to cutting short corn is provided in the small, round retarding spring. It may be set with the end tight against the binder deck. In this position, it holds the tops back, causing the corn to elevate in an upright position.

The lugs on the elevating chains serve as fingers that carry the stalks along. Chains that operate opposite to each other should be adjusted so that the lugs alternate rather than match as they move along the throat of the binder. In this adjustment, they are most efficient, and the danger of ears wedging between lugs and interfering with their work of elevating is eliminated. Note, in Fig. 4-56, the lugs in proper adjustment; the flat side of the lugs should always be run next to the corn, as shown.

Long steel springs are provided in the lower part of the throat to hold the corn against the lower chains. They are fastened to adjustable brackets and should be set with just enough tension to hold the stalks into the butt chains. In weedy conditions, more tension is applied to aid in elevating the extra quantity of material to be handled.

The Binding Unit The details of the operation and adjustment of the corn binder binding unit are practically the same as those given for the grain binder. Adjustments for tying troubles, twine tension, etc., are the same on both. A review of this text matter will furnish sufficient material for practical study of the corn binding unit.

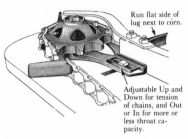

Run flat side of lug next to corn.

Adjustable Up and Down for tension of chains, and Out or In for more or less throat capacity.

Fig. 4-56. Top chain tightener is adjustable two ways

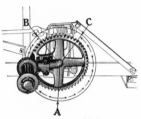

Fig. 4-57. Grain wheel adjustment for balancing corn binder, showing grain wheel set to rear between points A and B to keep stiff pole from whipping, or to keep enough weight on tongue truck. Set wheel to front between A and C on binder with stiff pole, but without carrier.

Field Operation The first field adjustment necessary is setting the binder to the height it is desired to cut the corn. In some cases, as in cutting corn infested with the European corn borer, it is desired to cut as close to the ground as possible, while many times high cutting is more practical. Height is controlled by cranks on both the main and grain wheels. The binder works best when the wheels are set at the same height. If additional traction is needed, it can be secured by lowering the main wheel.

The grain wheel axle is constructed so that the weight of the binder can be shifted forward or backward to balance the machine properly with any equipment (see Fig. 4-57). The wheel is shifted to the rear to prevent whipping of the pole, or to place proper weight on the tongue truck. It is shifted forward to relieve neck weight when the tongue truck is not used.

The binder is tilted with the tilting lever to adjust the position of the gatherers with relation to the ground. This setting is governed by the condition of the corn to be cut. If the corn is down, the gatherer points should be run close to the ground.

The butt pan, upon which the butts slide from the sickle to the binding head, is adjusted up or down at the rear with the pan lever. The binder should be operated with the pan as low as possible, raising it only when it is necessary to place the band closer to the butts.

Bundle Carrier   The power bundle carrier is set into operation by tripping a foot lever. It delivers the bundles beyond the path of the horses as they make the next round. This eliminates the waste caused by the horses tramping the corn and does away with the hard work of dumping the bundles and returning the carrier, which is necessary when the old-fashioned bundle carrier is used. A safety clutch in the carrier drive removes the possibility of breakage should the forward motion of the carrier be checked for any reason. The spring tension on the clutch is adjustable to meet varying loads that may be carried.

Haying Equipment

MOWERS

Every horse farm needs a good mower. Most of the major companies made horse mowers into the early fifties, and the late model mowers had mostly roller bearings and the gears ran in oil. They are very durable and a pleasure to operate.

Since it is impossible to get a new mower, the following checklist may be helpful in obtaining a good used one. Bearing in mind that most any horse mower at a farm sale is from twenty-five to fifty years old, here are a couple things to look for.

Check the castings very carefully. A mower with broken castings is very difficult to repair and in many cases it is a sign of misuse or a runaway. The mower frame is cast iron and difficult to weld.

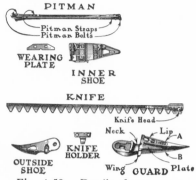

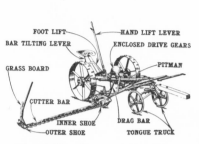

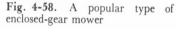

Fig. 4-58. A popular type of enclosed-gear mower

Fig. 4-59. Details of mower cutter bar parts

Open geared mowers are older and unless the gears are good they can be a headache. Repairs for these models are almost completely unavailable. The later model mowers that had the gears running in an oilbath had better bearings and they lasted longer.

Horse mowers were sold in varying sizes from one-horse mowers of 3½ feet, to two-horse mowers of 4½, 5, and 6 feet, to 7-foot mowers that need three horses. Most of the available mowers are 5 or 6 feet. Either one, in good running order, can be handled by a good team.

Probably the two most common horse mowers in our area are the Number 4 John Deere and Number 9 McCormick Derring. Maybe something else was popular in your area. In any event, you aren't likely to have a wide selection on really good machines. If I had my "druthers," I would rather see one of our machinery companies manufacture a good mower and manure spreader rather than any other two pieces of equipment, for they are needed on any horse and livestock farm.

Many horsemen prefer tongue trucks on their mowers. A mower is about as heavy on the neck yoke as anything you are likely to use with your horses and a truck takes that weight off the neck, saving shoulders. In our own case we have a set of old binder trucks on our mower.

The section on horse-drawn mowers in the John Deere booklet is the best source I know. So I will let them take it from here.

Mowers are in use in all sections of the country, and their operation, care, and repair should be a matter of general knowledge among farmers. Heavy draft, ragged cutting, and excessive breakage can often be avoided by using the maximum of care in the oiling, adjusting, and replacing of parts. A smooth-running, clean-cutting mower gives real satisfaction to the operator and requires less power from your horses. Fig. 4-58 shows a popular style of enclosed-gear mower with all main parts named.

The cutter bar and its parts, including the pitman shaft (see Fig. 4-59), make up the most vital unit in mower operation. These parts do all the work of cutting; draft, repair costs, and length of life of the mower depend upon the proper setting and care given them.

Register of the Knife   The knife is the heart of the mower. Its sections must be sharp and firmly riveted to the knife back; the guards, wearing plates, and knife holders must fit to it perfectly, holding it to a shear cut with the guard plates, if its work is to be efficient. Knife head guides must be properly set and bolted tight.

Register of the knife refers to the position of its sections in relation to the guards when the knife is at the outer end of its stroke and at the inner end of its stroke. The sections should be in the center of the guards when at the extremes of the strokes.

If the knife does not register on its outward stroke, that is, if the sections do not reach center of guards, part of the vegetation is not cut. The results are an uneven job of cutting, an uneven load on the entire mower, heavier draft, and often, clogging of the mower knife. An incomplete inward stroke will result in the same troubles.

To test and correct the register of a mower knife, raise the tongue to working position—thirty-two inches from underside of front end of tongue to the ground—and turn the flywheel over until knife is at outer end of stroke. It is necessary that pitman straps at both ends of pitman are tightened properly before making the test. If the sections do not center, an adjustment should be made. On most makes of mowers, register is obtained by adjusting the brace bar at the flywheel bowl. One complete turn of the brace bar will make ⅛-inch difference in register. In addition to this adjustment, forked washers are provided at both ends of the drag bar bearing on the mower shown in Fig. 4-58, so that knife will be properly centered without destroying the correct lead in the cutter bar. By transferring more or fewer washers from one end of the yoke to the other as may be necessary, and at the same time adjusting the brace bar, proper setting is obtained.

Cutter Bar Alignment   All new mowers have a certain amount of lead in the cutter bar; that is, the outer end is ahead of the inner end to offset the backward strain produced by the pressure of cutting and to permit the knife and pitman to run in a straight line. As the mower wears and parts become loose, the outer end of the bar lags back until the knife is running on a backward angle, causing undue wear and breakage of cutting parts. The outer end of the cutter bar should be ahead of the inner end 1 to 1¼ inches on 4½-foot mowers; 1¼ to 1½ inches on 5-foot mowers; 1½ to 1¾ inches on 6-foot mowers; and 1¾ to 2 inches on 7-foot mowers.

To determine the lead or lack of lead in a cutter bar, raise the end of the tongue (underside) thirty-two inches from the ground. Then tie a cord to the oil cap on the pitman box ("A" in Fig. 4-60). Stretch the cord over the center of the knife head, as shown at "B," Fig. 4-60; the amount of lead in the bar can be determined at point "C." The upper illustration in Fig. 4-60 shows a 5-foot bar with the proper lead—approximately 1¼ inches.

The lower illustration in Fig. 4-60 shows a bar with nearly 4 inches of lag—a condition that would result in heavy draft and poor work were it not corrected. With the cord tied to the oil cap on the pitman box, "D," and stretched over the center of knife head at "E," the position of the outer end of the bar at "F" is seen to be 3 inches behind the straight line, or approximately 4¼ inches behind the position at which it should be maintained for the correct amount of lead.

Lag in the cutter bar of the mower shown in Fig. 4-58 is removed and the bar brought up to proper position by turning an eccentric bushing ("A" in Fig. 4-61) to the left until proper alignment is obtained.

After hard usage, enough wear may occur to create excessive free motion of cutter bar. In such cases, new parts may be necessary for effective adjustment.

Pitman Adjustment   The mower operator must keep the bolts that connect the pitman to the pitman box and knife head at proper tension for good work. If pitman bolts are too tight, particularly the knife head bolt, the draft will be increased. The knife head must have a free ball-and-socket action in the pitman straps (see Fig. 4-59) to accommodate tilting of the bar and the up and down movement of the inner and outer ends of the bar in going over uneven ground. If the bar is tilted low, a tight pitman connection tends to hold the knife sections away from guard plates. This causes excessive wear and allows the grass to get between sections and guard plates.

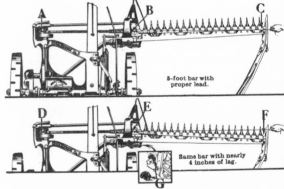

5-foot bar with proper lead.

Same bar with nearly 4 inches of lag.

Fig. 4-61.   Eccentric A is adjusted to left to take up lag in cutter bar.

Fig. 4-60.   Overhead view of a mower showing how to determine lead or lag in the cutter bar

If the pitman bolts are permitted to become too loose, or the strap rivets loosen, the pitman and knife are subjected to excessive vibration, which results in heating of pitman box, breakage of parts, and abnormal wear. Operating the pitman with the hand will usually show whether or not it is in proper adjustment.

Adjustment and Repair of Cutter Bar Parts (see Fig. 4-59)
When the pitman is properly adjusted and all cutter bar parts are set as they should be, the front end of every knife section rests smoothly on the guard plate, in position to make a shear cut. To maintain this ideal condition, guards and guard plates, wearing plates, and knife holders must be in good condition and correctly set. If these parts become loose or badly worn, the knife will flop around in the cutter bar, chewing and tearing the grass instead of cutting it, causing the mower to pull hard and increasing the possibilities of breakage.

The guard or ledger plates have a very important function in the cutting action of the mower. They act as one-half of the shear, the knife sections acting as the other half. If sections and plates are not sharp or do not fit closely together, the result is similar to that produced by a dull or loose shears in cutting cloth. Guard plates should be replaced when broken or worn dull (Fig. 4-62) and the guards aligned to give a shear cut on every plate.

A dull or improperly ground knife reduces the efficiency of the mower, results in ragged cutting, excessive and unnatural

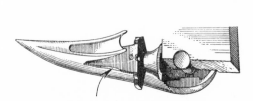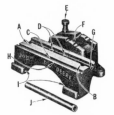

Fig. 4-62. The efficiency of the mower is seriously impaired by imperfect guard plates.

Fig. 4-63. A convenient block for removing and replacing guard plates, knife sections, flywheel wrist pins, and for straightening knives. A and B are holes used in riveting wrist pin to flywheel. C indicates a hole through which sheared rivets are driven. Removable, hardened riveting posts are shown at D. E is the guard plate riveting post. F indicates hole through which old rivet is driven. G is a groove for the knife back. When shearing sections, the knife back rests on edge H. The grooves, I, steady the knife. J is the rivet set used in completing the job of riveting.

wear, and extremely heavy draft. By actual dynamometer tests, a dull or improperly ground knife may increase draft of the mower as much as 30 percent over the normal draft of a new or properly ground knife.

The angle at which the sections work with the guard plates and the angle of the cutting bevel on new sections have been worked out by years of trial and experience; they are practically standard on all mowers. When grinding the knife, it is of utmost importance that these angles be retained if the knife is to be restored to its full efficiency. The angle at which the section meets the guard plate must be such that the grass will not have a tendency to slip away. The bevel of the section is highly important, as an abrupt edge will tend to dull easily and chew the grass, thereby increasing draft; too wide a bevel will cause the section to nick easily (see Fig. 4-64).

The type of knife grinder shown in Fig. 4-65, because of its better work, greater speed, and easier, simpler operation, is fast replacing the grindstone method of reconditioning knives. With this type of grinder, the operator simply slips the knife into slides, locates the setting with the gauge, clamps the knife into place, and brings the revolving stone into contact with the section by turning the horizontal adjustment screw. Up and down movement of the stone is controlled by the vertical adjustment lever. Most manufacturers

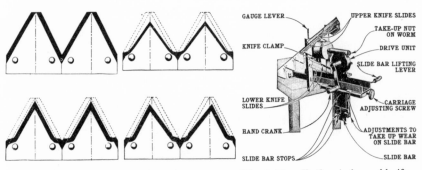

Fig. 4-64. The right and wrong ways to grind mower knives. Dotted lines show outline of new sections.

Fig. 4-65. Knife grinder and knife in upper knife slides

provide foot-, motor-, and engine-power grinders in addition to the hand-power grinder shown.

When knife sections have been ground to the point where the efficiency of the mower is impaired, or when sections have been broken, the worn or broken plates should be sheared off. With knife back resting solidly on the block, strike back edge of section a sharp blow. This operation will shear the rivets without damaging knife back. Driving out the rivets with a punch not only enlarges the holes, but weakens the knife back.

Aligning the guards is an important and exacting operation. A new knife, or a straight one that is not badly worn, should be used in testing and setting the guards. Insert the knife and set each guard up or down, as necessary, to make a shear cut between knife section and guard plate. Guards are malleable iron and can be bent without breaking by striking at the thick part, just ahead of plate when guard bolt is tight. Guard wings should also be aligned, making a smooth surface for knife back to work against. Position of guard points should not be considered—the plates and wings are the important units that must be aligned. See Fig. 4-66 for complete information on proper alignment of guards to produce a shear cut.

It is advisable to replace badly worn wearing plates (see Figs. 4-59, 4-62, and 4-66) when guards are repaired. The wearing plates hold the sections in correct cutting position, but when worn, they permit the sections to rise at front end, causing clogging and ragged cutting.

The knife holders hold the sections down against the guard plates. They must be set close enough to the sections to hold them firmly in position when cutting, yet not tight enough to cause binding and heavy draft.

When necessary to set the holders down, the knife should be pulled out—holders should never be set down with knife under holder. Starting at holder next to the outer shoe, set each holder down with a hammer, tapping it lightly. Then move the knife under holder to test the adjustment; if it tends to bind, leave knife under the holder and hit the holder on the flat surface between the two bolts. Proper setting of each holder must be made before moving to the next one.

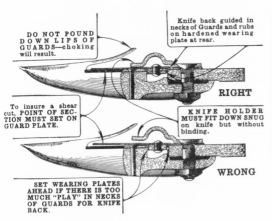

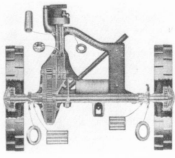

DO NOT POUND DOWN LIPS OF GUARDS—choking will result.

Knife back guided in necks of Guards and rubs on hardened wearing plate at rear.

RIGHT

To insure a shear cut, POINT OF SECTION MUST SET ON GUARD PLATE.

KNIFE HOLDER MUST FIT DOWN SNUG on knife but without binding.

WRONG

SET WEARING PLATES AHEAD IF THERE IS TOO MUCH "PLAY" IN NECKS OF GUARDS FOR KNIFE BACK.

Fig. 4-66. The right and wrong way for a mower knife to fit and operate in the guards

Fig. 4-67. Cross-sectional view showing oiling system, gears, clutch, and bearings of the mower shown in Fig. 4-58. The arrows indicate parts that are oiled automatically.

Lifting Spring   There should be enough tension on the lifting spring to cause the bar to rise easily and move steadily over the ground. With too much tension, the bar will not follow uneven ground, and the inner end may be held up after it has passed over a mound or other obstruction. When properly adjusted, the lifting spring carries the bulk of weight of the cutter bar on the wheels, increasing the traction and reducing friction between bar and the ground.

Clutch Adjustment   When clutch parts become worn, it is often necessary to make minor adjustments for good work. The clutch shifter rod is adjustable to take up wear and keep the clutch engaged full depth in drive gear. If the mower does not go out or stay out of gear when shifter lever is moved down, it is evident the clutch shifter rod adjustment must be shortened. This is done by loosening the lock bolt on the clutch pedal and turning the clutch throw-out sleeve to the left. After proper adjustment is made, tighten lock bolt and secure with cotter key.

When the clutch lever is up and the clutch meshes full depth with gear, the clutch shifter yoke should be free in the clutch and not bind against either side of the groove in the clutch.

Operation and Care   Mowers require a considerable amount of attention and care when at work. Following are a few hints for mower operators:

See that all moving parts work freely before putting the machine in the field. Keep all nuts tight.

Use plenty of good grade oil, and never let wearing surfaces become dry.

Oiling of the mower shown in Fig. 4-58 is greatly simplified because all gears are enclosed in running oil. In addition, the axle, wheel, gear, countershaft, and pitman shaft bearings are oiled automatically from the gear case, as shown in Fig. 4-67.

In dry, dusty, or sandy conditions, the cutting parts usually work best without oil.

The mower is in correct working position when underside of the tongue at the front end is thirty-two inches from the ground.

It is advisable to keep the horses close together by shortening the inside lines.

SIDE-DELIVERY RAKES

Both three- and four-bar side-delivery rakes for horses were made by all the major manufacturers. To find one that has not been used behind a tractor is not easy. It is a lot easier to find a ground-driven rake designed for use behind a tractor and then proceed to use it behind a fore cart. That is what we do and, actually, I think I prefer it to a horse rake. My rake is considerably heavier than any rake made for horse use. Some horsemen might find this objectionable and prefer the rake built for horses. Raking is something that shouldn't be done at top speed—it shatters too many leaves and the extra weight will slow the team down. Another advantage of using a ground-driven tractor rake behind your team is that you have a later model machine and parts do not present a problem. There is a good supply of ground-driven tractor rakes to be had, and fore carts are relatively easy to build, so unless a horse rake was really in mint condition I wouldn't get too excited about it. (On the other hand, if you know of one in mint condition, let me know—just in case.)

Here is what John Deere had to say about their horse-drawn side-delivery rake.

When the hay is cut, the flow of ground moisture is shut off, but the plant is full of water. The problem, then, is to reduce the moisture to a safe percentage for storing, and to do this in the shortest possible time.

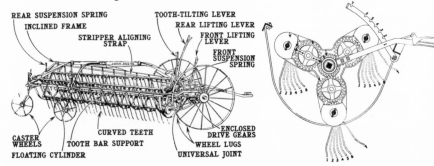

Fig. 4-68.   Side-delivery rake with the more important parts named

Fig. 4-69.   Rake teeth can be set in seven different positions with the tooth adjusting lever. Tooth positions 1, 2, 3, 4, 5, and 6 are working positions obtained by setting the lever in the six notches. When traveling on the road, the lever should be moved to position 7.

The leaves, or tops, are left exposed to the sunlight, as they fall back over the mower cutter bar. If allowed to remain in this position very long, the leaves dry up and shatter. When this happens, the natural flow of moisture from stems to leaves is stopped and the moisture is "bottled up" in the stems. This results in unevenly cured hay.

The function of the side-delivery rake (Fig. 4-68) is to lift the hay from the swaths and place it in loose, fluffy windrows with the green leaves inside, protected from the sun's rays. The leaves, shaded by the stems, are cured rapidly by the free circulation of air through the windrows. They retain their fresh, green color and the stems are thoroughly cured for storing.

If rainy weather catches the hay in the windrow, it is often necessary to turn it several times before it is thoroughly cured and ready for storing. The left front wheel is set in on the axle to allow enough of the reel to extend beyond for turning the windrow upside down when the left-hand wheel is run next to the right-hand edge of the windrow. This operation inverts the windrow, placing it bottom-side-up on dry stubble with the damp hay exposed for curing.

Field Operation   Side-delivery rakes, once they are adjusted to suit field conditions, are easy to operate. The operator simply drives his team or tractor and oils his machine when necessary.

The most important adjustment is setting the teeth in the proper position, or angle, in relation to the surface of the ground. This is done with the tooth-adjusting lever, with which it is possible to set the teeth in six different working positions (see Fig. 4-69). The teeth should always be set as high as possible and still pick up all of the hay. This setting causes the curved teeth to lift the hay gently, leaving the windrow as loose as possible and permitting free circulation of air.

In traveling on the road, the tooth-adjusting lever should be moved to notch seven. In this position, the teeth are raised above the strippers out of danger of being bent by hitting obstructions.

The front lifting lever should be adjusted so that the front end of the reel is low enough to pick up the hay, but never so low that the teeth strike the ground. A trial with the lever in the center notch will usually give an indication as to the position in which it should be set.

The rear lifting lever is properly set when the rear end of the reel is slightly higher than the front end. This aids in making the windrow loose and fluffy.

Care Is Important   When starting a new side-delivery rake, or when using one that has been stored, it is a good plan to turn the reel by hand to be sure it revolves freely and that the teeth do not strike the stripper bars. Then throw the rake into gear and turn the wheel by hand to see that the tooth bars and gears work freely. Breakage of parts which results in serious delay can be avoided by taking these precautions before entering the field.

All wearing parts should be oiled regularly. An occasional thorough inspection for loose nuts, worn bolts, and other parts will add to the efficiency of the side-delivery rake.

Some small farm and acreage operators with limited amounts of hay still use sulky rakes (or dump rakes) and hayloaders. The cost of baling has gotten to the point where it is possible that more small operators will be interested in making loose hay. Finding a good hayloader may not be too easy. Anyhow, for those of you interested in using either of these two pieces of machinery, here is what John Deere had to say about their models.

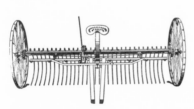

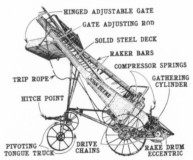

Fig. 4-70. The sulky rake is used in practically every section of the country.

Fig. 4-71. Combination raker bar-cylinder loader with the more important parts named

SULKY RAKES

The sulky, or dump rake, used in practically every section of the country, is built in both horse- and tractor-drawn types. Since the horse-drawn type is more common on farms today, a rake of that type will be used for discussion in this text. While it is easy to operate and adjust, many farmers work at a disadvantage when a slight adjustment would produce much better results.

The first requirement for good work is proper hitching. The rake shown in Fig. 4-70 is designed to work with the tongue thirty-one inches from the ground, measuring underneath at the front end. If this position is not maintained, the rake teeth will set at an improper angle, resulting in inferior work. If the tongue is too high, the teeth will have difficulty in clearing the hay after dumping; if too low, the teeth may fail to gather all of the hay.

Adjustments   Slight pressure on a foot trip lever causes the dump rods to engage in the wheel ratchets resulting in dumping of the rake. After the rake teeth have cleared the hay and started downward, they may be forced down quicker and held in position on the ground by pressure on the foot lever. An adjustment is provided at the hinge in this lever by which the wear can be taken up. If an adjustment is not made when the hinge becomes worn, the rake will be dumped with difficulty.

The height to which the teeth rise when the rake is dumped is controlled by adjusting a snubbing block bolt, located on the frame to the rear of the seat spring. If the rake rises too high and consequently does not get back to work as soon as it should, the block bolt must be screwed out of the block one or more turns. Turning the block bolt down permits the rake to rise higher when dumped.

If the rake repeats when it is dumped, the tension on trip spring is insufficient to hold the dump rod out of the wheel ratchets. More tension is produced by turning down the nut on the trip spring bolt.

When the wheel ratchets or dump rods become worn, the wheels and rods can be reversed, giving double wear.

Keep Nuts Tight   Because of the vibration attendant to raking, it is necessary that all nuts be kept tight. It is a good plan to go over the rake at regular intervals for this purpose.

Oil, used liberally on axles and wearing parts, will make for good work and lengthen the life of a dump rake.

HAY LOADERS

While most manufacturers build loaders of several designs, including heavy-duty types especially for loading green crops, the raker bar-cylinder type is generally recognized as the most efficient. For this reason, a loader of this type (Fig. 4-71) will be used for study of the hay loader.

In operation, the teeth on the floating gathering cylinder "comb" the stubble to pick up all of the clean hay and pass it on to the deck. Here, the slow-moving raker bars elevate the hay to the adjustable extension deck, or gate, from which it passes to the rack.

The most important factor in the satisfactory operation of a loader is the proper setting of the gathering cylinder. It does the best work when it is set in the highest position in which it will do a clean job of raking. If set too high, it misses some of the hay; if too low, it gathers trash and the spring teeth scratch the ground, throwing dust into the hay. Height of the gathering cylinder is varied by moving the position of the hand nut on the adjusting rod on each side of the loader. A spring placed behind each crank gives a floating action to the cylinder. In moving from field to field, the gathering cylinder should be raised to highest position by running the hand nuts all the way down on the adjusting rods.

The loader should be hitched as close to the rack as possible, but not so close as to cause it to strike the corners of the rack in turning.

The carrier extension or gate can be lowered for starting the load by releasing the lever. It is raised as the load goes higher by pushing up on the center of the gate.

Care of Loaders   Because hay loaders have wood and light chain in their makeup, they should be stored in a dry place if possible. If the loader is permitted to remain in the open, the rain and sun shorten its life and increase upkeep costs. Shelter should be provided whenever possible. The foretruck on the loader shown may be folded back to reduce height of deck for ease in storing. A long lever at front frame controls this adjustment.

The usual admonition regarding thorough oiling of farm machines and keeping all nuts tight can be repeated for all hay loaders. Slack seasons furnish an opportunity to overhaul the hay loader along with other farm machines.

Rotary Hoes

Partial as I am to the horse, I still recognize his limitations. The rotary hoe is an example. For a rotary hoe to be effective it *must* travel at high field speeds. As a horseman friend of mine once said, "I would just as soon drag a rooster by the tail across the field as use a rotary hoe with horses." That was overstating the case a little, but he had a point. The rotary does not do a good job at horse speed, so as far as I'm concerned, here is one item that is easy to pass up at farm sales.

The alternative—just harrow your corn an extra time with your spike tooth harrow after planting and before cultivation. The spike tooth harrow will kill a lot of weeds as the corn is emerging, but in all honesty, not as much as a rotary hoe operated at high speeds. But, you can't win them all.

And Finally . . . The Horse-Drawn Manure Spreader

If there is any piece of equipment more important than a good manure spreader on a livestock farm I don't know what it would be. Unlike most tillage tools, it is used off and on the year around. On dairy farms it is used every day. Until about three years ago the New Idea Company in Coldwater, Ohio, made new horse-drawn spreaders. We were fortunate enough to get one of their last ones. Because they did persist in the manufacture of horse-drawn spreaders long after most of their competitors had quit, you find quite a lot of New Idea 10A spreaders around the country. But all the majors made horse

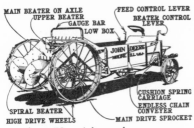

Fig. 4-72.   A horse-drawn manure spreader

Fig. 4-73.   Barn scraper shows: 1. Top link as cylinder connection; 2. Lower link as hinge point; 3. Three horsepower engine for hydraulic drive.

spreaders at one time, and they were good machines.

Here is what John Deere said about their horse-drawn spreader.

Types of Spreaders   A style of horse-drawn spreader in common use is shown in Fig. 4-72. It has three beaters. The upper and main beaters shred the manure; the spiral beater deposits it evenly over the entire width, making a well-defined line beyond the drive wheels.

The manure is carried back to the beaters by a steel slat conveyor, the speed of which is controlled by the feed lever from the driver's seat. From five to twenty loads can be spread per acre, according to the setting of the feed lever.

The operator must be sure to keep the feed lever forward, in neutral, whenever the machine is not in gear or whenever the beaters are not operating. If the feed lever is left in operating position when starting to the field with a load, the conveyor forces the load back against the beater, resulting in breakage in some part of the feed mechanism. The feed lever should be thrown into neutral, also, when turning sharply while spreading.

With the control lever, the operator shifts the main drive chain so that it is in contact with the large drive sprocket. The three beaters are driven by two chains, both of which are set into action by the drive sprocket. The beaters should not be put into gear in this manner while the machine is in motion. The control lever should be moved to the rear only when the spreader is standing still.

Building the Load   It is much easier on both the team and the spreader if the operator starts to load from the front end, finishing at the beater end. The shredding process, which is the work of the beaters, is less of a strain when the load is built in this manner, resulting in lighter draft and less wear on the machine.

Fortunately the demand for horse-drawn spreaders is so keen that a more serious effort has been made around the country to find, rebuild, and restore them than is true of most equipment. New horse-drawn spreaders are also being manufactured in Canada by the Bowman Manufacturing Co., Hawkesville, Ontario, Canada.

There are a lot of draft horsemen in the country who don't use their horses very much, but it is a rare one who doesn't haul his horse manure out behind a team.

This winds up the quotes and illustrations from the booklet entitled, *The Operation, Care, and Repair of Farm Machinery*, published by Deere & Co. I very much appreciate their permission to quote from this text. The company made a lot more horse machinery than I have referred to here, but I felt that these were the most important machines, and the most likely to show up at farm auctions.

In reviewing this old literature on horse-drawn machinery one cannot help but be struck by the simplicity of design, a sort of sophistication in itself.

Adapting New Machinery to Horse Power

Old machinery is fine if you can get it, but many farmers are faced with the problem of not being able to buy old horse-drawn machinery for their horses. At present, producers of new equipment for horses are few and severely overworked. In addition, many mixed power farmers also do not want to buy *two* pieces of equipment, one to use with their horses and another to pull behind the tractor. In these situations, conversion of tractor-powered machinery to horse power is a necessity. And it can be accomplished with surprising ease.

Conversion is usually not difficult if done with a little ingenuity; variations on a basic theme (such as the hitch cart discussed later in this chapter) are extremely common as a farmer adapts a piece of machinery or an idea for use on his farm. Among the most inventive at adapting machinery for horses are the Amish, many of whom have continued to farm with horses and have repeatedly faced the problem of conversion when their old machinery finally could not be repaired or when they needed a piece of machinery to do a new job around the farm. The following article, which appeared in the Winter 1976 *Draft Horse Journal* and is reprinted with permission of Sperry-New Holland, illustrates some examples of Amish ingenuity. The author, Dick Anglestein, is in a unique position to appreciate this quality of the Amish farmer since he is in the Public Relations Department of Sperry-New Holland, a large manufacturer of farm equipment located in the heart of Lancaster County, Pennsylvania, the historic home of the Amish in this country.

Quite a number of farms in Lancaster County, Pennsylvania, have gone from tractors back to horses. This phenomenon can't be attributed to any major movement away from mechanized farming. Essentially, it's the continuing resolve of Amish farmers to continue their way of animal-powered agriculture, which began on the county's rich, rolling farmland just about a half-century before the Revolution.

Their manner of farming not only has persisted for 2½ centuries despite the overall trend toward more and more sophisticated mechanized machinery, but also in the face of continually spiraling land prices. This is a general agricultural problem, no matter if it's powered by animals or their mechanized successors, however. What might be considered more unique is how the Amish farmers cope with modern mechanization.

They don't shun it completely. Using a good bit of ingenuity and basic mechanical skills, they adapt and remold the modern tools of agriculture to fit behind their teams of horses and mules. It's a blend of the past with the present, the old with the new. Through the years they've had to learn how to make or adapt farm machinery to animal power, as most of the rest of the world marched into mechanization. They don't view it as a particular problem, either. No more than holding to other beliefs of a life style that contrasts sharply with the surrounding worldly modernism. As one observer explains: "The plow doesn't know what pulls it. Neither does the baler or any machine for that matter. Simply, it's a practical situation of making a machine designed for mechanized operation suitable to animal power."

Here are a few examples of how the Amish do this.

Unusual even for an Amish farm is an animal-powered barn scraper (see Fig. 4-73). It is a standard three-point hookup with Category I three-point linkage. The drawbar hitch points become the hinge positions for movement of the blade. The top link is replaced by a standard ASAE remote control hydraulic cylinder, which raises and lowers the blade. A three-horsepower engine is belted to a hydraulic pump with a small reservoir. An open-center, double-action valve is utilized for raising and lowering the cylinder. Thus, down pressure can be applied for added penetration during manure cleanup operations.

Since horse-drawn plows are getting quite scarce, tractor trailer-type units are converted. They are hitched to a two-wheel cart with a drawbar for any trailer-type machine, a seat for the driver and tongue for the team (a hitch or fore cart). For planting, a four-row trailer-type corn planter, hitched to the same cart, is most likely used. But there are instances of a two-row no-till corn planter being used with a three- or four-horse hitch.

A Sperry-New Holland Model 33 flail-type Crop Chopper can also be adapted (see Fig. 4-74). At the front drawbar hitch point the front axle of an antique horse-drawn manure spreader is attached. The axle can be angled both for side position field use and roadway transport behind the animals. By a simple adjustment of braces, the hookup is easily modified to keep the wheels straight for right or left offset for transport and field position. The chopper is equipped with a small water-cooled engine, similar to that used on small combines or forage blowers. Equipped with a speed reducer, the engine modifies the RPMs approximately to that of the PTO

Fig. 4-74. PTO coupler is pointed out on Sperry-New Holland Model 33 Crop Chopper

Fig. 4-75. Spreader cart hitched to team

speed and also changes the direction of rotation in keeping with the PTO. Since the fastening of the engine is accomplished by only four bolts and the PTO coupler, it is interchangeable on other equipment, such as when it is time for haying. Using an overhead chain hoist in the implement shed, Amish farmers switch the engine to a hay conditioner or a Haybine mower-conditioner in less than a half-hour. For those Amish farmers not utilizing a Haybine to combine their mowing and conditioning in one operation, a six- to eight-horsepower engine is mounted on an old ground-drive mower. The drive is disconnected and the engine operates the pitman, taking the load off the horses.

For raking, again the two-wheeled driver's cart or "Amish tractor" is used. A modern Rolabar rake is hitched to the drawbar. Slower propulsion with animals saves more of the alfalfa leaves and more protein per acre is gained. A Sperry-New Holland Model 273 baler, equipped with a small Wisconsin engine, packages the hay.

With the Amish reluctance toward the use of rubber tires, an extra factor must be added to the machine's adaptation. Due to their conversion to steel wheels, absorbing the shock loading—normally handled by the rubber tires—becomes a major concern. To absorb the shock, two methods may be used. Conventional leaf springs may be utilized. Also, coil springs are incorporated into the spokes of the steel wheels to absorb the shock and prevent axle failure. (It is interesting

Fig. 4-76. Ground-drive Sperry-New Holland manure spreader is equipped with driver's cart containing 1. Steering lever and 2. Brake pedal.

that a version of the coil spring design was a part of the buggy the astronauts drove across the surface of the moon. The Amish were using this method of absorbing shock quite a few years before modern science found an application in space exploration.)

An ingenious design for animal power can be found in the conversion of a Sperry-New Holland Model 202 manure spreader (see Figs. 4-75 and 4-76). The driver's cart is made from the front end of a late model Ford automobile. Both the coil springs and shock absorbers are retained. The steering tie rod is connected to a lever in the manner of a tractor hillside plow hitch. This greatly simplifies the maneuvering of the spreader close to buildings and eliminates the need for backing the animals. The conversion utilizes the car's hydraulic braking system and master cylinder, which is connected to a foot pedal, for helping to control the spreader over hilly terrain.

The Fore or Hitch Cart   The "Amish tractor" mentioned repeatedly in the previous article is one of the most useful pieces of machinery found on a horsepowered farm and is a virtual necessity to the mixed power farmer. The following article, reprinted from *Draft Horse Journal*, is by Cumberland-Lyle Bare, a vocational agriculture teacher from Dunkerton, Iowa. Cumberland runs a mixed power farm himself, and is interested in adapting and rebuilding new farm equipment for horse power.

The fore cart has become an essential piece of horse equipment for many people who really want to use their horses as a source of power. They are especially handy on a mixed power farm. A fore cart enables you to use available tractor machinery with your horses. Anyone who has attempted to line up a complete set of good useable horse-drawn machinery knows how difficult it is. With a well designed cart you can use a two wheel tractor spreader, a tractor plow, and tractor disks. If you really want to go all the way you can pull a baler with a motor on it and even a corn picker, or if you hire your ear corn picked and hay baled, the fore cart will come in handy hauling in loads from the field. It is a quick way to hitch and use your horses to the maximum in cutting power costs in this age of high priced petroleum.

Farmer ingenuity seems to have a field day where hitch carts are concerned. I don't believe I have ever seen any two that were exactly alike. Each was adapted to a particular situation or purpose. I'll give some recommendations based on my observations of their use and then you can let your imagination go to work.

A scale drawing of my own hitch cart is included (see Fig. 4-77). The drawings are non-professional and don't include an end view. My cart does not have brakes because the cart itself is too light for them to be very effective. A team can drag it easily with the wheels locked.

I would suggest building a cart with adjustable tread if I were planning to plow with it. It should be adjustable from fifty-eight inches to eighty inches to fit different requirements. An adjustment similar to the one used by tractors with a wide front end would be ideal.

The seat on my cart is from a 1937 A John Deere tractor. The seat is forty-eight inches from the ground and I wish it were at least one foot higher. Here, it would raise you out of the dust and you could watch your lead horses better with the added height when you are using five or six strung out on the cart. The two-foot by four-foot platform gives you standing room. Make sure your seat is solid and safe. On horse machinery the seat was usually in the rear so if you had to bail

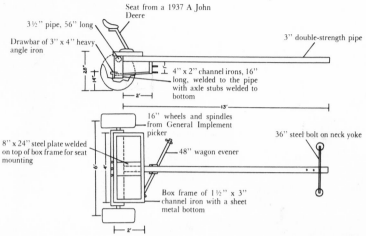

Seat from a 1937 A John Deere

3½" pipe, 56" long

Drawbar of 3" x 4" heavy angle iron

3" double-strength pipe

4" x 2" channel irons, 16" long, welded to the pipe with axle stubs welded to bottom

2'

13'

16" wheels and spindles from General Implement picker

8" x 24" steel plate welded on top of box frame for seat mounting

48" wagon evener

36" steel bolt on neck yoke

Box frame of 1½" x 3" channel iron with a sheet metal bottom

2'

Fig. 4-77. Fore cart or hitch cart

out the implement was ahead of you. This is something to keep in mind in using a fore cart.

The tongue on my cart is extra long with holes drilled to move the neck yoke in or out to fit the team. I like a bolt-on neck yoke because it is impossible to have the tongue drop. It makes the fore cart safer for both team and teamster. The neck yoke is a thirty-six-inch metal type. I use a forty-eight-inch wagon evener with stay chains and only give the evener about ten inches of movement. You have to make your team work together with this arrangement.

The drawbar is as close to the center of the cart as I could make it. This enables you to keep some weight on the tongue even if you are pulling a heavy two wheeled spreader. A drawbar extension makes it more maneuverable with a four wheel wagon or implement with no tongue weight.

The Horse-Drawn PTO Self-Unloading Wagon In the February 1973 issue of *Draft Horse Journal,* Jennis B. Hofer of Freeman, South Dakota, ran an ad showing him feeding cattle with a team, using a converted PTO self-unloading wagon. Later on that year the South Dakota Draft Horse and Mule Breeders picnic was held at his farm, at which time he demonstrated the use of the wagon.

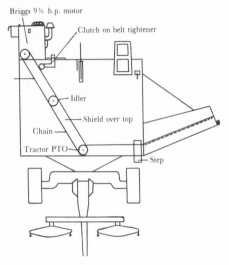

Fig. 4-78. Self-unloading feed wagon

Others have expressed interest in this idea and its application so I wrote Jennis for the particulars. A good idea deserves imitation and I'm sure this one will have wide application.

Here's a portion of Jennis's reply to me concerning the wagon, along with a drawing of the wagon and its important parts (see Fig. 4-78).

The only thing I changed on this feeder wagon was putting the motor on and the clutch which is a V-belt with a tightener. I have an idler in the middle for the span is too long from motor to PTO shaft stub. Otherwise everything comes out perfectly all in an arm's length from the seat.

This was wishful thinking on my part before I started on it. I never thought it would come out this perfectly. It takes a powerful team of honest pullers. The box holds 150 bushels and the weight is over 2400 pounds empty without running gear.

Chapter 5

Feeding, Care, and Housing

Feeds and Feeding

So now you have bought a team and have them at home. They probably aren't exactly what you had in mind when you started down this road. Maybe they aren't the same color or breed you had in mind—or *any* particular breed. Never mind that. You will come to appreciate that walking up together is a lot more important than being the same color, and if they are what a first team should be in terms of training and temperament the bonds between you and this team will soon be just as close as if you had ordered them from J. C. Penney's perfectly tailored for size and color. Your problem now is one of care and feeding. The late A. B. Caine, horseman at Iowa State in the thirties, wrote an extension circular entitled *Care and Feeding of Horses* in 1938. We are pleased to reprint portions of that bulletin here, in the hope that it will be as helpful to you as it was to horsemen of that era.

This is, of course, the age of complete commercial feeds, pelleted rations, and other feeds available at your local feed mill or dealer. This may be well and good for the family with a saddle horse or pony and no home-grown grains and roughages, but for the small farmer with a team or more of work horses or mules they are a luxury. There are some very good and useful feed supplements for draft horses on the market, but in the main you are going to have to rely on home-grown feedstuffs for your draft animals. These sections will be devoted to feeding what you can grow with the labor from your draft animals.

The successful feeding of horses requires a knowledge of the adaptability of the common feeds and a thorough understanding of feed requirements under various conditions. Those who have studied feeding problems know that the skill used in feeding is responsible, to a large extent, for the efficiency of horses. Improper methods of feeding are not only expensive but in many cases materially affect the period of usefulness.

When selecting rations a few pertinent facts regarding feeds should be kept in mind. Some of the important considerations are the following:

1. The most economical rations are those made up of home-grown feeds. Most farmers can raise all the feeds that are needed for satisfactory and efficient rations.
2. Rations should be made up of a variety of feeds, each one supplying some necessary nutrient.
3. Feeds should be palatable and adapted to the needs of horses for growth, work or reproduction.
4. A certain amount of bulk is needed in all rations.
5. Rations that have approximately the correct proportion of proteins, carbohydrates, fats and minerals are usually more efficient and cheaper.
6. Select only feeds that will not in any way prove injurious to horses.
7. The economy of the ration is important, because 60 to 70 percent of the cost of keeping horses can be charged to feed.

SOME PRACTICAL SUGGESTIONS IN FEEDING

Horsemen may vary considerably in selection of feeds and in some methods of management but they recognize a number of factors that are essential to success. Some of the important things to keep in mind in successful horse production are:

1. Regularity in feeding. Horses are beasts of habit and fret if the feeding schedule is changed from day to day.
2. Rations should be adjusted according to the needs of horses. Brood mares require more feed than geldings, colts must have a liberal supply of muscle and bone building nutrients, and work horses need energy producing feeds.
3. Horses should be watered frequently and liberally.
4. All changes in rations should be gradual rather than abrupt.
5. Feed only clean, bright feeds.
6. Use pastures liberally for all horses. Turn work horses on pasture at night and on all workless days.
7. Provide ample salt at all times.
8. Reduce the grain ration a half to a third on workless days.
9. Keep the horses' teeth in good condition. A veterinarian should examine the teeth once or twice a year.
10. Keep horses free from parasites.

CONCENTRATES

Oats—the standard grain for horses and can be fed safely to all horses, including both work horses and breeding horses, and are valuable for fitting horses for show or sale. They can be used as the entire grain ration or fed in combination with almost any natural or commercial feed.

Corn—a carbonaceous concentrate, is extensively used as a feed for work horses. It should be used as a part of the grain ration because it is usually cheap in price and has a high feeding value. Corn is better adapted to the needs of mature work horses than it is to colts, brood mares or stallions. It is a heating feed and it is usually best to reduce the amount of corn fed during hot summer months. Legume hays are excellent feeds to use with corn because of the protein and mineral matter they furnish.

Barley—another carbonaceous concentrate used in many sections as a part or all of the grain ration for horses. Its feeding value is not as high as corn or oats but it can be used to good advantage, and if the price is not too high it can be substituted for corn. It is a very hard grain and should be rolled, ground or soaked for best results.

Wheat—usually too expensive to be fed and it is not a safe feed in the hands of an inexperienced feeder. Some horse breeders feed stallions and brood mares grain rations that contain up to 20 percent wheat because of the value derived from the wheat germ. Wheat should be rolled or ground and fed with oats, bran or other grains, or it can be mixed with cut hay.

Soybeans—concentrated and must be fed in limited amounts, but give satisfactory results. A high-protein feed, they can be used with a carbonaceous grain or roughage. With corn and timothy hay, the addition of about 5 percent of ground soybeans would make the ration more effective. Soybeans are rather hard, and horses sometimes refuse to eat them unless they are ground or crushed.

Wheat bran—a bulky, protein-rich concentrate and a cooling, laxative feed which can be mixed with the regular grain ration or fed as a mash. It is too bulky to feed in large amounts, but for limited feeding and to keep a horse's digestive system in good condition, bran is excelled by few, if any, feeds. The substitution of bran for a large part of the regular grain ration on workless days is a practice followed by many successful horsemen.

Bran is a valuable feed to use for mares before and after foaling and for stallions during the entire year, unless allowed the use of a pasture during the summer.

Bran mashes are frequently fed with splendid results. Many horsemen give a mash every Saturday night, or the night before any workless day unless their teams are turned on grass. A better practice could not be followed. A mash is made of about two quarts of bran with enough water added to make the mixture the consistency of a thick gruel.

Linseed meal—a nitrogenous concentrate with a high protein content that can be fed with carbonaceous grains or roughages. It is somewhat laxative and therefore can be fed with feeds that are constipating. Oilmeal is used in conditioning horses for spring work, especially those that have been running out in cornfields and are in poor condition. It seems to act as a tonic in that it causes early shedding of long hair, gives life to the skin, and improves the general appearance. It is a valuable feed for fitting horses for show, sale, or market, because it produces a glossy hair coat so much desired in show and sale animals.

Usually not more than one to 1½ pounds, mixed with the grain, are given daily. Some feeders do not bother to weigh the meal but just add a small handful once or twice a day.

Cottonseed meal—a highly nitrogenous concentrate used rather extensively as feed in the South. It is not especially palatable and should be limited to not more than one or two pounds daily. Best results are obtained when it is fed with a laxative feed. In the South, the animals that are fed cottonseed meal are usually turned on grass. In some cases equal parts of cottonseed meal and linseed meal have given more satisfactory results than when cottonseed meal was fed alone.

In an experiment conducted by the Iowa Agricultural Experiment Station and reported in Bulletin 109, Kennedy, Robbins and Kildee found that: "Cottonseed meal has somewhat better results on the whole than oilmeal. The ration containing it was fully as palatable and as efficient in maintaining the health and weight of horses, it was less laxative and a little cheaper with cottonseed meal at thirty dollars a ton." Further they found: "The health, spirit and endurance of work horses were the same when fed corn with a moderate amount of oilmeal, or gluten feed or cottonseed meal, as when fed a corn and oats ration supplying a similar nutritive ratio."

ROUGHAGES

Timothy hay—one of the most commonly used roughages in horse feeding, and is the standard to which other roughages are compared. It is probably the safest hay that can be fed to horses. Timothy is a carbonaceous feed, fairly rich in carbohydrates and fats but lacking in digestible protein and minerals. Whenever this hay is fed, special care should be taken to add protein and minerals to the ration. Oats, bran, soybeans, linseed meal or cottonseed meal are valuable protein feeds to use with timothy, while alfalfa, clover or soybean hay are roughages that will help to balance timothy.

Timothy has long been a favorite of horsemen, especially city users, because it is usually free from dust and mold. It is not a "washy" feed, which is regarded as an advantage for saddle, show or race horses; in fact, timothy is considered the most valuable roughage obtainable for light horses.

From Iowa farmers' viewpoint, there are several drawbacks to timothy:

1. It is not a heavy yielding feed and is hard on the soil.
2. It is not a very desirable roughage when fed with corn, as both feeds lack in quantity and quality of protein and minerals.
3. It is not very well adapted to the feeding of colts, brood mares and stallions, though safe to use.

Experience and experiments have shown that there are roughages other than timothy which yield more per acre, build up soil fertility, are better suited to balancing corn and can be fed advantageously to horses and other farm livestock.

Alfalfa—probably the most palatable of all hays for horses. It is high in digestible protein and some minerals and is especially useful to feed with corn, barley or oats. It is a high yielding feed and builds up soil fertility.

In feeding alfalfa, care must be taken not to overfeed. Horses will eat more than they should if given an opportunity. A good rule to follow is to feed daily one pound of hay for each

100 pounds of live weight. If more roughage is needed, straw, prairie hay, timothy or any other nonleguminous hay may be added.

Alfalfa may become dusty when cured and should be sprinkled before feeding. Alfalfa cut when fairly mature seems to be best suited for horses; it is less laxative than that cut sooner.

Clover hay—ranks next to alfalfa in value for horses. It is palatable, slightly laxative and has a fairly high protein content. It is well suited to the feeding of horses of all ages that receive considerable corn or other carbonaceous grains as part of the ration. Clover is sometimes rather dusty but can be safely used if sprinkled before it is fed.

Medium red clover is the most commonly used. Other varieties, such as mammoth or sweet, are usually coarse and a considerable quantity is wasted. In feeding clover, about the same precautions should be followed as with alfalfa; that is, feed a limited amount and have the hay as bright and clean as possible. A mixture of clover and timothy hay is a very desirable roughage for horses.

Soybean hay—generally contains more protein and total digestible nutrients than alfalfa or clover and can be used for feeding horses of all ages when corn or corn and oats are used as concentrates.

The stems are rather coarse and horses will not eat all of them, but the finer, more nutritious portions are readily consumed. Soybean hay is frequently used to fatten horses and mules for market.

Prairie hay—another carbonaceous roughage that is widely used as horse feed. Like timothy, prairie hay is not high in digestible crude protein and must be supplemented with nitrogenous feeds. It can be used for all classes of horses with safety but is not effective for colts, brood mares and stallions unless fed with either a protein-rich hay or concentrates.

Oat hay, barley hay, soybean straw—if the regular hay crop winterkills, oats or barley can be grown and used for horses with good results. The grain should be sown at a trifle heavier rate per acre and cut after it has headed out but before the grain is ripe, usually in the milk stage.

These hays are palatable and can be used for horses of any age. Horses may not consume the entire stalk; the remainder can be used for bedding. If fed with corn, some protein should be added.

Soybean straw is useful for wintering horses. It contains more than twice as much digestible crude protein as oat straw and is a valuable roughage when horses are running in stalk fields.

Oat, barley and wheat straw—straw from small grains is found on nearly every Iowa farm. The principal use made of straw is for bedding, but some of it can be used for wintering horses. Oat straw is regarded as the most valuable because of its somewhat higher nutritive content and palatability, but any straw of good quality can be fed.

Under no conditions, however, should straw be used as the sole winter ration because of its low protein and mineral content. At the South Dakota Station it was found that horses wintered exclusively on oat straw were permanently injured. It is often used as a part of the roughage ration when alfalfa or clover is fed. As has been stated previously, alfalfa or clover should be limited to one pound per day for each 100 pounds of live weight, but it is often advisable to feed a little more roughage, such as straw.

Corn fodder and corn stover—commonly used for idle horses but are not so well suited for work horses. These roughages are low in protein and should be fed with other feeds. Fodder and stover are difficult to feed in the barn because of their bulky nature. Leaves and the top portion of the stalk may be eaten, but the larger, coarser portion is usually refused and must be removed from the mangers. When fed out in the fields the refused portions can be used as fertilizer.

Bright, clean fodder is usually most economically fed if it is cut or shredded; more will be consumed, and what is rejected can be used for bedding. If the shredded fodder is dusty, it is a good practice to sprinkle it before feeding. Fodders when carelessly handled become moldy, partially spoiled, unpalatable and sometimes unsafe to feed.

Corn silage—not one of the principal roughages for horses but it can be used successfully if fed with care. Its use is mainly as a succulent feed to be used as a supplement in limited quantities. This feed should be introduced gradually into the ration and always with a dry roughage. The amount fed should not exceed ten to twelve pounds daily per animal. It is dangerous to feed moldy or frozen silage. Silage should be made from fairly mature corn. (Personally, I feel the risks of feeding corn silage to horses outweigh any advantages.)

SALT

Salt is needed by horses of all ages. The sodium and chlorine which make up salt are necessary for the proper digestion of the ration. Salt may be fed free-choice, given at regular intervals, or fed with the grain. The first method is preferred, since not all horses consume the same amount of salt, and it is difficult for the feeder to know exactly how much is required. As a rule, horses will eat from ½ to two ounces per day, depending upon their size and age, the work performed, humidity, temperature, the nature of feed and the character of the soil on which the feeds are produced or on which the horses are kept.

Where goiters frequently occur it is a good practice to feed iodized salt, especially to brood mares, stallions and colts. Iodized salt can be purchased on the market or the iodine may be added if care is taken that the salt and iodine are carefully and thoroughly mixed. The usual amount of potassium iodide to add is .05 pound with 100 pounds of barrel salt.

Iodized salt should be kept in covered containers, as it is thought that some of the iodine evaporates when kept in ordinary sacks or open bins.

MINERALS

Calcium and phosphorus are two of the most important minerals that are lacking in common feeds but can be easily and cheaply supplied. Ground limestone and spent bone black or bone meal will take care of the calcium and phosphorus deficiency. Using a variety of feeds lessens the necessity of feeding a complicated mineral mixture.

The following mixture, a simple combination that adds most of the minerals needed to improve the common rations used, has been fed to colts and brood mares at Iowa State College:

Iodized salt, twenty pounds; finely ground limestone, forty pounds; spent bone black or bone meal, thirty-five pounds; commercial iron oxide, three pounds; sulfur, two pounds; total, 100 pounds.

The amount horses will consume depends upon their ages and the character of the feed. Some horses will eat as much as one ounce daily. Horses are particular about eating anything that has a strong odor, and that is why spent bone black is suggested in place of bone meal.

WATER

Adequate supplies of water and sensible watering systems throughout the year, but especially during the heat of summer, will do much to insure both the comfort and well-being of your work stock.

Horses which have been deprived of water for a long period of time, or those which have undergone severe or prolonged exertion should generally be watered before they eat. It is dangerous, however, to allow an animal to drink heavily while very warm. If the horse is hot when he comes in from the field, give him a moderate drink at that time, and water more freely after the animal has cooled off.

It is not a good practice to water heavily just before putting horses to heavy work.

Horses on a protein-rich diet, such as alfalfa hay, will drink more water than those fed a carbonaceous diet, such as timothy.

Though not always practical or possible, it is an excellent idea to have water available in the field and to water them frequently during the day; this is especially true during the hard, hot work of oat harvest, for example.

Many feeders maintain that horses should always be watered before feeding in order to prevent a flushing of the grain through the stomach and into the small intestine. Like watering in the field; however, this is not always practical. Thus individual convenience and attendant circumstances will largely determine the watering practice to be followed. In any event, once a plan or system is put into effect, it is well to adhere to this plan.

One of the times when a horse requires and appreciates a drink most is after he has finished his nightly allowance of roughage. Every horse should be allowed to drink at this time. A small night pasture, where they can be turned out to cool off and drink at leisure during the night is best of all.

The average water consumption per draft horse is from 10 to 12 gallons a day. Water is one of the most essential things in the ration of a horse, and yet its functions are frequently overlooked or taken lightly. Water aids in digestion, carries off waste products from the body, and flushes out and cools the system of this equine power plant.

Give your horses the same consideration you give yourself during the heat of summer. If you have sense enough to not drink heavily yourself just before heavy work, and to not gorge yourself when you come in all steamed up, then make sure your horses do likewise. And if you like an occasional drink of water in the field, it's a safe bet your faithful partners would appreciate the same. Moderation is the key, for both man and beast.

FEEDING WORK HORSES

The methods of feeding work horses vary in different sections of the country, and there is no one best way of feeding under all conditions. Available feeds, character of work to be performed and climatic conditions all have a bearing on how horses should be fed.

The amount of feed required for work horses depends upon the nature of the work, the size of the horses, age, sex, season of the year, their individuality, and the rate of speed at which they work.

The ration for work horses must consist of a fairly large amount of concentrated feeds that are rather easily digested. A variety of feeds may be used, but the most popular are grains or concentrates that are easily digested, nutritious, palatable, and cheap in price.

When the work is extremely heavy, it is necessary that the concentrate be heavily fed and that the roughage portion of the ration be limited. As the work becomes lighter the grain can be decreased and more hay added, because horses doing light work can get along on from a third to a half as much grain as when they are working hard.

Oats, 3 parts
Corn, 2 parts
Clover and timothy hay

Oats, 2 parts
Corn, 3 parts
Alfalfa hay, 1 lb. for each 100 lbs. of live weight

Oats, 2 parts
Barley, 2 parts
Corn, 2 parts
Mixed hay

Fig. 5-1. Suggested rations for work horses

PASTURES FOR WORK HORSES

The ration for work horses for summer feeding can be somewhat different from the winter ration. It is a good practice to feed less heating feeds, or at least smaller amounts of the concentrates with a higher carbohydrate and fat content. Some farmers feed about 75 percent corn in the winter and 25 percent or 50 percent in summer.

From about the middle of May until cold weather in the fall, it is good practice to turn the horses on pasture at night after giving them their regular feed. They will eat some grass but not enough to harm them. The grass is cooling and laxative and keeps the digestive system in good condition. The horses also have an opportunity to rest better out in the cooler night air. Another advantage is that the damp grass helps to keep their feet from drying out. Labor requirements are also reduced by having the horses out during the night, and it has been found that they will get along with less feed than when kept in the barn.

When the horses are brought in in the morning they should be fed their regular grain ration, but usually very little hay is needed. In fact, if the pasture is good and horses eat considerable grass they will be better off with no hay at all in the morning.

On Sundays or other workless days the grain should be reduced to a third or half the regular amount. In the summer, put horses on pasture and if they seem contented and satisfied just leave them there and do not feed them more than one grain feed.

FEEDING IDLE HORSES

Mature, idle horses can be fed more cheaply than work horses. If horses are idle in the summer, they should be turned on pasture, because with average pasture conditions in Iowa, idle horses do very well on grass alone.

The most economical way to winter idle horses is to turn them into the stalk fields and meadows. This utilizes considerable non-salable roughage, saves labor in handling horses and hauling manure, reduces housing costs, and keeps them in good, healthy condition, providing, of course, that the feed is plentiful. Cornstalks and straw are not adequate to winter horses in good condition.

The addition of a little legume hay makes a great difference in the way horses will go through the winter. Alfalfa, clover, limited amounts of sweet clover, and soybean hay are valuable supplements to stalks and straw. The legume hays add protein and minerals and make the ration more nearly balanced. Stalks and straw are very deficient in both minerals and protein, and horses seldom do very well when these nutrients are lacking in the ration. Under most conditions the addition of eight or ten pounds of legume hay will keep them in first-class condition.

No hard and fast rule can be applied to all cases. The requirements of horses of the same weight, type, and breed differ greatly. The suggestions in Fig. 5-2 are given as general guides which can be used for average horses at various kinds of work.

It should be remembered that the kind of hay fed determines the amount of grain to feed and vice versa.

Idle Horses: principally roughage, cornstalks, fodder or some other cheap roughage, with 8 to 12 lbs. of alfalfa, clover, timothy, or soybean hay

Light Work: 1/3 to 3/4 lb. of grain and 1 ¼ to 1 ½ lbs. of hay for each 100 lbs. of live weight

Medium Work: 3/4 to 1 lb. of grain and 1 to 1 ½ lbs. hay for each 100 lbs. live weight

Heavy Work: 1 to 1 ¼ lbs. grain and 1 lb. hay for each 100 lbs. live weight

Fig. 5-2. General rules for regulating the amounts of feeds to be fed horses when idle and at work

---

How to best divide the daily ration is not thoroughly understood by many feeders, who feel that horses must be allowed to gorge themselves on hay at each feeding time. A simple rule to follow is to divide the three feeds about as follows:

Morning feed—⅜ of the grain and ¼ of the daily
allowance of hay
Noon feed—⅜ of the grain and ¼ of the hay
Night feed—¼ of the grain and ½ of the hay

It will be noted that most of the hay is fed at night when the
horses have ample time to digest roughage, and more grain is
fed during the day when more concentrated feeds must be
more readily available. Overfeeding of roughage is one of the
most common mistakes made in horse feeding and it is a very
wasteful practice.

MORRISON'S FEEDS AND FEEDING

One text that should be in every stockman's library is Frank
B. Morrison's *Feeds and Feeding* (Ithaca, New York: The
Morrison Publishing Co.), first published in 1898. The first
abridged version was published in 1917 to be used as a text for
students in agricultural short courses. It was immediately successful, and has been constantly updated. The seventh edition, published in 1937, was entirely rewritten and reset, as
was the eighth edition in 1949. This happens to be the one we
have on hand, so I don't know how many editions have
followed. Currently out of print, it continues to be regarded
as the basic text on feeds and feeding of beef, dairy, swine,
sheep, and poultry, as well as horses. Written in understandable language, it deals with the fundamentals of animal nutrition and treats feedstuffs used throughout the country, rather
than those just common to one state or locality.

Since it has enjoyed widespread usage as a text book, old
copies are usually not too hard to come by. I have not seen the
most recent editions so am not prepared to say how much attention is devoted to heavy horse nutrition. Whatever the
case in that respect, the material is basic, and this book
belongs in the home of everyone who is concerned about economical and efficient rations for horses or other species.

Horse Pastures

It is important to always remember that horses are basically pastoral animals; they are never happier and healthier than when on pasture. Pastures, especially permanent pastures, have become a casualty of modern agriculture in much of the Midwest. When you decide, however, to use live horsepower you will have to rearrange your thinking to provide for pastures. Pasture is probably more important with horses than with any other domestic livestock. Good pasture is essential in continuing low maintenance costs.

Following is an article we originally printed in the *Draft Horse Journal* of May 1965, by C. J. Heidenreich, at that time with Purdue University.

Good pastures offer horsemen the best and most economical source of feed. Most horsemen agree that the better the quality of pasture, the greater the prospects for health and soundness. Well-managed pastures, grown on fertile soils under favorable climatic conditions, are an excellent source of high quality feed. In general, good pastures supply protein, vitamins (especially carotene, the substance from which the horse synthesizes vitamin A), and minerals including those so important for soundness of limb, calcium and phosphorus. High-quality growing pasture furnishes all the essential nutrients, except salt and water. Only under conditions of rapid growth, heavy work, gestation, and lactation may increased energy supplementation be needed. Furthermore, pastures afford the opportunity for exercise which is an essential if horses are to stay sound in their legs.

Soundness of bone is much more important in horses than any other of our farm animals. This is due to the fact that sound legs are essential to function in the horse. Also, the horse often has stress and strains inflicted upon his limbs during work which other animals do not. Since the longevity of horses exceeds that of other farm animals, good bone development is necessary to sustain the animal through many years of usefulness.

The pasture can only be as good as the soil on which it is grown. If pastures are to furnish the maximum nutritional requirements soil must be considered. Soils differ in their plant food reserves. The success of the horse industry surrounding Lexington, Kentucky, may be partially attributed to the high limestone content of the soils and the calcium-rich bluegrass produced on such soils; not all soils have such high mineral reserves and in order to meet the needs of the horse from pasture forage, fertilization may be required. Continuous removal of crops and forage from the land has often depleted soils of essential elements. Since proper bone development and soundness in horses depend on proper mineral levels and balance, fertility levels are very important in the soils upon which forages are to be grown for horses. The importance of limestone, a calcium source, is understood when we consider that the horse's body is 6 to 9 percent bone, and bone is 25 percent ash, with 85 percent of the ash as tri-calcium phosphate.

PASTURE PLANTS

Several factors should be considered regarding the plants grown in the pasture. The plant species used should:

1. Be adapted to the soil moisture status, fertility level, and climatic conditions of the area in which they are to be grown.
2. Have insect and disease resistance. Use disease resistant varieties.
3. Be palatable to horses and have a high nutrient content. Plant species vary in their nutrient content even when grown on similar soils.
4. Have a long productive season. The longer the growing season, the better. Horses graze practically year round.
5. Be resistant to grazing injury. Low-growing species have a better chance of escaping injury under grazing pressure, especially from horses.

6. Produce a tight, dense turf. Plant species should develop a turf which can resist the action of running horses with hooves which are sharp and tend to "tear up" the turf. The root system should also penetrate deep enough to avail the plant of water and mineral reserves.

It is quite obvious that no single plant meets all the requirements needed to develop a top quality pasture in all aspects as outlined above. Kentucky bluegrass has long been a byword among horsemen. Drought susceptibility has often marred the reputation of bluegrass although research indicates that its total yield through the growing season is equivalent to other grasses when properly managed. Grasses such as Alta fescue and timothy may produce somewhat higher yields, but are of limited value due to their low palatability and digestibility late in season. Fig. 5-3 shows the yield of various grasses throughout the growing season.

Time of Cutting

	May	June	August	Sept.	Annual Total
	Pounds of dry matter per acre				
Alta fescue	1,429	1,155	482	547	3,613
Timothy	1,352	1,742	142	137	3,373
Kentucky bluegrass	1,228	1,092	490	539	3,349
Orchardgrass	1,531	944	397	449	3,321
Reed canary grass	1,325	761	425	420	2,931
Bromegrass	995	1,155	262	96	2,508

Fig. 5-3. Seasonal distribution of total yields of grasses under simulated grazing management. (Fertilized at 600 lb. per acre of 10-10-10. From Duell, Rutgers University Extension Bulletin 350-A.)

To assure high initial yields due to seedling vigor when pasture is first being established, orchardgrass may be included with Kentucky bluegrass. Orchardgrass will also give the pasture increased drought resistance and will not be discriminated against by horses when mixed with bluegrass.

The addition of a legume in the pasture is highly recommended. Either alfalfa or Ladino clover among others can be used although alfalfa can not tolerate heavy grazing pressure from horses. The addition of a legume assures high quality grass yields by supplying adequate nitrogen through atmospheric nitrogen fixation. Sufficient lime, phosphorus and potassium must be available or supplied, however, to promote good legume growth.

On drier sites, it may be worth considering Birdsfoot trefoil in place of Ladino clover. The deeper root system of trefoil renders it more drought resistant. Be sure to use a prostrate type of trefoil as these withstand grazing better than the more upright varieties. A good pasture mixture contains: a legume, a grass with good seedling vigor, and Kentucky bluegrass. Fig. 5-4 gives two mixtures which can be recommended.

Type of Species		Fertilizer at Seeding	Fertilizer for Maintenance
Well-drained soils			
Kentucky bluegrass	10 lb.		500 lb. 9-10-30 in spring. If
Orchardgrass	6 lb.	500 lb. of	legume declines to less than 30%
Ladino	1 lb.	5-10-10	of stand use 700 lb. of 10-10-10 as
Poorly drained soils			needed to maintain them.
Kentucky bluegrass	10 lb.		
Reed canary grass	8 lb.		
Ladino	1 lb.		

Fig. 5-4. Recommended perennial horse pasture

To realize the greatest returns from pasture, rotational grazing, clipping, and dragging are good management practices well worth the effort expended. Quality pastures grown on fertile soils and well managed, produce high quality feed that just can't be beat for raising healthy, productive horses.

REGIONAL PASTURING

Indicative of the importance that the Horse & Mule Assoc. of America attached to pasture is the fact that almost half of their booklet, *Care, Feed, & Management of Horses & Mules* is devoted to the part pasture plays in good horse husbandry. Following are some sections from this booklet concerning pasture; especially interesting are the regional recommendations:

Planning Summer Pasture Crops   From the time bluegrass is four inches high, horses and mules will do better if turned out on it all night every night, even when at work. They then have a chance to stretch and roll and to fill up on green grass, which is more palatable to them than hay at this time of the year. It is also an advantage to allow them out on Sundays, holidays, and rainy days. Pasture is the best and cheapest of all feeds for horses and mules.

Sweet clover (hubam) sowed early in April will be a foot high by June 1 in many sections and will pasture two horses per acre where horses are turned out every night. Biennial white or yellow sweet clover, sowed with oats, barley, or wheat, in the spring, will make a fair amount of fall pasture and will make an abundance of feed by June 1 of the following spring. Sweet clover furnished more feed per acre than almost any other pasture crop available, but, only should be used as a supplement to other pastures. If sweet clover alone must be used for pasture for some time, the animals should have some oat straw available also, and must have some hay when at work.

Barn lots should be well drained so that horses may have reasonably dry footing, even immediately after a rain. It is desirable to have a slope for drainage, preferably toward the south, since sunlight is good for the horses and aids the drying. Many successful farmers have hay racks in the barn lots, where oat straw and some hay is placed for the horses to eat when out in the lot, the idea being to have the horses and mules turned out in the barn lot during the spring whenever idle, in order that they may get fresh air and sunshine with access to good roughage before pastures are sufficiently far along to permit usage.

On a number of well-managed farms, horses and mules also are turned out in the barn lot at night during April and May after they have had their evening feed. The animals go out and roll, stretch, feed for a while from the hay racks, and then lie down and rest more comfortably than if they were tied up in the barn. This reduces the work of cleaning stables to a negligible point, as the horses and mules are in the barn for only about two hours in the morning, an hour at noon, and two hours or so at night.

Whenever possible it is a good idea to have a small pasture paddock or two near the barns for use as nighttime grazing during the work season. Ideally, this should be reserved exclusively for the work animals' use at nights and on Sundays and holidays. If they are to be idle for longer stretches than that, they should be turned out into larger pastures. It will be argued by some that their land is too valuable to be used in this way. In reply, I can only say that the contribution such night pastures make in keeping work stock fit and comfortable during the work season is also of great value.

Permanent Pastures on Every Farm   In all sections of the United States effort should be made to have some permanent pasture with good stiff sod which will furnish winter and early spring pasture. To supplement this, various grasses in mixtures may be provided. These are discussed under the head of "Supplemental Pasture" in paragraphs following. Where no permanent pasture is available, temporary spring pastures must be resorted to, but it should be understood clearly that these are a stopgap only, until such time as some permanent pasture can be made available.

Annuals for winter forage should be grown where there is likely to be a shortage of hay or straw. For these, heavy yielding forage crops should be chosen.

It is important in building luxuriant pastures that bare spots on the land should be disked lightly, seeded, then cross-harrowed with a spike-toothed harrow, slanting slightly and loaded with plenty of weight. This covers the seed which has fallen in the disk marks. Many farmers report that after disking, seeding, and harrowing, they spread five or six loads per acre of sheep manure over such pasture holding stock off thereafter until about June 1. Horses and mules are then turned on it. Where soil is sour it is essential to add lime before seed is sown, for clover will not grow in sour soils. Use horse manure on plowed fields, not on pastures for horses.

One very successful farmer declares: "Old pasture treated in this way will produce twice as much feed as other similar pasture untreated."

With a view to making this information of specific value to farmers and stockmen, wherever located, we have grouped states into districts where pasture conditions are in some measure identical. The recommendations which follow are applied to such specific districts. It will often be found helpful under special soil conditions to write directly to your agricultural college for further recommendation.

District No. 1   Eastern Nebraska, eastern Kansas, Missouri, Iowa, Illinois, Indiana, and Ohio
Early Pasture—Bluegrass—frequently termed "June grass"—is the best of all permanent pastures in this district. One or two of the nearby pasture paddocks should be in bluegrass, as it will furnish feed earlier in the spring than any other pasture grass or combination of grasses.
Supplemental Pasture—To take the place of or relieve bluegrass pasture during June, July, and August, one small paddock should be in supplemental pasture. For this, hubam sweet clover (fourteen pounds per acre) sown as early in the spring as possible is good; or the following mixture—oats, three bushels; red clover, four pounds; timothy, five pounds; sweet clover, five pounds—seeded as early in the spring as soil and weather conditions will permit, gives a large amount of pasture from very early until very late in the season, and

pasturing of the oats offers favorable conditions for a rapid and sure development of grass.

Where desired, sudan grass may be sown in another of the small pasture paddocks. Sudan is a warm weather crop and should not be seeded until corn planting is over; it makes rapid growth and in six weeks' time will afford abundant pasture. In fact, one acre will pasture four horses or mules at nights and on Sundays and rainy days. About thirty pounds of seed to the acre are sown. In the southern part of this district, either biennial sweet clover (fourteen pounds of seed to the acre) or Korean lespedeza, sown with small grain in the spring, will furnish a great deal of pasture after the grain is cut, and comes to full growth the following season. Sweet clover seed always should be scarified.

Sweet clover can usually be pastured by May 1 of the second season, and enough stock must be turned on it to keep it eaten back sufficiently to prevent its attaining a height of more than eight or ten inches. The Korean lespedeza becomes available a little later—about July 1—but furnishes abundant pasture from then until September 10, and will reseed itself under the most severe grazing. A reasonable seeding, therefore, of Korean lespedeza will furnish a stand for a long time.

In the southern part of this district, then, bluegrass for early spring and late fall, sweet clover from May 1 or 15 to July 15, and Korean lespedeza from July 1 to September 10 give a combination of pasture crops which will furnish maximum feed from a minimum acreage. Where lespedeza does not do well, sudan grass may be used instead. It will be available the latter part of June and furnishes an extremely heavy pasture growth.

In District No. 1, amber cane sorghum (the sweet variety), drilled in rows just wide enough apart to permit cultivation (about 30 inches) will yield an enormous amount of forage for winter. Planting should be delayed until about June 1, or till after warm weather has come, and the crops should be cut before the seeds have ripened thoroughly; in any event, before frost. The yield per acre is enormous and furnishes a most economical source of winter feed.

District No. 2   Minnesota, Wisconsin, and Michigan
Recommendations substantially the same as for District No. 1, with the exception of lespedeza for supplemental pastures.

District No. 3   Pennsylvania, New York, and New England
Same as District No. 1, with the exception of lespedeza, save for altitudes of more than 1,200 feet, where sorghum and sudan grass are not likely to do well for winter forage. In such cases, after making sure that the land is limed sufficiently to permit the growth of legumes, use fifty pounds of oats and sixty pounds of Canada field peas to the acre; or, if the land cannot be limed, use thirty pounds of vetch instead of the Canada field peas. It is wise to use half winter and half spring vetch.

These combinations, cut just before the heavy yield per acre, are high in nutritive content to take the place of the sorghum or cane, though the yield per acre will not be as heavy.

District No. 4   Maryland, Virginia, West Virginia, Kentucky, and Tennessee
Recommendations same as for southern part of District No. 1. Bluegrass does so well in these states that it often eliminates the necessity for supplemental pasture, but it is well to have some in case the season turns out to be dry.

District No. 5   North Carolina, South Carolina, Georgia, Alabama, Mississippi, Louisiana, and Arkansas
Permanent Pasture—Bluegrass where available. It seldom is. Where it is not available, a combination of Bermuda grass, white clover, and lespedeza appears to furnish the best permanent pasture for spring and fall grazing.

Supplemental Pasture, for summer months—Same as in District No. 1. Planting can be in February or March and the grain and grass combinations will be far enough along to furnish good feed by May 10 or shortly thereafter.

On account of the mild climate in these states, winter grazing should be provided, as this not only furnishes cheap feed but also prevents soil leaching. For such winter pasturage, rye on account of its hardiness and vigorous growth has been used very largely. One of the best mixtures consists, per acre, of: rye, one bushel; hairy vetch, fifteen pounds; crimson clover, ten pounds. It is desirable to plant early—as soon as possible after September 1. On fertile land the growth of pasture may be improved by lessening the amount of rye and adding winter wheat, oats and barley, making a mixture per acre as follows: winter wheat, ½ bushel; rye, ½ bushel; oats, one bushel; barley, ½ bushel; hairy vetch, fifteen pounds; crimson clover, ten pounds.

This makes a splendid grazing mixture and if planted in August or early in September will usually do to turn on the latter part of November. It is necessary, however, to keep the stock off the fields when the soil is soft from rains.

In some sections, remarkable results are being secured in production of winter hay planted in the fall. A mixture that is giving good results in Georgia is the following (per acre): fulghum oats, one bushel; any prolific winter wheat, ½ bushel; hairy vetch, fifteen pounds; crimson clover, ten pounds.

This should be planted comparatively early and cut at the dough stage. The crop comes off from ten days to two weeks ahead of normal oat cutting, yielding from two tons up per acre. The land occupied by it may be planted to sorghum or cow peas prior to the general oat harvest, with assurance of another good hay crop, to be cut in the early fall.

In the western part of this district, on sandy or hilly upland soils, winter rye with winter wheat, winter vetches and sweet clover as companion crops, seems best adapted for winter pasture; and, if not fully grazed off, can be cut for hay in the spring before the land is turned under for spring planted crops.

Farther south, on rich alluvial soils, a combination of fall-sown grains and legumes, consisting of rye, ½ bushel; winter wheat, ½ bushel; oats, one bushel; barley, ½ bushel; hairy vetch, fifteen pounds; sweet clover, ten pounds, furnishes a still better combination affording more luxuriant pasture.

In all of the states of this district, bluegrass generally does not do well; but Bermuda grass, a native grass called "carpet grass," white clover, and lespedeza furnish a permanent pasture that is abundant, nutritious, and a fair substitute for the bluegrass grown farther north.

Supplemental Pasture, for winter months—The winter grown grain-hay named above, and cow peas, soybeans, or amber cane sorghum, all furnish abundant roughage. The horses and mules should be permitted access to such dry forage to supplement their winter grazing.

This district with its heavy rainfall is preeminently suited to the production of good pastures and abundant forage, which should be used to the maximum, keeping grain feeding as low as is consistent with the satisfactory maintenance of the draft animals when they are at work. No grain should be fed when animals are idle. Soft ground due to heavy rains is the principal obstacle to full use of pastures, but can be overcome, in a measure, by using permanent pastures when land is too wet for the temporary winter pastures to be used.

Johnson grass and Bermuda hay may constitute a part of the roughage, although they are not as valuable as the legume hays which should constitute a fair proportion of the ration.

District No. 6   Texas and Oklahoma

Early Pasture—Bluegrass is available as permanent pasture in a few places in the eastern part of these states, but to rather a limited extent. Bermuda grass, white clover, and lespedeza, where they can be grown, furnish good permanent pasture. Also, the native prairie grasses common to the plains are valuable for permanent pasture. On farms, however, more reliance must be placed upon the necessity of getting greater yields per acre than the prairie grass affords.

Supplemental Pasture—Winter wheat and sweet clover (twelve to fourteen pounds of seed per acre) drilled in during August, are highly recommended for winter and early spring pasture by very successful farmers in this district; and a mixture of oats, barley, wheat, and winter vetches also is recommended as a good cover crop which furnishes useful winter and early spring pasture for horses and mules.

Sudan grass is the chief reliance for pasture during June, July, and August, and where sweet clover can be grown in nearby fields you have an ideal combination, as the mules will pasture on one for a while and then on the other. It appears advisable to plant the sudan in rows wide enough apart to permit cultivation, as the increased yield is held to justify the additional labor involved.

The planting of sudan grass with cow peas or sweet clover in thirty-inch alternate rows furnishes very successful supplemental pastures. The cow peas should be used with the sudan in sandy sections, but where sweet clover does well, use it instead of cow peas.

Reports from southern Texas are to the effect that some farmers have successfully maintained ten head of work animals on three acres of such a pasture combination from May 15 until September 1 without feeding any additional roughage. It is advisable, however, to allow the animals access to hay or straw in addition to such pasture.

The sweet sorghums are considered to make the best forage and the red top or shumake sorghum drilled thickly in rows thirty inches apart to permit cultivation produces an enormous amount of good forage from a very small acreage. Idle work animals will winter well on this forage and the winter pasture combination suggested above.

District No. 7　　Western Kansas, eastern Colorado, and western Nebraska

Recommendations substantially the same as for Texas and Oklahoma, except for the fact there is no permanent pasture, save for the native prairie grasses.

Winter Forage—Same as District No. 1.

District No. 8　　Wyoming, South Dakota, North Dakota, and Montana

Permanent Pasture—In the eastern half of North and South Dakota, alfalfa or sweet clover with brome or slender wheat grass are about the most desirable pasture mixture, producing the highest tonnage per acre, with power to withstand climatic conditions. In all other sections where these will not grow the native prairie grasses only must be relied upon for permanent pasture.

Supplemental Pasture—The same grain pasture combination as in District No. 1, with the addition of some plots planted to sudan grass wherever experience indicates it will grow.

Winter Forage—Same as in District No. 1.

District No. 9   Oregon, Washington, Idaho, Utah, and western Colorado

There are no permanent pastures with the exception of native grasses that have been left on rough land.

Supplemental Pasture—Hubam sweet clover, sown early, or biennial sweet clover sown the preceding fall—where soil conditions permit of the growing of such clover. Where clover will not grow, sudan grass planted as early in the spring as it is warm enough affords practically the only summer pasturage. As soon, however, as the winter wheat is cut, the stubble fields may be utilized for pasturing horses and mules; other stubble land not plowed in the fall will afford late fall pasture.

Winter Forage—The wheat or other small grain growing next to the fence usually is cut with the binder while still somewhat green. After curing in the shock, it is hauled in and stored for winter feed. It would be crushed down and wasted by the combine if not cut in advance. It is customary also to cut the grain in the ravines, draws, or coulees at the same time, as these areas remain green long after the rest of the grain is ready to cut. It is therefore advisable to cut this with a binder and get it out of the way before undertaking to combine the rest of the field.

For other winter forage, it is customary, where harvester combines are used, to employ a chaff holder, permitting the long straw to blow out separately. Chaff is then dumped into piles and later hauled in in basket racks and stacked for feed-ing. This makes good feed, would represent waste if not used, and reduces the amount of grain-hay used to about half of what would otherwise be needed.

While much fall plowing is done in these states, it is seldom possible to do all of it in the fall. Consequently, enough stub-ble remains unplowed to pasture the horses and mules nights and when not at work, from September until snow falls. Even in winter it is found practicable and desirable to turn the ani-mals out on the stubble about nine or ten o'clock in the morn-ing and let them stay out until four o'clock, for the sake of the exercise they will get in roaming over the stubble fields, where they will also pick up some feed.

In addition, the horses and mules have access to the chaff stacks (which usually are in racks in well-drained barnyards) both before going out to pasture and when coming in. They usually are stabled and tied up at night, at which time they have access to some grain-hay, whether it be wheat bundles or sheaf oats.

District No. 10   California
California is a district unto itself. It is customary to sow practically all small grain in the fall, and the winter rains make the valley lands so soft that it is impracticable to graze during winter months, except where native grass on rough land is found near farms or ranches. A good many farmers own or lease such rough pasture lands on the hills within a few miles of their holdings and turn their work animals out to winter on pasture alone, and with good results. For spring and summer, native pasture grasses are used where available and for sup-plemental summer pasture, same as District No. 9.

District No. 11   Nevada, New Mexico, and Arizona
Permanent Pasture—The only permanent pastures avail-able in these states are the native prairie grasses on rough land. Where winter rainfall is sufficient, winter wheat, oats, or barley may be sown with some sweet clover. This usually will afford early spring pasture, extending up to about July 1.

Temporary Summer Pasture—For temporary summer pastures, sudan grass should be planted as soon as warm weather comes.

Supplemental Feeds—Amber cane sorghum or kafir corn will furnish feed for winter forage where there is enough rainfall to make a crop of any kind. On irrigated lands, the grain pasture mixture recommended for District No. 1, and access to small areas of alfalfa, will furnish an abundance of spring and summer feed, while the grain mixtures recommended for winter grazing in District No. 5 are also adapted to irrigated sections in New Mexico and Arizona.

Bear in mind that these recommendations were developed some forty years ago during which time our plant breeders and agronomists have not been standing still. You may wish to check with your area agronomist or extension agent before making your pasture seeding selections.

FENCING THE PASTURE

As Professor Caine mentioned earlier in this chapter, there is considerable economy in turning out the idle horses. In fact, horses not at work should be kept almost entirely on pasture or other good roughage. Of course, care must be taken that the picking not be so poor that they lose flesh and do not have the required strength and vitality when returned to work.

There are two additional reasons for pasturing horses as much as possible. First, they will stay fresher in the legs, grow a larger hoof, and have less trouble with swollen legs and stiff joints than horses that are stabled constantly. Second, horses that share a night pasture during the work season will usually work more quietly and handle better in multiple hitches simply because they know one another better.

Fencing is of special importance for horses, because a wire cut or blemish reduces the sale value of a horse far more than with a cow, for example. The best fence is a good, woven wire fence with a barb on top. Board and rail fences are not practical in most cases, but are fine if well constructed and if the lumber is available at a cost you can afford. The most common type of fencing for horses is probably the four barb fence. This type of fence can be reasonably safe, providing:

1. There are no blind corners where a vicious horse can drive his companion (blind corners should be taboo with any type of fence, for that matter).
2. The wires are all stretched tight.
3. Horses are not pastured on the opposite side (there is considerable danger with strange horses fighting one another over such a fence).
4. The bottom wire is well off the ground.

Probably the most frequent cause of injury comes from horses pawing over the bottom barb. In this respect, a three-wire fence with the bottom wire two feet from the ground, or even a two-wire fence with the bottom barb being 2½ feet off the ground and the top wire four feet off the ground, are safer for horses than the conventional four- or five-wire barb fence. They are, however, not nearly as good for cattle and useless for sheep and hogs.

Our own place is fenced with woven wire and a top barb, but not only because of the horses. Our fences have to be both horse-safe and sheep-tight, and this type of fence allows maximum latitude—you can pretty well put horses, cattle, sheep, or hogs wherever you please.

Electric fence is probably the most common temporary type of fencing arrangement these days and horses will respect a good electric fence. Stallion paddocks frequently have a hot wire around them in addition to the conventional fence.

Conditioning Horses for Spring Work

No matter how well your horses have wintered, some sort of conditioning is necessary in the spring to prepare them for their spring and summer work. The following section from A. B. Caine's *Care and Feeding of Horses* is pertinent here, and I have also included some suggestions on spring pasture for heavy horses from the Horse and Mule Association's circular, *Care, Feed, and Management of Horses and Mules.*

Horses that are wintered out are healthy and in good physical condition but are usually thin and have very long hair, and some extra feed is needed before they are ready for work. Horses that are conditioned are able to convert their strength and energy into full power each day, while thin horses cannot do this because they haven't strength enough and are often too poor to even work efficiently.

The careful farmer who is looking ahead makes a special effort to have his horses gaining in weight for several weeks before the actual field work begins.

If horses can be kept in the barn at night, it is easy to increase their feed to get them in condition for spring work. Some farmers, however, do not care to take their horses out of meadows and stalk fields until the weather breaks in the spring. This is often too late to start the conditioning process, but horses can be fed grain while still running in the fields. Bunks can be used in which oats, corn, bran, barley, or other concentrates may be fed. From the standpoint of labor and housing costs it is best to leave the horses out as long as possible but they would probably fatten faster and shed their long hair if kept in the barn at night. A yard with an open shed for shelter is also a very suitable place to condition horses for spring work. Local conditions probably will determine how horses are handled in the spring, and it may not be of great consequence whether they are stabled or left in the fields, but it is very important that they have extra feed and gain in condition before they start working.

Get Rid of Winter Hair   Well-fed horses usually shed early, or at least they start as soon as warm weather comes, while thin horses often fail to shed until well along in the spring. Long-haired horses cannot work as efficiently and are more susceptible to disease. They sweat profusely while working, which has a tendency to weaken them, and if they are allowed to stand when wet with sweat, they often take cold.

Clipping   Clipping to get rid of long hair in the spring is sometimes advocated and may be advantageous in some special cases but not as a general practice. Sometimes only the legs are clipped, but this is not a good practice with draft horses. The feather on the legs serves as a protection if kept clean.

If horses are clipped the manes and foretops should not be removed. It takes a long time for them to grow out and not look shaggy. If there is any chance of selling horses to be handled by a dealer or to go to a central market they should never have any hair clipped from their legs, manes or foretops. Such animals sell as second-hand horses.

Clipping the shoulders of long-haired horses and mules just where the collar fits on seems to help prevent sore shoulders because it keeps the hair from matting on the collar. This condition, if unchecked, sometimes irritates the skin and starts a collar sore.

Care of the Teeth   Horses should have their teeth examined at least once or twice a year by a competent veterinarian. This is especially advisable if horses fail to respond to grain feeding in the spring. Slobbering is often caused by a sharp tooth gouging the cheek or tongue. In other cases a tooth often grows longer than the others, which interferes with the proper mastication of feeds.

Some of the teeth troubles might be corrected by a farmer if he had the necessary equipment, but the safest way is to call a veterinarian who understands abnormalities and knows how to correct them.

Care of the Feet   Horses' feet need constant care. Too often they are allowed to grow abnormally long, which causes the weight to be improperly distributed on the foot. Untrimmed feet usually break off, leaving the foot unbalanced, which causes a strain on the tendons and sometimes results in unsoundness or may interfere with a horse's action.

With a hoof knife, overgrowth of the frog and sole should be pared off, removing loose and cracked material. The frog, however, should never be cut back too much or its protective function is reduced. Next, take hoof cutters and nip the hoof wall down to about the same level as the sole. With a rasp smooth off the rough places. Make sure that the heel and toe are the right length to give the foot the correct shape. When the bottoms are finished, hold the feet in front of the horse and with the rasp round off the walls and smooth up the horny portion.

Feet that are regularly trimmed seldom have quarter cracks or cause much trouble. The frequency of trimming depends upon how the horses are used, but usually a little shaping up can be done about every sixty days. Practically all horses that have been running out during the winter need their feet trimmed before being placed in harness.

Foals seldom need their feet trimmed before they are three months old. If their feet are not wearing evenly at this age, a hoof knife or rasp can be used to level them up. In fact, much can be done to straighten crooked feet and sometimes incorrectly shaped pasterns and legs by trimming the colt's feet.

Grooming   Daily grooming of work horses is essential for good condition. Horses on pasture do not require grooming but horses that are highly fed and doing active work need grooming to keep them clean and to remove impurities secreted by the skin. Many horsemen believe that daily grooming is as essential as proper feeding to keep stabled horses in good condition.

Excretion of worn-out materials through the skin goes on more fully in highly fed horses that are worked hard and thoroughly groomed.

The healthy or unhealthy condition of the skin is shown by the appearance of the hair. If the skin is unhealthy, the hair is harsh and dry. Careful daily grooming will remedy this condition by cleansing the skin of secreted material and allowing the glands to function unchecked.

Horses' legs should receive special attention and should be cleaned carefully. Currycombs must be used cautiously on the legs, but brushes can be more vigorously used. The fetlocks and back of pasterns should be thoroughly brushed so that the dirt will not cause a skin irritation which may develop into scratches if neglected.

Horses shed their hair coats in the spring and fall. In the fall, longer hair grows as a protection against cold weather, while in the spring, the long hairs are replaced by shorter ones for warmer weather. Grooming assists in removing the loose hair and at the same time keeps the skin clean and healthy. Ungroomed horses seem to be more susceptible to mange and parasites because the insects are not disturbed and breed more rapidly.

Short, glossy hair coats, which are desired by all horsemen, are the results of good grooming. Glossiness in the hair is the result of the absence of dirt, increased secretion from the oil glands and partly the mechanical action in polishing the hair.

For grooming the mane, foretop and tail, a small wool card is very useful. The card will separate the hair, but will not cut it off as will a currycomb. If the mane and tail are too long and thick, they should be thinned out by using a pocketknife or pulling some of the extra hair out with the fingers.

A woolen cloth with a little oil on it is very useful for cleaning horses' heads and in removing the light dirt from the body which the brush does not remove.

Washing is not commonly practiced in caring for horses as water will not easily penetrate the hair. Water seems to retard the action of the oil glands and leaves the coat harsh and dry. The legs are frequently washed to remove mud or manure stains, but after washing they should be immediately dried by use of sawdust or cloths. After drying, the legs should be carefully brushed.

Spring Pasture for the Horse   Pastures should not be utilized until the grass is fairly firm, since green, washy grass is apt to scour the animals. For the first week it may be well to turn the horses or mules out on pasture for only an hour at night and then put them back into the dry lot. As one farmer expressed it, "I do not want the horses to have too much green grass for the first week or ten days, but try to taper them into it gradually." After becoming accustomed to it, the horses may be turned out on pasture all night.

In the case of horses that are shod, hind shoes should be pulled before such horses are turned out, particularly if the shod horses have not been running together with the others or are not thoroughly accustomed to one another. Serious injury to some of the animals may result if this is not done.

By late March or the first of April, good farmers reinforce their bluegrass pastures for grazing. Many advise disking lightly with disks set fairly straight, and sowing various grass seeds suited to the locality, which then are harrowed in. Where sweet clover or alfalfa do well, these are sown; while some brome grass, timothy, red top, bluegrass, and other grasses known to do well in any given locality may be put together in a mixture to be sown on such pastures.

Health Problems of Draft Horses

Although I have discussed some health problems that you might encounter with your horses elsewhere in the book, several deserve attention here because they are related to poor feeding practices on the part of the person who is keeping the horses.

AZOTURIA

Azoturia is probably known to more horsemen by its other two names, Black Water and Monday Morning Disease than as Azoturia. (Some of you probably thought Monday Morning Disease was confined to factory and office workers. Well, as is so often the case, there isn't really that much that is new under the sun and a lot of the common maladies of industrialized society have similarities to those in our agricultural past.)

At any rate, equine Monday Morning Disease is characterized by a sudden stiffening and paralysis of the muscles, usually in the hind legs, profuse sweating, and black or coffee-colored urine. It usually makes its appearance shortly after exercise is begun after a day or more of idleness. It occurs chiefly in animals on full feed, in good condition, and most often in the spring before they are hardened to everyday work.

The 1942 Yearbook of Agriculture which carried an excellent section on animal health problems says the cause, so far as was known, was that a working animal, particularly one on a high carbohydrate diet, stores a large amount of glycogen in the muscles during periods of idleness. Such an animal may develop an excess of lactic acid—one of the by-products of animal starch—in the muscle tissue. Excessive lactic acid is thought to cause deranged muscular activity, circulatory sluggishness, and muscular exhaustion.

The obvious control is to cut back on carbonaceous feeds during idle periods, giving some laxative feed such as bran, and allowing the animals to exercise naturally in a pasture or paddock.

If this does happen to one of your work animals, call the veterinarian promptly. The horse will require absolute rest and it may be necessary to erect a sling of some sort to keep him on his feet. This disease was probably a good deal more common with city horses than their country cousins because of differing management practices. That is a supposition on my part, but it seems to make sense.

COLIC

This is the most common horse disease and has killed and disabled more horses than any other. It is a rather loose term, applying to a wide range of symptoms and diseases having one thing in common—acute abdominal pain. This covers quite a range; namely, bloat (gas), impaction, or a complete stoppage, extreme constipation, twisted intestine, obstruction of the bowels, calculi in the urinary tract, etc. Any one of these, or combination thereof, is called colic.

The causes are as varied as the manifestations but most of them stem from poor management in some form or another. I'll list them as follows:

1. An abrupt change in ration, such as a sudden and complete switch from corn to oats as the weather heats up, from old grain to new crop, from good quality roughage to poor, etc. All ration changes should be gradual.
2. Overeating. Standing around idle on a full stomach is a predisposing condition. Also a waste of feed.
3. Drinking excessively directly after severe or prolonged work or immediately after feeding grain. That is why elsewhere in this book I suggested that while you water your horses after work, you not let them gorge themselves, and that you water before grain.
4. Extremely fibrous roughage can lead to impaction. I've noticed that in our area a lot of hay that is mostly just overmature stems and weeds to begin with, is sometimes passed off as either "horse hay" or "stock cow hay." Now it is true that horses and stock cows don't require the high quality roughage of lactating dairy cows or ewes, but that doesn't make them candidates for junk.
5. Older horses frequently cannot masticate their food properly after about ten or twelve years of age; this accounts for quite a bit of colic in older work teams. These horses suffer from habitual indigestion and you should have a vet float their teeth. Once a year is often enough.
6. Fatigue: Overworking a horse on a hot day can bring on an attack of colic. This condition is most likely to occur in the spring before the horses have become hardened in and their feed has been increased. (See earlier suggestions about conditioning horses for spring work.)
7. Dusty, moldy, sour, filthy, and frozen feeds. Such feedstuffs have no place in a horse's diet.

8. Exposure during cold, wet, and stormy weather may set off a round of colic.
9. Internal parasites leading to an intestinal blockage.

The treatment for colic is somewhat variable. Get a veterinarian as soon as you can to administer medication. The use of a stomach tube affords immediate relief of most acute stomach colics through the escape of gas. Until the vet gets there, walk the animal slowly. Do not let the horse lie down; he will probably try to roll to relieve the pain and this can make matters a great deal worse if he twists a gut in the process.

PARASITE CONTROL

Parasites, both external and internal, are as sure to be with us as death and taxes. So you may as well have a control program in mind if you are going to work horses and mules. A complete catalog of the parasites that find horses a suitable host is beyond the scope of this book. Besides, it might scare you into buying a tractor instead of a team.

Young horses probably suffer the most from parasite infection—and it is with them that the results are most damaging. Parasites interfere with the normal growth and development of young animals and with the functional efficiency of the mature horse as a work machine.

The damage done by parasites is often insidious, setting the animal up for other ailments. The general symptoms of a severe parasitic invasion are an unthrifty appearance (long haired, dull eyed, etc.), weakness, lack of appetite, lack of growth in the case of young horses, coughing, and mane and tail rubbing. The symptoms are as variable as the parasites are universal.

As with most things dealing with animal life, preventive medicine is the cheapest. I'd suggest the following measures:

1. Manure disposal. This is a great breeding ground. Fresh manure should not be spread on pasture areas

where the horses will graze. Either compost the manure before spreading on such pastures (eggs and larvae are killed by the heat generated by composting) or spread on cropland that will not be grazed.

2. Keep the stable area clean. In small corrals where the horses are kept, pick up the manure frequently.

3. Do not overstock pastures, and rotate pastures when possible.

4. Do not feed hay on the ground, if you can avoid it.

5. Spilled grain in the barn that the horses have masticated should be thrown out with the manure.

6. Clip your pastures if they get overgrown and use a chain harrow or spike tooth harrow laid pretty flat to break up the manure piles.

7. Provide fresh, clean water. Stagnant ponds as a drinking source are about as undesirable as manure piles in the paddock.

8. Don't pasture the horses in low, marshy areas if it can be avoided.

9. Worm them all twice a year; severely infected horses will need it more often than that, but we are talking here about a control program. The best time for treatment with a broad spectrum wormer is about a month or six weeks after the first killing frost. By this time the flies are done in and most of the eggs have hatched. The horses should be wormed again in the early spring.

Consult your veterinarian on the worming medicines available. Wormers are available in several forms: liquids, gels, granules, and powder. Many of them can be given in the feed, but horses are very sensitive to any change in the taste of their grain and some simply won't take their medicine. This is why many horsemen prefer to give them the recommended dosage by stomach tube—you know they get it that way. Some of the newer wormers are designed to be mixed with the grain and appear to be much more palatable than older types. It is a good idea to change wormers; don't rely on the same one repeatedly because parasites often develop resistance to specific wormers. Your veterinarian can make helpful suggestions to you in this regard.

Some anthelmintics should not be given to pregnant mares, weak animals, or in connection with some other drugs. This is a question for your vet, too.

External parasites such as ticks, chiggers, lice, mites, and flies are sometimes a bigger aggravation to the horseman than internal parasites. The same cleanliness and sanitation rules concerning manure, feed, and water apply here. Check your horses frequently for lice, ticks, mange (caused by mites), etc.

Fresh wounds should be treated with suitable medication. There are various chemical controls for external parasites. Some horses don't much care for the idea of being sprayed; in those cases you can use a wipe-on application. In the case of severe cases of lice or tick infestation or mange you will probably have to use an insecticide. Mange is very contagious from one species to another and some to man, usually by direct contact but also by way of equipment.

Anyone wanting more specific information on the appearance, life cycle, damage, and control of the common parasites is advised to purchase *The Common Parasites of Horses* recently published by the Division of Agricultural Sciences, University of California. It costs four dollars and is available from Cooperative Extension, Division of Agricultural Sciences, University of California, Davis, California 95616. I think it one of the best things recently published on equine parasites.

Strongyles and Botflies   In our region strongyles and botflies are two of the most troublesome. Clifford Nelson, extension veterinarian at Iowa State University, has this to say on the subject of those two parasites:

Immature ascarids and strongyles migrate through the intestinal wall into blood vessels. Once in blood vessels they mi-

grate through other organs. This makes the animal susceptible to infections leading to coughing, pneumonia, colic, and
plugged or partially clogged blood vessels.

Botflies cause excitement among horses and the larvae
cause digestive upsets, retarded growth, and poor condition
from stomach rupture or perforation.

Many years ago when horses were more widely used for
farm power, a routine bot treatment kept the parasites from
becoming a widespread nuisance. Today, says Nelson, the
neglect of horse owners is causing a rapid increase in botfly
populations.

The adult botflies are most bothersome for horses during
August and September when the female fly deposits eggs on
the horse's front legs, chest, neck, belly, and sometimes hind
legs. The yellow-colored eggs are glued to the hairs and when
the horse licks or bites the area, the developing bots begin
their journey inside the horse.

Inside the horse's mouth, the young bots penetrate the mu-
cous membranes of the mouth and tongue and, after about
four weeks, they migrate to the stomach where they attach to
the lining of the stomach wall.

Researchers and veterinarians are questioning the amount
of damage the bots inflict on the horse stomach. However, the
stomach lining is certainly irritated, and bot larvae can
produce an ulcer or rupture of the stomach wall. Occasionally
a large bot population will block the digestive tract, says
Nelson.

When the bots are fully grown, they detach themselves and
move through the intestines, eventually to be passed out in
the droppings. As the larvae begin their migration in the
spring from the stomach, they are slowly transformed into
nonfeeding pupae.

Once outside, the pupae burrow into the ground. After
several months they emerge as adults to begin anew their
one-year life cycle.

Effective control depends on treatment and interruption of
the life cycle. Eggs may be washed from the horse's hair with
a warm water solution containing an insecticide.

HOT WEATHER PROBLEMS

If you are going to do serious farming with horses it follows that you are going to work them in the heat during the growing and harvesting season. This calls for a kind of restraint and common sense that tractor farming does little to cultivate. Howard Johnstone, horse farmer from near Dover, Kansas, says, "I pay attention to the U. S. Weather Service killing heat livestock warnings, but it is the hot, still, and humid day that is the horse killer. If it is a dry heat, with a good breeze, the horses work." In any event, hot weather calls for caution on the part of the teamster.

Sunstroke and heat stroke are always possibilities during extreme weather. Sunstroke is caused by the direct rays of the sun falling on the animal and heatstroke from a high temperature and poor circulation of air in the immediate surroundings. The animals in the middle of multiple hitches are in a position of poor air circulation, and therefore more subject to heatstroke than those working on the outside. This is one of the advantages to hitching tandem.

Sweating during hot weather indicates that the cooling system is working. Puffing may be a serious warning, especially if the horse has ceased to sweat, and overheating may result if he is pushed at this time. A rest, a swallow of water, or a sponging of the mouth at this time will often restore normal respiratory action and avoid serious consequences.

If a horse stops sweating, has labored breathing and a strained, wild, depressed, or anxious expression on his face, accompanied by trembling and apparent exhaustion, you have the serious consequences of sunstroke or overheating.

Prompt measures must be taken. Cold packs of ice or real cold water should be applied, but to the head and forepart of the body only. Small doses of some stimulant may be given. Quinine is an old remedy and if available and ready at hand should be given as soon as the attack is noticed. It acts as a tonic and lowers the temperature. If given by hypodermic needle under the skin, forty to fifty grains is sufficient for a dose; if the powder form is used about a teaspoon should be given in capsule or ball. It is best to call a veterinarian who may have a better suggestion, but since one is not always available you may have to take other measures as soon as possible. Unless treatment is prompt, death is the usual result. Horses that have once been overheated are afterward unable to stand severe work during the hot months of summer, usually become unthrifty, do not sweat freely, and pant if the work is hard and the weather warm. A horse that survives such an attack should not be put back to work for three or four weeks.

The animals most likely to have such an attack are those that are overfat, soft, or unthrifty, long haired, and out of condition. Horses answering these descriptions should not be worked hard on a hot day.

The hottest weather occurs in July and August. Horses, even old-timers, that have been worked wisely and steadily from March through June will be in much better condition to take the heat of these two months. Conditioning is all-important.

Another obvious way to circumvent the heat is to get started early, press the work during the cool of the morning, ease up during the heat of the day, and—nature of the work permitting—go at it again toward evening. Haymaking, of course, does not lend itself to this arrangement, but many other tasks can.

Housing for Horses

Horse housing need not be elaborate. In our own case our horses have the use of a good shed, open to the south, and located on a hill which affords excellent drainage out of the shed. They spend very little time in the two double tie stalls we have in the barn. (I understand that blueprints for tie stalls are still obtainable from Cornell University's Agricultural Extension Service, Ithaca, New York, for fifty cents.) Even when at heavy work, they are turned out at night. Last winter, a fairly severe winter, I think we took them in only about a half dozen times overnight. If they are accustomed to getting grain when they come in it is certainly no trouble to get them to come in in the morning when you wish to work them.

By and large, the more time the horses can spend outside the healthier they are, and the less manure you have to haul.

Nonetheless, you must have some stalls for them for the working season and for extremely inclement weather. Following are some suggestions by Cumberland as they originally appeared in the Winter 1975 *Draft Horse Journal*.

There are probably almost as many variations in horse housing as there are people using horses. They range from a cow barn with the floor as a manger to the very elaborate show barn. If a horse is dry and has light, well-ventilated housing he will thrive. Your own convenience and satisfaction can complete the job of adequate housing.

Fig. 5-5. Double stall for work horses. Note the open partition which permits free circulation of air, the slope of the clay floor, and the swinging pole. The bedding is thrown forward to the middle for sanitation.

There are nine factors to consider in housing: 1. location, 2. width, 3. ceiling height, 4. alleys, 5. standing stalls, 6. box stalls, 7. floors, 8. harness storage, and 9. feed and hay storage. Any one of these factors can take much of the pleasure out of working horses if it is overlooked.

1. The location should be close to where you hitch up and also have easy access to a small night pasture. The more time you can keep your horses outside on pasture the lower your costs will be. Our night pasture is ten acres and I know you spend too much time catching horses in that size of pasture.
2. The width of the building should allow seventeen to eighteen feet for one row of stalls with ample room for a feed alley, stall and manger, and a walkway behind the horses. This, of course, will depend on the building that is available.
3. Ceiling height should never be less than eight feet and nine feet is better. A horse needs air space and head room. You don't need a warm barn for horses. A dry, well-ventilated horse barn can be very cold to you but just right for the horse.
4. Allow at least three feet for feed alleys. If your horses face out and are in a double row, allow ten feet for the litter alley. If they face in, keep six feet between the wall and the stall. This is a safety factor and a horse needs six feet to back out and turn.
5. There are some standard dimensions for standing stalls that you might vary according to your personal requirements. The standard width for a single stall is five feet. The double stall is eight feet with some nine-foot double stalls used for big horses. A horse uses seven feet of standing length and the manger is two feet wide with the top of the manger three feet six inches from the floor. The sides of the stalls should be four feet high, the full length of the stall. A six-foot guard rail that extends two feet on top of the stall does not need to be as heavy as the lower section. The stall should be nine feet from the front of the manger to the rear of the stall.
6. Box stalls should be twelve feet by twelve feet. I feel that to utilize the space they should also be able to be used as a double tie stall if needed.

7. Floors made of concrete with two-inch planks on top are the most satisfactory. The often recommended clay floor is fine if you have a lot of time for maintenance. We have not had problems with floors of concrete with ample bedding.

8. The storage of the harness is always a problem. The handiest place is behind the horse but it is also subject to manure fumes and deterioration there. A harness room is a fine idea and if you don't use the harness often it is the best place for it. Have it as close as possible, however. The easier it is to use your horses, the more you will use them.

9. Feed and hay storage is usually solved by a feed room in front of the horses for grain, and hay storage overhead. If I were building a new barn I would not plan any hay storage overhead. It is too expensive. A pole barn with hay clear to the floor in front of the horses is the cheapest.

Now that I've told you how it should be, I'll tell you how our barn is set up. I don't particularly like it, but I'm used to it. The barn is thirty-two by forty feet with the horses across the north end. We have four double tie stalls, eight feet wide. I don't have a box stall and I don't have room for one, anyway. We have kept a stallion in a double tie stall with no problems. He was well broke and earned his keep, but today I would not recommend it because you probably wouldn't work him as hard as we did. We have a narrow door that has cost enough straps and buckles so that a seven-foot sliding door could have been put in years ago and it would have been a profitable investment. Harness storage is a problem that I have not solved yet. With the increase in harness cost, I am really unhappy with it behind the horses.

One factor not stressed enough previously is the importance of light and proper ventilation for good sanitation and the health of the horse. Where windows are relied upon for both light and ventilation they should be high up from the floor, and open inward from the top. Ventilation is required both winter and summer. A system with floor-outlet ventilators will tend to carry off foul air and regulate the temperature of the barn, especially in colder latitudes. In some cases, exhaust fans may be desirable depending on the structure of the barn. In any event, use a system of ventilation that keeps the barn as fresh as possible and does not subject the horses to a direct draft.

Whether you use plank on concrete, as suggested by Cumberland, or the clay floor recommended by the USDA, sanitation is very important. The stalls must be well bedded and should be cleaned daily if you are housing the horses continuously. Wet mucky stalls predispose your horses to the development of thrush and similar foot ailments.

The big objection to clay floors is that they present more difficulty in keeping them level and clean. To be satisfactory, clay floors must be kept smooth, with slightly more slope for drainage than is required by other types of floors. A clay surface, with its elasticity, certainly offers some advantages to the horse, if not the horseman.

Chapter 6

Shoeing and Foot Care

Care of the feet was touched on briefly in an earlier section of the book (see Chapter 3). The foot is so important to the horse that I believe it merits a chapter of its own. A lame cow may milk for you (not as well as if she weren't lame, but nonetheless, she will still milk), but a horse that can't travel is useless.

As Jack MacAllan, master farrier at Michigan State University, said in the 1937 *Belgian Review*:

> The art of horseshoeing can only be learned by practical experience. If the foot of the horse were not a living object, this practical experience would not be absolutely necessary for efficient workmanship. As a hoof is constantly growing and changing its form, the duty of a horseshoer is not merely to apply a shoe upon a hoof but to reduce the excessive horn or wall to proper proportions. There are many injuries caused by good looking work based on wrong principles. The injury to feet resulting from shoeing may not be apparent at once; it may be and often is of a slow and gradual nature and not credited to its true cause until the horse is rendered an incurable cripple. It seems evident then, that the horseshoer should possess not only skill to place a shoe upon a foot, but should have a correct idea of the structure and functions of the foot as well as a thorough knowledge of the form and variations of the same.

197

Excessive growth of horn on foal's feet causes badly formed feet and soon reacts injuriously upon the leg, affecting the joints and tendons.

Agreed! Shoeing is no job for the casual amateur. There are many good farrier schools operating in the United States, though I doubt that very many of them include shoeing heavy horses in their curriculum. Be that as it may, I would no more recommend that you as a novice draft horseman do your own shoeing than I would recommend that you be your own dentist. Hire the professional. It is money well spent. Unless, of course, you want to become a farrier. And if you do, you won't become one by reading a book.

That does not, however, give a draft horse owner license to be ignorant of the structure of the hoof and of knowing what *should* be done, even if he isn't competent to do it himself.

A general knowledge of the anatomy of the hoof is the first step in knowing how to care for it. (See Fig. 6-1 for a diagram

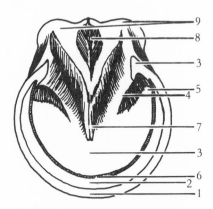

Fig. 6-1. Ground surface of a normal front hoof
1. Ground border of wall (horny wall)
2. Laminae of wall
3. Heel
4. Bar
5. Sole
6. White line (junction of wall and sole)
7. Point of frog
8. Cleft of frog
9. Bulbs of the heels

of parts of the hoof.) The two parts that will concern you the most in shoeing or trimming the hoof are the horny outer wall and the frog. The horny wall is the tough, outer surface which serves to protect the inner, sensitive parts of the foot from injury. The frog is the shock absorber and acts as an elastic cushion. It is pliable, fleshy, and peels off as it grows, and should be large, pliable to the fingers, and "alive" if it is to do its job.

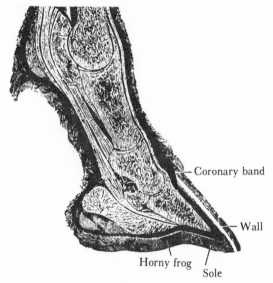

Coronary band

Wall

Horny frog

Sole

Fig. 6-2. Vertical section through middle of forefoot. In trimming or shoeing the foot be careful not to injure the inside, sensitive structure.

The USDA Bulletin 1535, *Farm Horseshoeing*, printed in 1927, offers the following description of the growth of the hoof.

The horny parts of the hoof consist of the wall, sole, frog, and bars, and are made up of insensitive, horny cells (see Fig. 6-2). The growth of the hoof, however, is from the sensitive inside of the hoof. The wall grows from a fleshy band, the so-called coronary band, which lies on top of the wall (hair line). It grows in a straight, downward and forward direction. The average rate of growth is estimated to be about ¼ to ⅜ of an inch a month in a normal animal. The wall is that portion of the hoof to which the shoe is nailed. The horny sole grows from the fleshy sole and grows solid to a certain extent. As it continues to grow the old sole will crack and check, and a network of small, black lines will be formed all over the bottom of the sole. The horny frog grows from the fleshy frog and is a cushiony, elastic wedge between the bars and the edges of the sole in front of the bars. In unshod hoofs the bearing edge of the wall, the sole, frog, and bars are on a level, and each of these structures assists in bearing the body weight. The bars are extensions of the wall from the heel along the sides and to the point of the frog. The purpose of the bars is to assist in absorbing the shock when the foot strikes the ground. As the function of the bars is important, they should not be cut away in trimming the hoof. Contracted heels will result if the bars are cut away.

Trimming the Hoof

The hoofs of most colts require nothing more than timely and intelligent trimming, especially if they are running on grass, as they should be, and getting adequate exercise. As Jack MacAllan said, "A colt with well-formed legs only requires that his feet be kept in good proportion." Unfortunately not all colts are so endowed by nature, so MacAllan goes on to say that a colt with defective conformation requires the foot being put into form to correct these faults. "This can only be done over a period of time. In cases where the knees are thrown unduly forward, a shoe with a thick toe and thin heels will assist in bringing them back to the desired position. When the hocks are turned excessively inward, the use of a shoe with the inner web higher will counteract the condition. A shoe with the outside higher will have a tendency to throw the joints closer together. For young colts whose bones are not yet hard, an in-toed condition may be corrected by trimming the inside of the hoof lower than the outside; if he is out-toed, lower the outside of his foot. It must be emphasized that these alterations of the foot must be gradual and maintained over a long period. An extensive or too forcible (abrupt) an alteration will set up consequences worse than the condition. I do not wish to infer, however, that all defective conformations of the leg and foot are due to neglect of the feet in youth."

The USDA bulletin offers this advice on trimming the colt's feet:

The newborn foal has a rather pointed, narrow hoof, which is very soft, and the bottom is covered with a thick cushion of soft, horny material. This, however, falls off in a few days, and the development of the permanent hoof begins. The horny sole begins to grow in an arch shape, and the new wall grows down from the coronary band. In a few weeks there is a distinct difference between the old and the new horny mass in that a complete ring forms around the hoof. The new hoof is circular and spreads considerably at the sole surface, and the leg assumes its natural shape. The foot becomes more slanting from the fetlock joint down, and during the first few weeks there is very little to be done to improve the standing position of the legs.

A little later, however, when much can be done toward developing normal conformation by the proper trimming of

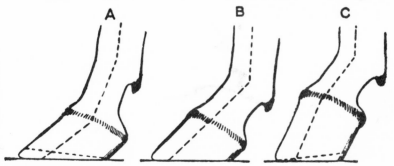

Fig. 6-3. Legs and hoofs in profile: A. Side view of foot axis broken backward as a result of too long a toe. The amount of horn to be removed from the toe in order to straighten the foot axis is denoted by a dotted line. B. Side view of a properly balanced foot, with a straight foot axis of desirable slant. C. Side view of a stumpy foot with foot axis broken forward as a result of overgrowth of the quarters. The amount of horn to be removed in order to straighten the foot axis is shown by a dotted line.

the little hoof, one should observe the development of the legs. When the colt is three months old one can begin using the hoof knife for trimming the feet. To do this work properly, first observe the standing position of the front legs from the side. If the leg is placed too far forward it is an indication that the toe is too long (see Fig. 6-3). By close examination of the hoof it will be found that the heels are curving under and that the toe is growing in a straightforward direction. If the hoof is trimmed in the manner described, the legs will take their proper position.

Now, observe the hind legs. One will usually find that the legs are too straight from the fetlocks down because the heels are long. If the heels are pared down, the legs will usually be "base wide" or in a spreading position. As the colt matures, this condition usually corrects itself. By closely observing the colt occasionally, possibly once a month, and keeping the hoofs properly trimmed, one can do much to promote the development of a normal conformation, which brings good returns to the owner.

The colt should have abundant exercise on dry ground. The hoofs will then usually wear gradually, and it may be necessary only occasionally to rasp and round off the sharp edges around the toe in order to prevent the breaking away of the wall. Colts in the stable, however, cannot wear down their hoofs; therefore, the feet of such colts should be rasped down every few weeks. The soles and clefts of the frog should be picked out every few days and the entire hoof washed out thoroughly.

I have repeatedly mentioned the need for good pasturage for colts and the importance of exercise. Nutrition also plays a part. A vitamin A deficiency often accompanies abnormal hoof growth. If this is the case, a correction of diet can go a long way in solving the problem.

Fig. 6-3, showing the legs and hoofs in profile, gives you an idea of what a properly trimmed hoof should look like, whether on a colt or mature horse. Most of what has been said about the care of a colt's feet applies with equal force to that of a mature horse or mule. The important thing, at any age, is to make sure that the animal is standing normally, bearing his weight in such a way as to make for correct leg posture.

Shoeing

As for shoeing, the first decision is to decide whether you should. Most farm horses working on a soft or sandy loam, comparatively free of stones, simply don't require shoeing if they are kept trimmed and have good feet to begin with. In other words, don't incur the expense of shoeing unless you need to.

Horses that work on rough and stony ground or spend a lot of time on hard-surfaced streets and roads can give continued service only if well shod. Horses working on hard and stony ground will not only have greater traction with shoes, but the shoes will also protect the foot and prevent the horse from picking up stones which can penetrate the breaks and clefts in the hoof, working into the sensitive parts of the foot and causing lameness.

Pick out any stones in the hoof if you can. I had a mare with gravel, once, and we got it out. It was pretty high up, but I soaked cotton balls in peroxide and put them in the hole every day, letting the pus drain each time I changed the cotton until it healed. It takes a long time for the gravel to work up to the coronary band, it's painful to the horse, and lames the animal for quite a while. I have seen cases of gravel working up through the entire hoof, erupting at the coronary band. This is painful and incapacitates the horse.

About the only shoeing we ever do on our farm is temporary and corrective in nature; most of our horses work barefoot all the time. But if you do work your horses under the more rigorous conditions described above, hire a competent farrier and have him reset the shoes at least every six weeks, every four weeks in some cases. Leaving shoes on longer than that without resetting and refitting can result in injury to the foot.

The first few times you take your draft horses to a local farrier, you might have to explain what you want done. Any farrier whose work has been confined to light horses will confront a different set of problems with heavy horses. First, and most obvious, is the size and weight of the animal—roughly twice as much in many cases. Second, this obviously is reflected in the size of the foot to shoe; light horses not only have smaller feet but are relatively more narrow at the heel. The light horse is used at higher speeds, thus there is more concussion. The draft horse is used for tractive purposes and needs a relatively bigger foot to give him that traction. In the one case you are shoeing for speed and in the other, strength. Most farriers coming on a heavy horse for the first time will probably not be inclined to leave enough foot, though that is by no means always true. It is a question of degree and type of usage, and the plain fact of the matter is that many new draft horse owners—unless they are located in an unusual community—will rely on farriers whose principal trade is with the lightlegs. We do—and get along fine.

Now, I hope you're beginning to understand a little of the complexity of the farrier's art and to see why horseshoeing is not something you can learn from a book. Having said that, however, I'd like to stress that there is no reason why you can't learn to do your own *trimming* without a farrier's diploma, and I will go ahead and reproduce the balance of the USDA's bulletin on farm horseshoeing. Because even if you aren't going to make a career out of it, you should still be familiar with the tools, procedures, and desired results, if for no other reason than to know when to change farriers.

TRIMMING THE FOOT FOR SHOEING

Before beginning the trimming of the hoof one must observe the standing position of the limbs, particularly from the fetlock joint down. The position of the foot must correspond to the angle of the leg, as indicated in Fig. 6-3. If the standing position of the foot is too slanting it is an indication that the toe is too high, and a line, the so-called foot axis, is broken backward. Reducing the toe will change the angle and bring the foot axis into a straight line.

After the standing position has been observed, raise the foot and begin with the hoof knife to remove the overgrowth of the sole, starting at the quarter. This overgrowth is indicated by cracks and checks and loose material (see Figs. 6-4, 6-5, 6-6). It should be removed down to the solid sole. The solid sole should not be touched under any circumstances, as the horse needs this as a protection for the inner organs of the foot.

Fig. 6-4. An untrimmed foot

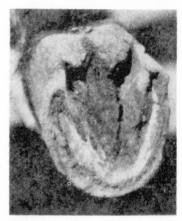

Fig. 6-5. An untrimmed foot. Note the long heels.

After the sole is cleaned, the wall extending far beyond the sole can be reduced to its normal length with hoof cutters, as shown in Fig. 6-7. The amount of cutting is determined by the upper edge of the trimmed sole; in other words, the hoof cutters will follow the upper border of the trimmed sole all the way along the hoof, and by so doing give the heel and toe the proper length (see Figs. 6-9, 6-10, 6-11, and 6-12).

After this is done the hoof rasp should be held in a level position and the hoof sole rasped so that the wearing surface is in a level plane, as shown in Fig. 6-8. One can observe this plane level in the position illustrated on the title page of this bulletin, which shows also the proper method of holding the

Fig. 6-6. A bad break in the wall, caused by neglect in trimming and shoeing.

Fig. 6-7. Proper use of the hoof cutter

Fig. 6-8. Proper position of rasp in leveling hoof

Fig. 6-9. A hoof which has been properly trimmed on one side; the other half is untrimmed. Note the difference especially in the amount of trimming necessary to balance the foot properly. Note the bars.

horse's foot. The handy shoeing outfit illustrated consists of a box, hammer, clinch cutter, large pincers for pulling shoes, hoof knife, and hoof cutters, and a pair of small pincers for pulling and cutting nails.

FITTING THE SHOE

The hoof is now ready for the fitting of the shoe. For ordinary farm work the shoe does not need to extend much beyond the end of the wall. The type of shoe, whether calked or plain, depends largely on the work which the animal performs. The plain shoe should be even with the end of the wall. If a calked shoe is needed, it is necessary that the shoe be a trifle longer. In fitting the shoe it is necessary to give an

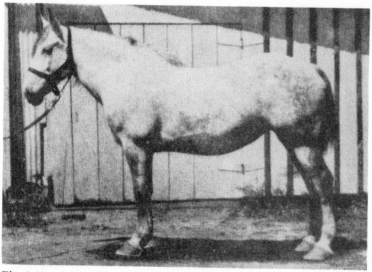

Fig. 6-10. Mare with untrimmed feet. Note the long, slanting position of the foot from the fetlock to the ground.

absolutely even fit, as the outline of the hoof shows. In other words, fit the shoe flush with the outline of the outer border of the wall. The heels of the shoe should be well under the heels of the wall; this is very important, as the heels of the hoof must rest on the iron in order to permit proper hoof expansion and contraction. Good nailing consists in having the nail holes of the shoe well punched in the same slanting direction as the wall.

NAILING

The method of nailing is shown in Figs. 6-12 and 6-13. The nail should be of proper size to fit the shoe. The nail is held with the thumb and index finger, the other fingers lying against the wall to guide the direction of the nail, and the shoe is held in position, the hand resting on the shoe to hold it in proper position in driving the outside nail first (see Fig. 6-13).

The nail should be driven just outside that portion of the wall known as the "white line," so called because of its well-defined "white" appearance. Be careful not to allow the nails to go inside this line into the sensitive portion of the foot. The proper course of the nail is shown in Fig. 6-12. After the first nail is driven it is best to make sure that the shoe is in its proper place. Then the nail on the opposite side is driven, and so on until the nailing is completed.

In tightening the nails, a clinching block or the pincers should be held underneath the nails, and the head driven with the hammer tight into the crease of the shoe. In clinching the nails, as shown in Fig. 6-15, the foot is brought forward on the knee of the operator, and the nails are cut close to the wall, and with the rasp a clearing cut is made underneath the nail on top of the wall. Cut or twist off end of nail with pincers or claw of hammer, place the clinching block underneath the nail, and with the hammer bring the nail over in a small, bending form so as to form the clinch. With the hoof rasp smooth or rasp over the rough spots on the outside. Rasping the outside of the wall should be avoided as much as possible. Fig. 6-16 shows a plate shoe, well fitted.

Fig. 6-11. Trimmed feet. Note the corrected position of the feet and compare their position with that shown in Fig. 6-10.

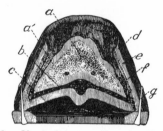

Fig. 6-12. Vertical cross section of well-shod hoof showing correct position of nails: a. pedal bone a'. outer layer of pedal bone b. sensitive sole c. horny sole d. horn wall e. outer layer of laminal sheath f. laminal sheath g. nail

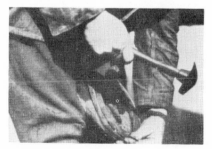

Fig. 6-13. Proper method of nailing a shoe on. Note position of hands.

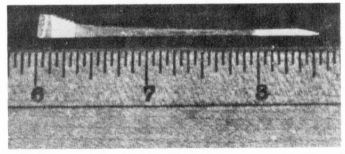

Fig. 6-14. The nails used for shoeing horses have one straight side, and the other side is beveled at the point. In driving a nail, the straight edge should always be held to the outside, the beveled point to the inside. This will guide the nail out through the wall. The nail should be driven just outside the "white line" described in the text.

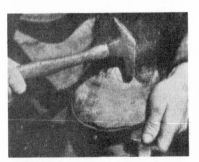

Fig. 6-15. Proper method of clinching the nail. Note position of hammer and clinching block.

Fig. 6-16. Plate shoe, well fitted

Fig. 6-17. Well-shod feet

Fig. 6-18. Ready-to-wear shoe. Plain shoe.

Fig. 6-19. Ready-to-wear shoe, with toe and heel calks

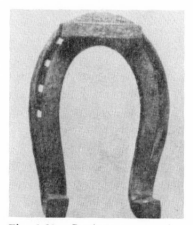

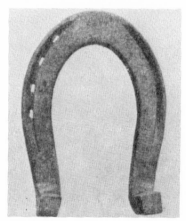

Fig. 6-20. Ready-to-wear mule shoe, with toe and heel calks

Fig. 6-21. Ready-to-wear mule shoe, with heel calks

READY-TO-WEAR SHOES

Horseshoe manufacturers are now making and distributing horse and mule shoes of all types (see Figs. 6-18 to 6-21) suitable for shoeing farm work stock. In many places they can be obtained at the general store or from the local hardware merchant. (This is no longer true, unfortunately.)

In using the ready-to-wear shoe it is important that the farmer exercise particular care in measuring the feet of horses or mules to be shod before he purchases the shoes. The following system of measurement should be applied: after the feet are trimmed (one front foot and one hind foot), measure the width of the foot, in inches, and the length of the foot from heel to toe, making sure, however, that an allowance of at least ½ inch is made in the length of the shoe beyond the wall of the foot at the heel.

RUBBER SHOES AND RUBBER HOOF PADS

Because horses are often worked on hard-surfaced streets and highways, the use of rubber shoes and rubber hoof pads has become common. These modern devices not only relieve sore and lame horses, but many times prevent corns and other foot sorenesses and lengthen the usefulness of horses used on hard surfaces. This type of shoeing is also valuable in preventing slipping on such surfaces and reduces to a minimum the number of injuries to horses caused by falling. Hoof pads and rubber shoes should be used as a preventive rather than as a cure for the many leg ailments caused by the constant use of horses on hard-surfaced roads.

Rubber pads are not recommended for horses that work on the farm, as the soil works its way under the pad, causing lameness by extra pressure in the navicular joint. Whenever rubber pads are used, pine tar with a thin layer of oakum should be applied to the sole to keep it moist and prevent contraction.

Shoeing for shows is an art in itself. As such, it is of interest to only a relative handful of people, and I don't feel has any place in a book directed at novices.

Common Diseases of the Hoof and Their Treatment

Before leaving the subject of hoofs, we must discuss the importance of cleanliness in the stable. The heels of horses that are forced to stand in filth are weakened by the constant moisture surrounding them and become breeding grounds for a variety of dangerous diseases. If properly handled, hair on the legs becomes a preventive of cracked heels, and if the skin around the heels is kept dry and warm, no heel troubles will arise.

During wet weather or early spring and winter, the last duty of the horseman at the end of the day should be to examine the legs and give them a final rubbing. The mud can then be easily cleaned off the legs. The hoofs should be examined and the cleft between the sole and frog cleaned out.

In our library of out-of-print publications is a fine little booklet called *How to Care for the Feet of Your Horses and Mules* published by the Phoenix Manufacturing Company, Joliet, Illinois, in the early forties (since out of business as far as I know). The closing section of their booklet is a fine, brief review of the common diseases of the hoof and their treatment.

It is better to prevent foot ailments than to be faced with the necessity of curing them.

Frequent pasturing on good grassland is an excellent foot conditioner for farm animals. This is nature's own remedy, and the benefit of having frequent periods of contact with fresh, dewy pasture grass can hardly be over-estimated. The feet are kept moist, and cuts and abrasions heal quickly.

While horse and mule foot ailments are sometimes caused by injuries sustained in an accident, failure to provide some element in the simple, everyday care needed is usually the underlying cause.

Especially dangerous is the practice of leaving shoes on a work animal's feet for too long a time. Corns, sidebone, and sore tendons are common results of this practice. These conditions usually require treatment by a veterinarian. In refitting shoes which have remained on the feet too long, an experienced horseshoer should be employed, since special preparation of the hoofs is sometimes necessary, and shoes of special design are frequently required. In extreme cases, it is helpful to spread pine tar over the sole of the foot and around the frog. Pack the foot with oakum or cotton and apply a leather pad to cover the entire bottom of the foot. This pad is nailed in place under the shoe when the horse is shod. It should be left on until normal growth has returned to the sole and wall.

Hoofs which are improperly trimmed often cause curbs, spavins, and ring or sidebones on the hind legs, and splints, sidebones, ringbones, corns, and quarter cracks in the front legs and hoofs. Painstaking care when trimming or rasping the hoofs will eliminate the cause of most of these ailments.

Diseases of the feet and legs of horses and mules often have their inception in faulty conformation of the bones. An improper diet, deficient in minerals and vitamins, is another cause, and strains, bruises, and improper shoeing are sometimes contributing factors.

BRITTLE HOOFS

This is an abnormally dry and brittle condition of the hoof, usually brought on by stabling too long a time on hard, dry floors. When in this state, the hoof wall chips, cracks, and breaks off readily. Difficulties in shoeing frequently develop.

Treatment—Wherever possible shoes should be removed, the feet trimmed and reshod under a veterinarian's direction. In re-nailing shoes, extra thin nails should be used, carefully placed in the strongest parts of the hoof wall. Apply a mild blister to the coronet daily. This treatment will stimulate blood circulation in this area, causing a heavier, more normal growth of horn. Application of a hoof ointment, containing turpentine, tar, and wax, is also beneficial.

SPONGY HOOFS

This condition is the exact opposite of brittle hoofs. The hoof structure becomes extremely soft, spongy, and non-resistant. It is sometimes present in the feet of animals which are kept on wet, marshy ground. Or it may be due to an inherited tendency, since this condition is a common characteristic of certain breeds.

Treatment—Keep animals away from wet, marshy pastures and wet stalls. The feet must be kept dry. Particular care should be taken to keep feet clean, since canker and corns frequently develop in spongy hoofs. Excessive paring of the sole and hot-fitting of shoes should be avoided.

CONTRACTED FOOT

This is a contracted, tightened condition of the foot, chiefly noticeable at the heel. When present, the foot does not have its normal flexibility. Contraction of the foot is usually present with brittle hoofs and spongy hoofs. Flat feet with low, weak heels, so shod that the frog does not press normally on the ground, frequently become contracted, especially during long periods of hot, dry weather. Excessive paring of the bars may also be a contributing cause of this ailment.

Treatment—Correct any conditions in the animal's care which have brought on the ailment. Rasp thin the quarters of the hoof. This will permit the foot to expand. Animals with long-standing cases are generally better off without shoes for a while. This permits natural pressure on the frog and forces spreading of the heels. With the advice of a veterinarian, special expanding shoes may be applied in some cases. Hoof ointments may be used to soften the horn, which usually becomes extremely hard and inflexible.

THRUSH

Thrush is a disease of the frog, most commonly found in the hind feet. It is almost invariably caused by unsanitary conditions in the animal's stall. Horses will not get the disease if their stalls are kept clean and well bedded, and if their feet are cleaned out daily. The first indication of the disease is often the disagreeable odor caused by the discharge from the cleft of the frog. This discharge at first is thin and watery, but later becomes dark, with a tarry consistency. Thrush should be checked quickly as it nearly always leads to severe lameness.

Treatment—First trim away all diseased parts of the horn so that an antiseptic may be applied to the affected parts. Sulfanilamide powder is the best antiseptic for this purpose. Liberal quantities should be applied to the diseased parts. Absorbent cotton stuffed into the cleft of the frog will usually keep the antiseptic in place, although a leather boot may be used if necessary. Powdered bluestone or copper sulphate applied in the same manner as the sulfanilamide powder is another excellent treatment for thrush.

Obviously the stall condition which brought on the disease should be corrected immediately.

CORNS

Corns are usually caused by faulty foot conformation—the result of improper trimming or shoeing. Wide, flat feet with low heels, high, contracted heels or long, overgrown hoofs encourage the development of corns. Direct injury to the foot, excessive moisture or excessive dryness, and prolonged contact with stable filth are frequently contributing causes.

Treatment—If horse is shod, remove the shoe. If the corn has festered, make drainage possible, then poultice the foot until the corn shows indication of complete drainage. The sole should be pared only enough to insure complete drainage of the corn. On the advice of a veterinarian or practical horseshoer, bar shoes may be put on after careful leveling of the hoof.

CANKER

Canker often is not discovered in its early stages as the disease progresses slowly and practically without pain at first. Ordinarily it begins in the frog and, if not checked, spreads rapidly to the sole or even to the sensitive laminae.

The affected parts sometimes grow into a deformed fungoid mass, and fetid cheese-like material accumulates in the surrounding tissue. The cause of the disease is not exactly known, but it is believed that conditions which produce thrush are also conducive to canker.

Treatment—Remove all pieces of sole or frog which cover diseased parts. Cleanse thoroughly with warm or hot water. Cut away all unnatural growth, follow by application of a hot iron. Apply a pad soaked in a solution made by mixing equal parts of sulphate of iron, sulphate of zinc, and sulphate of copper. Pack foot with oakum and encase in a boot. Dressings should be changed twice daily. This is a serious foot ailment, and all treatment, if possible, should be under the direction of a skilled veterinarian.

Other serious foot problems are sidebone, ringbone, founder or laminitis, and bone spavin. These have already been discussed in some detail; see Chapter 3.

Chapter 7

Harness and Hitching

You bought this team to work. To do so efficiently they must have properly fitted collars, hames, and harness. Following is the text from Circular 408, published by the University of Kentucky in 1945. This should prove helpful to you in getting the most out of your "equine motors." Also included in this section are illustrations from the current Detweiler's Harness Shop catalog showing various harness parts and an illustration of the straight faced, full sweeney, and half sweeney collar from the University of Minnesota bulletin, *Using Horses on the Farm.*

FITTING THE COLLAR

To avoid sore necks or shoulders, each work animal should have a collar that is used only on that horse. This is as important to work animals as individually fitted shoes are to a marching soldier.

There are three types of collars: regular, half sweeney, and full sweeney. A "regular" collar will fit long, flat, slender necks (see Fig. 7-1); "half sweeney" collars fit necks that are a bit heavier, and slightly thick at the top (see Fig. 7-3); and "full sweeney" collars are intended for stud-like necks, very thick near the top (see Fig. 7-2).

All-leather collars are best, but other kinds are serviceable for three or four years and sell at lower prices.

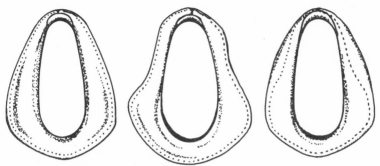

Fig. 7-1. A "regular" collar for long, slender necks
Fig. 7-2. A "full sweeney" collar for thick necks
Fig. 7-3. A "half sweeney" collar for heavier necks

Fitting a collar to a new work animal should be done by testing with different collars till one is found that fits (see Fig. 7-4). If it is not practical to take the animal to the harness shop, try on collars that belong to other animals until one is

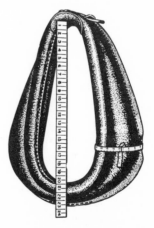

Fig. 7-4. Fitting a collar to a horse. When fitting a horse with a collar there should not be any more space between the horse's neck and throat of the collar than will allow your four fingers, when laid flat on inside of throat of collar, to pass through freely.

(Courtesy of Detweiler's Harness Shop)

Fig. 7-5. How to measure a collar. Place the rule against the collar pad and measure to the inside of the rim of the throat as illustrated. This collar measures 20 inches. For size of draft draw a tape line around the collar at its heaviest part, as illustrated. This collar has 17½-inch draft.

(Courtesy of Detweiler's Harness Shop)

found that seems about right, then measure for length as shown in Fig. 7-5. Collar sizes depend on length. A size 18 measures eighteen inches from top to bottom just inside the rim when the collar is buckled. Small animals take size 16 or smaller, very large draft horses size 24 or larger.

A collar of the right size, when buckled on and pressed or drawn strongly back against the shoulders, fits snug enough against the neck so that the fingers only, held flat, can be passed between the rim of the collar and the sides of the neck. Fig. 7-6 shows a collar that is too wide; the whole hand goes in, instead of just the fingers.

When the collar is pressed back against the shoulders, it should be long enough for the flat hand to be turned up as shown in Fig. 7-7. Thus turned, the hand crowds against the throat. Measured with a ruler, there should be about two inches free space between throat of horse and collar when the collar is drawn strongly back against the shoulders by a pull on the tugs—all a man can pull—or when the horse steps forward against the lead till the collar is firmly pressed against the shoulders.

Fig. 7-6. Improperly fitted collar. This collar is too wide.

Fig. 7-7. Properly fitted collar. The collar shown in Fig. 7-6 has been made to fit by using a collar pad.

Getting the right length of collar is very important. If it is too short, as shown in Fig. 7-8, or too long, as shown in Fig. 7-9, trouble will result. Too short a collar presses down on top of the neck and up against the throat when a load is being pulled. It makes the neck sore on top, and on heavy pulls it chokes the horse by pressing against the windpipe. Such choking may cause a horse to fall, and will discourage him from pulling with his full strength. In addition, too short a collar brings the point of draft too high, and sores high up on the shoulder may result.

Too long a collar, on the other hand, brings the point of draft too low and too near the shoulder point. This will make a sore very quickly, for it causes constant friction as the

Fig. 7-8. Improperly fitted collar. This is too short and narrow for the horse.

Fig. 7-9. This collar is too long for the horse; however, the hame has been properly fitted to the collar.

shoulder point moves forward and back. Too wide a collar, even when long enough, will create pressure too far away from the neck and too near the shoulder edge, and will cause a sore there.

The collar should be snug at the top where it rests on the neck—not too tight nor too loose. There should be space on the sides to run the fingers clear to the collar cap at top of collar, but no more. Collars that are too narrow at the top will pinch the neck and chafe it, causing sores on the sides near the top. If the collar is too wide at the top, it will work back and forth sideways chafing the top of the neck and causing a sore to start there.

Another frequent cause of sore necks is too much weight on the neck yoke, as when a mowing machine or other implement has too light a driver to balance the weight of the tongue. The solution is to fasten a weight—a stone or concrete block—under the seat, so the combined weight of teamster and added object will balance the weight of the tongue, taking all weight off the neck yoke when the driver is on the seat.

Fig. 7-10. The hame on this collar is improperly fitted. The top hame strap is too loose, and the hame drops too low.

Fig. 7-11. Improperly fitted hame. The gap between hame and collar will cause a sore shoulder.

This takes off the downward pull on top of the neck of work animals. It is important to do this at the outset so sore necks will not start.

After a collar of the right size and shape has been found, the face of it must be fitted to the exact shape of the horse's neck and shoulders, regardless of whether it is a new collar or an old one to be used on a different horse. One good way is to soak only the face of a leather collar for an hour in a couple of inches of lukewarm water in a tub. If there is no tub large enough at hand, lay lukewarm wet cloths over the face to soften it. When softened, put the collar on the horse, adjust the hames and harness carefully, and work the horse moderately. The damp collar will adjust itself to the exact shape of the horse's neck and shoulders. If the collar face is *not* leather it should *not* be soaked (face only) for more than half an hour.

Check the fit of collars frequently. Collars that fit when work starts in spring often prove too large (especially too wide) when horses grow thinner from hard work. A pad should then be used to make the collar fit. Pads are usually two inches longer than collar sizes—thus a twenty-two-inch collar would call for a twenty-four-inch pad. Pads must be open at the throat. Be sure the pads are new each season, clean, and of the correct size to make the collar fit properly.

FITTING THE HAMES

Correct hame adjustment is extremely important. If the hames do not lie in the collar seam for the full length of the collar, they do not fit. If the top hame strap bows across the top of the collar as in Fig. 7-10, rather than lying straight across the top as in Fig. 7-11, the pull of the tugs will spread the hames at the top and cause sore shoulders. If the hames are either too long or too short, they cannot be adjusted to fit the collar. The only remedy is a set of hames that does fit the collar. Hame sizes depend on the length from the loop where the top hame strap is used, to the bottom loop, measured as a taut bowstring would be. The sizes correspond approximately to collar sizes. A twenty-three- to twenty-four-inch hame will fit either a twenty-three- or twenty-four-inch collar. Even these must be correctly adjusted. In Fig. 7-11 the top hame strap is one loop too low, causing the hame to be away from seam (see fingers between hame and collar). If the hame strap at top is put one loop too high and left loose as in Fig. 7-10, it will cause the hames to drop too low, leaving a gap between hame and collar at bottom, shown by fingers in Fig. 7-10. This is apt to cause a sore near the shoulder point. If the hames are buckled too close together at the top they will cause the collar to pinch the neck and chafe it, making sores on the sides, near the top.

Too long a hame—for instance, a twenty-four-inch hame on a twenty-one-inch collar—will cause a sore shoulder. If the hame is drawn snug in against the seam of the collar at the bottom, the point of pull on the hame is above the true point of draft on the shoulder and will make a sore high up. If the hame is allowed to drop, so there is a gap between hame and collar at bottom, as in Fig. 7-10, it will make a sore near the point of the shoulder. Too short a hame—say a twenty-one-inch hame on a twenty-four-inch collar—will make a sore near the point of the shoulder, if the hame is drawn close to the collar seam at the bottom. But if it is set up high (adjusted to fit close to the seam at top rather than at bottom of collar) it will make a sore high up and near the outside edge of the shoulder.

CARE OF THE COLLAR, NECK, AND SHOULDERS

Good horsemen keep the horse's neck, shoulders, and collar clean at all bearing surfaces. Be sure the mane does not work back under the face of the collar. Stop occasionally to give horses a breathing spell, and at that time raise the collar away from shoulders, wipe off dust and sweat, and give the shoulders some opportunity to cool. At noon hour it will take a few minutes to remove the harness and collar, but it will pay, as it gives the shoulders an opportunity to cool. Look frequently to see whether the hair is wearing short at any point, as this is the first sign of chafing, leading to an open sore. If the hair is wearing short, correct the adjustment of collar, pad, or hames at once.

At the close of the day's work, washing the shoulders of the work stock with a strong salt-water solution will help keep them in healthy condition. As soon as the collar is removed, wipe the leather face clean with a damp cloth, and then wipe lightly with another cloth soaked in harness oil. Do not rub oil on the collar cap, but keep it clean and smooth. If pads or non-leather collars are used, wipe clean but do not use oil. If unbuckled, the collar should be held with both hands and the left arm passed under the throat of the horse, to prevent any strain on collar throat while the collar is unbuckled. The collar should be buckled before being hung up.

Collars always should be hung bottom-side up, face out, as shown in Fig. 7-13, on a peg with round edges, so that the weight is on the throat of the collar, not on the cap. The cap is the separate curved piece of pressed sole leather which rests on top of the neck to protect it from chafing. Every morning when the horse is harnessed wipe your hand over the face of

Fig. 7-12. Putting a collar on a horse over the head

Fig. 7-13. Collar part, properly hung

the collar again to make sure it is smooth. These things take less time than it takes to tell them, but are the little things that go far toward keeping shoulders in perfect condition if collar and hame adjustment are right to begin with.

Many farmers who are especially successful in avoiding sore necks or shoulders on their work stock carefully do the fitting themselves and do not allow collars to be unbuckled again till readjustment is necessary. Such men take collars off and put them on over the head as shown in Fig. 7-12. This may seem odd to those unaccustomed to it, but horses quickly become used to it and the owner has the satisfaction of knowing that the collars are being used exactly as adjusted.

This plan works well with horses, but not with mules. Their long, sensitive ears make them object strongly and it is difficult to persuade them to accept collars over their heads.

Because the collar is widest at point of draft it should be put on upside down, as in Fig. 7-12, turned over about eight inches back of the poll, then slipped back to shoulders. In taking off, reverse the process. The halter, not the bridle, should be on the horse in either case.

LONG LIFE FOR HARNESS

Giving long life to harness is simple. All that is necessary is to keep it clean and well oiled with a good harness oil. Best results are attained by taking the harness apart, unbuckling all straps, washing each with a very mild soap and warm water, rinsing each strap in clean water as soon as it is washed, and hanging it up to dry.

By the time all straps are washed and rinsed, the first straps will be dry enough to oil. A sponge or soft rag will hold enough oil to make hand rubbing effective. Some harness shops oil harness by placing it in a wire basket and dipping in a large tank of warm harness oil for 15 to 20 minutes, then suspending it above the vat till the oil drains off. This is fairly effective, but the person who takes his harness apart and washes it thoroughly before oiling gets a much better job, for dried sweat and dirt prevent oil from penetrating to the leather beneath.

Longer life of harness also is obtained where harness is hung in a harness room away from the ammonia fumes rising from stalls. This seldom is considered practical for lack of time, and harness generally is hung on two pegs or hooks on the wall about eight feet behind the work animal it is used on. Drape the hames over one hook and the breeching over the other.

It is impractical to wash, oil and repair harness in cold weather unless a warm room is available. Leather and oil must be warm for a good job.

CLEANING OLD HARNESS

You might be able to pick up old harness at sales rather cheaply. Such harness is generally neglected and requires a great deal of work to refurbish. This brief article from *Percheron News*, October 1946, offers some suggestions for restoring old harness. This might be the only course open to you if there is not a harness maker in the neighborhood. A location in close proximity to an Amish settlement is certainly an advantage to anyone wishing to use work horses.

When cleaning old and hardened harness, first take it all apart, unbuckling every strap. The pieces should be soaked in a tub of lukewarm water for half an hour, then spread out on a smooth board and scrubbed until thoroughly clean. Touch up any red spots due to wear or clean with some harness blacking (shoe blacking will do). Hang the straps as rapidly as they are finished over a convenient pole where they can dry.

It is important not to let the leather become wholly dry before oiling. The straps should hang in a warm room for two or three hours after being cleaned until all surface water is dried out, but while they are still pliable and still feel moist to the hand they should be spread out flat on a piece of board and have oil or dubbin worked into the fibre of the leather. Dubbin worked in with a brush is one of the very best treatments that can be given to harness leather. It surpasses tub dipping or mere rubbing of the straps with oil because the brush works the dubbin into the leather more thoroughly.

Dubbin is made by mixing tallow and neat's-foot oil half and half. A little more tallow is needed in the summer than in the winter. The tallow should be melted in a kettle (preferably a double boiler) at a temperature not exceeding 110° or 115°F. After it is entirely melted, cool to about 100°F., and add the oil. Let stand for a few minutes. It will be about the consistency of a fairly stiff mush. Dip into a smaller vessel for use as needed, brushing it back and forth on the leather with a stiff paint brush and working it carefully into both sides. The harness should be allowed to stand over night and then wiped off with a cloth.

Hitching Your Team

After you have a team of your own in the barn, a set of harness, and collars that fit reasonably well, you're ready to "hook 'em up." Always speak to the horses when entering the barn, just to let them know you are there. Before entering the stall, speak to them again, asking them to get over. A draft horse that doesn't know what "get over" means has an inadequate vocabulary.

Enter on the left side of the horse. Fast, jerky movements, indicating nervousness or impatience, will be reflected in the horse. So take it easy.

In harnessing your new team you will put the collars on first. If they are accustomed to the collar over the head routine, fine; otherwise unbuckle the collar and slip it on from under the neck. After you get better acquainted with them and they with you and are completely satisfied as to the collar's fit, you can begin putting the collar over their heads. But remember, a collar is not the same thing as a pair of your own shoes; if *they* fit, they fit winter and summer, whether you gain weight or lose it. Not so with a collar—as a horse gets worked down, his neck gets slimmer, and you may need to either change collars or use a pad.

After buckling the collar, go back to the hooks on which your harness is hung inserting your right arm under the breeching. Hoist the harness more or less onto your shoulder, and grasp the hames, one in each hand. Approach the horse from the left, lifting the harness over his back and putting the hames over the collar. Get the hames seated down into the collar and adjust.

Hook the breast strap into the other bottom hame ring, hook up the belly band, hook the hold-backs or side straps, and crouper. Now, if the harness you have bought for this pair of horses fits without adjustment, it will be a miracle. If it doesn't fit, don't worry—harnesses are wonderfully adjustable. Go to work and make it fit, using a leather punch if necessary. In due time, by letting it out here and taking it up there you can achieve a good fit.

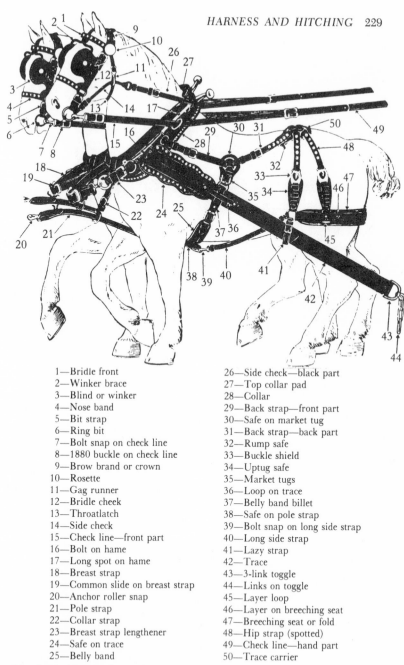

Fig. 7-14. Names of team harness parts
(Courtesy of Detweiler's Harness Shop)

1—Bridle front
2—Winker brace
3—Blind or winker
4—Nose band
5—Bit strap
6—Ring bit
7—Bolt snap on check line
8—1880 buckle on check line
9—Brow brand or crown
10—Rosette
11—Gag runner
12—Bridle cheek
13—Throatlatch
14—Side check
15—Check line—front part
16—Bolt on hame
17—Long spot on hame
18—Breast strap
19—Common slide on breast strap
20—Anchor roller snap
21—Pole strap
22—Collar strap
23—Breast strap lengthener
24—Safe on trace
25—Belly band

26—Side check—black part
27—Top collar pad
28—Collar
29—Back strap—front part
30—Safe on market tug
31—Back strap—back part
32—Rump safe
33—Buckle shield
34—Uptug safe
35—Market tugs
36—Loop on trace
37—Belly band billet
38—Safe on pole strap
39—Bolt snap on long side strap
40—Long side strap
41—Lazy strap
42—Trace
43—3-link toggle
44—Links on toggle
45—Layer loop
46—Layer on breeching seat
47—Breeching seat or fold
48—Hip strap (spotted)
49—Check line—hand part
50—Trace carrier

The same is true of bridles. Make sure the blinds are in a position to do their job, that the bit fits comfortably; in brief, that the bridle has been adjusted to this horse.

Okay, lead the horses out of the barn and take down the lines. At this point, double check to make sure that all buckles

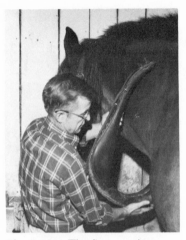

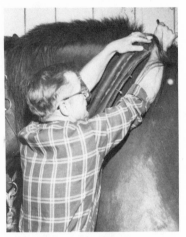

Fig. 7-15. The first step is to put on the collar. If your horse isn't trained to have it put over his head you will have to unbuckle the collar at the top and put it on him thusly. When doing so, support the collar with your hand on the bottom side; don't let it flop —this will help to keep it from breaks that can be irritating to the horse and damaging to the collar.

Fig. 7-16. Buckle it at the top and see that the strap is through the keeper. You should be able to insert your fingers between the horse's neck and the bottom of the collar. This is also the time to make sure that you don't have a lot of mane hair jammed under the collar; arrange it so that it doesn't serve as an irritant.

and snaps are secured. Hook up your overcheck or side check and drive the team around a little in the lines, making sure that everything is all right before putting the horses over the tongue.

Always secure the neck yoke first. If you are in doubt about your horses or if a colt is involved and you are using a slip-on neck yoke rather than a bolted-on neck yoke, it is a good idea to secure it to the tongue. The reason is simple, you can imagine what a mess it would be with the tongue banging along into the ground and the trace chains hooked into the singletrees. If the horses jump ahead before you have your tugs or traces hooked and the tongue bangs to the ground, startling them, you can have your hands full. In any event, *always secure the neck yoke first when hitching and unfasten it last when unhitching.*

You will have to figure out which link to hook them in by trial and error. Tongues vary in length. If they walk up

Fig. 7-17. In most cases harness is hung on two hooks, with the top hame strap carrying the load on one hook and the back strap, trace carrier, and hip strap on the other.

In picking up the harness, insert your right arm under the trace carrier, back and hip straps. Slide it under the backpad and take the hames, one in each hand with the harness mounted on your right arm and/or shoulder.

Fig. 7-18. With the collar on the horse and the harness on your right arm, you're now ready to harness the horse.

together like a pair of soldiers on parade, you will drop the same number of links for both horses. Few teams go off quite this well. That's one reason there are several links in your trace chains—to keep the doubletree at right angles with the tongue, you may have to drop one or two more links for one horse or the other.

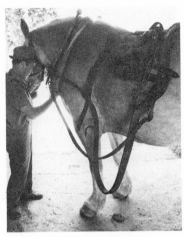

Fig. 7-19. Approaching the horse from the left, place the harness on the horse and seat the hames into the collar. Having properly fitting hames is important. (See section on proper fitting of hames and collars.)

Fig. 7-20. Having the hames seated, buckle your bottom hame strap, making sure the hames are snug into the collar, that your hame straps are tight and, again, use the keepers.

Know where your lines are. Loose lines dragging behind you can get tangled up in the wheels or other moving parts. This can be very serious.

If you are going to tie up your team while still in harness, tie them with their halters, not with their bridles, and make sure you tie them to an immovable object. If a horse is tied to something that will move rather easily if he pulls back, he may get frightened, and you have the seeds of a disaster.

MULTIPLE HITCHES

In the 1920s and 1930s the multiple hitch was the horse and mule man's answer to the tractor companies. By using more horses on larger machines, they reasoned, you could cover more ground, and thereby blunt, to some extent, the challenge of the tractor companies. In 1976 I think it reasonable to assume that the chief agricultural interest in horses and mules is for the smaller operator. Today, the Bonanza-type farmer is not about to use animal power seriously. And on the small farm the majority of jobs are two-horse jobs. To use our own eighty-acre operation as an example—we plant our corn with an old John Deere 999 two-row planter, seed our oats with a rubber tired wagon and IHC endgate seeder, haul our manure with a New Idea 10A spreader, cultivate our corn with a couple of old IHC single-row cultivators, all two-horse operations. Mowing (with a six-foot Case mower with tongue trucks) and windrowing with the side delivery rake are

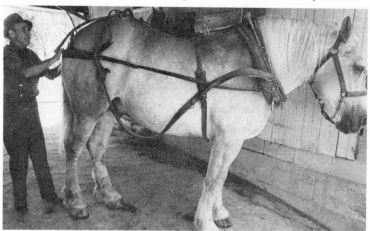

Fig. 7-21. With your hames secured, arrange the rest of the harness on the animal.

Fig. 7-22. Take your breast strap and hook it into the hame ring on the right (or off) side of the horse.

Fig. 7-23. Hook up your belly band.

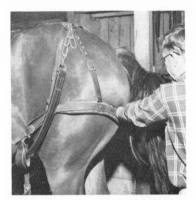 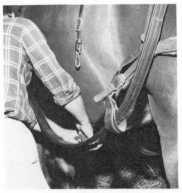

Fig. 7-24. Put the tail over the breeching. Adjust crupper if you are using one (this harness doesn't have one).

Fig. 7-25. Snap in your side straps (sometimes called hold-backs), checking their length; they are adjustable.

likewise two-horse operations. We have an eight-foot Oliver disk which we use three abreast on stalks and four in plowed ground. We use three abreast on the harrow.

Hitching three or four horses abreast calls for no special equipment or expertise. Anybody who can hitch two can hitch three or four abreast. You simply tie back from the bit ring of the outside horse to the hame ring of the inside horse, tie the lines up or take them out on the middle horse, and drive your outside horses with two lines. At least that is the way we do it. One of my neighbors has a fit every time he sees this. When he hitches four abreast on the disk he likes to have four lines in his hands. He is welcome to it. He likes to handle a lot of leather. But maybe he is right—I never claimed to be an expert. Extra cross lines for each of the inside horses are no doubt better than either of these methods mentioned. Use your faster walking horse or horses in the middle.

The only time we get into a situation where we use the bucking-back and tying in, common to the true multiple hitches, is in plowing. We have two plows, both Emersons, a sixteen-inch sulky and a two-bottom twenty-eight-inch gang plow (two fourteen-inch bottoms). When plowing is easy we use three abreast on the sulky, or four hitched two and two tandem-style on the gang. Alfalfa sod calls for the four hitched tandem on the sulky. Inasmuch as we never use a tandem disk

Fig. 7-26. Insert the bit in the horse's mouth, adjusting the bit so that it is comfortable for the horse.

Fig. 7-27. Buckle the throatlatch so that it is comfortable.

Fig. 7-28. Snap your over-check into the ring on the side check, making sure you have it under your lines. (I do this after I have the horses outside and am putting them together, rather than in the barn.) Now you take your team out, take down their lines, and snap their lines into the bit rings. The inside line on each horse goes to the bit ring of his mate, the outside line into his own outside bit ring.

Fig. 7-29. When putting a team in for the noon hour or at any other time when they are not going to be un-harnessed, I think it a good idea to un-snap the long side straps or hold-backs. Otherwise, especially in fly season, if they kick at a fly on their belly, they get their foot caught. When taking the bri-dle off, let the horse "spit" out the bit, don't yank it out. If you hang up your harness carefully it will be easier to harness the next time. It is also a good idea to wipe off the face of your collars with light harness oil on a rag before hanging them up.

or implements in combination such as a tandem disk followed by a harrow, and because we have only four work horses and relatively little work ground, we are probably fairly typical of the majority of today's horse farmers. We do, however, have many Amish friends and know some non-Amish farmers who farm large units with horsepower and *do* make use of the larger multiple hitches which we will present in this section.

The advantages of the multiple hitch are as follows:

1. It enables one man to accomplish more work per day. With horses in hard-working condition you can expect to plow up to one acre per day per horse, using the hitches herein illustrated.
2. It eliminates side-draft. This increases the power approximately 15 percent to 20 percent and pulling straight away from the plow helps to prevent sore shoulders, necks, legs and sides.
3. It equalizes the pull on each horse.
4. It prevents crowding and enables horses to remain cooler and be more comfortable.

You will need bucking-back straps or ropes and tying-in chains as shown in the illustration (see Fig. 7-30). For tying-in a light chain five feet long with a bolt snap on each end is used. One end is snapped into the *halter* ring of the horse in the rear, the other end is snapped to the inside trace of the horse diagonally ahead. If the rear horse is slow, the chain can be shortened up to make him quicken his pace. The rear horses wear halters, so the lead chain can be attached to the halter ring rather than the bit to prevent jerking on the mouth. This tie chain should have enough play so that the horse can swing his head freely, but should be short enough to compel him to do his share of the work and to turn readily. *Never fasten tie chains to a bridle; they are apt to break and cause a runaway.* Always use strong halters on horses controlled with tie chains.

The buck strap or rope, made on the same principle as a line, is run through the hame rings and snapped into the bit. From the withers the buck strap runs downward fastening to the draw chain back of the horse's hind leg. One buck strap and one tie chain are required for each horse, except the leaders. If the horse is not next to a draw chain, his buck strap fastens to the tug of a horse which has already been bucked back to the draw chain.

Just as you can "encourage" a slow horse behind by shortening up his tying-in chain, you can slow down a rear horse with a tendency to travel too fast by shortening up his buck strap.

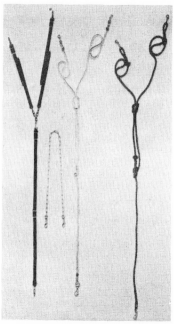

Fig. 7-30. From left to right, buck strap, tie chain, and buck ropes. Dimensions of buck strap—inside check 48 inches, outside check 54 inches, short connecting chain 10 inches, and lower portion of buck strap which runs to draw chain 96 inches long, arranged so it can be shortened as desired. Extra heavy snaps are used on this strap, regular bit snaps on the check reins. Straps should be as strong as the heaviest lines.

The tie chain is 72 inches long, plus snaps. Use heavy snaps and double back, snapping to chain if bad horse or mule is being handled; there are no snaps which will stand such a heavy strain.

The buck rope (center right) adjustable through figure eight loop. Upper portion used as inside and outside check 108 inches long; lower portion adjustable 96 inches long. Use extra heavy, large eye snap on either strap or rope where it fastens to draw chain. Ropes, where used, should be waterproofed by soaking in warm paraffin. Straps should be kept well oiled with some good harness oil, as dry leather lacks tensile strength. The buck rope shown at the extreme right is a homemade one, of ½-inch Manila. Snaps are spliced in.

Once the adjustments are made, and the horses get used to it, you can go right along driving with only two lines, praise the Lord. Use your fastest walking horses in the lead, and expect to make some adjustments after you get to the field. Not every horse is going to walk up in place until the proper adjustments have been made on the buck ropes and tie chains, and until they figure out what is expected of them.

Taking an outfit such as this to and from the field is not quite as impossible as it first appears. You simply drive your leaders and, taking the tying-in chain from your off (right hand) wheel horse (that's the horse in the wheel position in your hitch), lead them.

Tying-in and bucking-back equipment can either be homemade or secured through many of the harness shops presently doing business.

To illustrate multi-horse hitches, there can be no better source of reference than a couple of booklets published by the now defunct Horse and Mule Association of America.

The first one is their pamphlet called *The Hitch Booklet*, for three, four, five, and six horses. Using the "tied in" and "bucked back" system previously described, all the eveners can be homemade (dimensions are given in the diagrams). This log chain and pulley hitch can be rigged up by most any farmer. Needless to say, the prices quoted for some of the materials have changed. But then, this pamphlet was published in 1926!

Experiments have proved that there is a "true center of draft" on plows. In simple language this means that it takes less power to pull the plow when the team is hitched directly forward of that point than when it is hitched further away from or nearer to the furrow.

On a two-bottom gang plow, twelve-inch bottoms, the true center of draft is usually nineteen or twenty inches from center of furrow; on the same, but with fourteen-inch bottoms, it is generally from twenty-two to twenty-three inches from center of furrow.

This makes it impossible to hitch four, five, or six horses abreast on such gang plows and to have the center of evener directly forward of true center of draft unless part of the horses work on plowed ground. This is hard on such horses; if, on the contrary, the horses remain on solid ground except for the furrow horses, the point of hitch comes far to the left of the center of draft (in a right hand plow) and causes side draft, which increases by 20 percent or more the power required to pull the plow, besides causing crowding, trampling, overheating, etc.

To escape this, it is necessary to hitch the horses or mules tandem. The leaders can be equalized against the wheelers by a chain and pulley, as in the four-horse hitch illustrated, or by a chain and lever equalizer, as outlined in the three-, five-, and six-horse units.

For pulleys order ten-inch Hartz single steel tackle blocks, No. 608 and specify that they shall be furnished without hook or becket. Chain should be $5/16$-inch special steel logging chain, which will run in these tackle blocks and which has the necessary tensile strength. Length should be thirteen feet on pulley hitch, ten feet on lever hitch.

The lead eveners must be heavy enough to keep the angle of trace down so that traces will come out at right angles to the shoulders as on the wheel pair. With two ahead the eveners should be weighted till they and the weights total about fifty pounds. With three in the lead, the total should be about seventy-five pounds. In very hard plowing more weight may be needed. Stand off at one side, watch the horses plowing, and add weight until the angle of trace on leaders is the same as on wheelers. This does increase the tension on the tugs of the leaders, but brings the traces at right angles to their shoulders and enables them to work so much more efficiently that the extra tension on the traces of leaders is more than offset. Furthermore, the tandem hitch makes it possible to hitch at true center of draft, reduces the pull required to a minimum, and gives the horses a straight forward pull with ample room in which to work.

Driving is simplicity itself because the wheelers are "tied in" and "bucked back," hence, automatically controlled. Light link halter chains with snaps at the end are best to tie the wheelers to the traces ahead; ropes or straps can be used to "buck back." Allow some slack and the horses will quickly adapt themselves to the system, and in less than half a day they will learn to "drive themselves" better than any driver can. The slowest horses should naturally be put in the wheel group, but a light air rifle with compression cut down, loaded with dried peas will be found to be more useful than a whip. A tin can hooked on the plow to carry a few clods will do if the driver is a reasonably straight thrower. The essential thing is to speak to a laggard and follow your command with a reminder, without disturbing the other horses or mules.

All these hitches can be made at home. Working dimensions are given. Singletrees of the right length can be purchased; doubletrees and eveners should be made from hard wood if available, although yellow pine will do if a few extra pieces are handy for occasional repairs. All singletrees shown here are twenty-eight inches long (see Figs. 7-31, 7-32, 7-33, 7-34).

By the early thirties the depression had sidelined thousands of tractors as farmers returned to horsepower in earnest, and the Horse and Mule Association refined, demonstrated, and pushed the multiple hitches on every front. In 1934 they came out with a much larger pamphlet called, *Horses-Mules, Power-Profit*, that was devoted in its entirety to the use of multiple hitches. The tie-in and buckback system was still basic, but the association was now pushing a set of four eveners, iron bound to withstand strains up to 18,000 pounds, and adaptable to multiples from three to sixteen horses.

Three of these four eveners are pictured, along with the straight clevises that they called for, in Figs. 7-35 and 7-36. Interestingly enough, Quality Craft, Rt. 3, Independence, Iowa 50644, still manufactures these four eveners for multiple hitches. Made out of seasoned oak and varnished, they are one of the horse farming items that is again available in new form. The clevises may be available in some harness shops, as are the eveners.

FOUR-, FIVE-, AND SIX-HORSE HITCHES

The four-horse hitch shown here (see Fig. 7-37) is designed

for a fourteen- or sixteen-inch sulky plow in very tough plowing such as an alfalfa or sweet clover field. A forty-two-inch wagon evener is used in the lead; also a log chain strong enough to hold up under heavy work and of such length that horses in wheel team will not bump their knees on lead eveners. Be sure to use at least a forty-two-inch evener in the lead; using a shorter evener—say a thirty-two-inch—will prevent the plow from cutting a full width furrow. The hitch works equally well on a wagon when attached underneath the wagon pole to the front axle by means of a crotch chain. This makes the wagon pole of ample length and helps take the side whip off the pole when teaming is being done on rough ground. It also works well on a grain binder or small combine, as it gives good air space, makes turning easy, and reduces side draft. The equalizers on the rear horses draw at an angle, with the outside ends higher, adjusting themselves to the angle of the horse's shoulder. This puts the inside ends of the equalizers at the point where the draw chain attaches, from four to six inches lower than the point at which the hitch attaches to the implement. Buckstraps and tie chains *should not* be used with this hitch on wagon; lines should be used on both lead and wheel pairs because the draft is not constant.

The six-strung-out (see Fig. 7-38) is a good hitch, notwithstanding the fact it seems awkward in driving for the first time. There is an abundance of air space between the horses and each horse works as freely as if he were on the road. Many think that the lead horses must exert the greatest amount of energy, due to the fact they are farthest from the load. However, they have the same power effectiveness as the wheel team if the angle of trace is correct.

True enough, the horses do not have to pull any more pounds when the angle of trace is wrong, but it is more difficult for them to secure a footing; this does not hold true on a stuck load, for then you want your team to raise up and carry part of the load for a short time. In the use of farm machinery this is not true, for, if the horse lifts up, the machine will have to be so adjusted as to counteract the lifting force, increasing the load on the horses.

This six-horse hitch will require a wider headland than or-

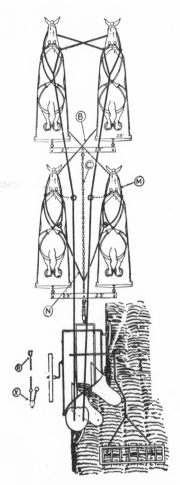

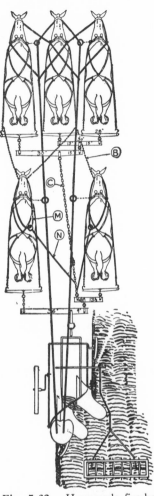

Fig. 7-31.   Homemade four-horse pulley hitch

B. Halter tie chain
C. Draw chain, about ten feet long
M. Bridle reins with ring riding loose where it loops
N. Buck strap tied into loose ring on bridle reins, thence to draw chain. Prevents rear horses pulling too far forward.

Fig. 7-32.   Homemade five-horse plow hitch

R. Forward end of draw chain and clevis. Draw chain about thirteen feet long, adjusted enough so that rear horses cannot step on doubletree of leaders.

X. Weld large ring in chain three feet from end. This allows flexibility between front and rear pair, yet prevents rear team from going too far ahead if buck straps should loosen.

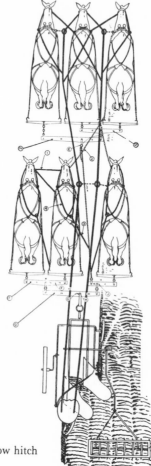

Fig. 7-33. Homemade six-horse plow hitch

dinarily, but there are enough good points to counteract this disadvantage. After a team becomes accustomed to the hitch, the turn can be made without slowing down, and without crowding or trampling on feet. It makes a good hitch for a wagon or for moving a heavy load, since every horse must pull and no horse can shirk his share of the burden. When used on a wagon, however, do not use tie chains and buck straps; use lines instead, at least on the wheel as well as the lead pair, because the load is not constant, and you must hold the wheelers back at times.

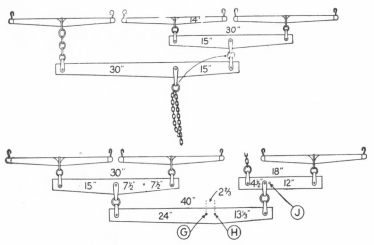

Fig. 7-34. Working plans of homemade six-horse plow hitch which can be adapted as a five-horse hitch.

Hitch the plow clevis at H for six horses. To change this for use as a five-horse hitch—two ahead, three in rear—shift clevis to J, back of furrow horse (which is 1 ½ inches to the right of the hole where the clevis is now attached), and change plow clevis to G on the large evener; then use an ordinary 4-foot evener on the lead pair.

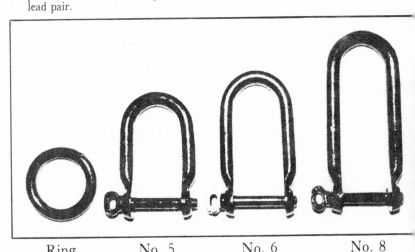

Ring   No. 5   No. 6   No. 8

Fig. 7-35. Rings and clevises

For evener 24 .... No. 5 and two No. 6s

For evener 30 .... One each No. 5, 6, and 8

For evener 43 .... One No. 5 and two No. 8s

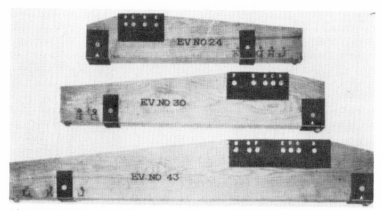

Fig. 7-36. The eveners (designed for ordering by number) are iron-bound to withstand strain up to and exceeding 18,000 pounds. The maximum strain apt to be encountered with a twelve-horse team is 12,000 pounds.

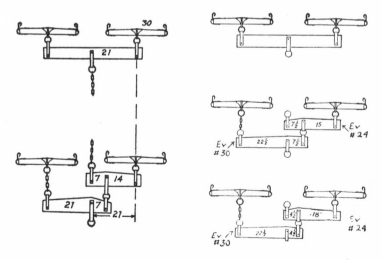

Fig. 7-37. Showing details of four-horse hitch for sulky plow

Fig. 7-38. The lead and swing pairs in this six-horse hitch form five-horse tandem hitch for gang plow.

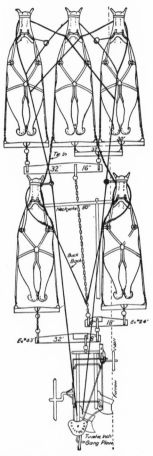

Fig. 7-39. Five horses on a
twelve-inch gang plow

Fig. 7-40. Six-horse unit in
detail

The five-horse hitch (see Fig. 7-39) is immediately
popular where it is given a fair trial. The rear horses work
nearly as far apart as do the outside leaders. Neck yoke on the
wheel team must be so built as to extend about eighteen
inches longer on the horse working on unplowed ground than
on his mate. The advantages of this hitch are that it gives
ample air space to the rear team (which is the harder of the
two to keep cool) and enables the teamster to get a good view
of all his horses; it also allows plenty of room for lines, and, in

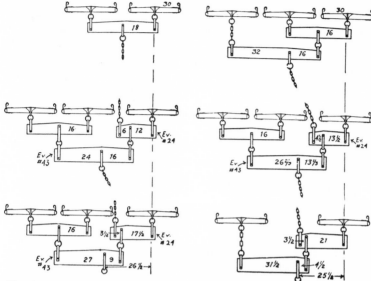

Fig. 7-41. Eight-horse hitch (two, three, and three)

Fig. 7-42. Eight-horse hitch (three, three, and two)

Fig. 7-43. Jiggs Kinney, one of the present-day generation of horse farmers, who farms near Columbus Junction, Iowa, using ten head (three, three, and four) on a combination disk and harrow.

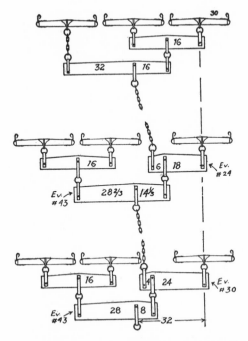

Fig. 7-44. A good hitch for a three-bottom plow (fourteen-inch shares) in heavy soil. This hitch can be changed to an eight-horse hitch for a three-bottom gang by substituting singletree for the rear doubletree and changing rear evener from 28 by 8 inches to 42 by 6 inches.

turning short at the end of the field, makes it almost impossible for lead team to punch rear team with its doubletrees; also causes little trampling and crowding on turns.

This hitch for five can be used on a sulky plow in adverse soil conditions by shortening the short rear equalizer (ev. 24) to 4½ vs. 13½ as in Fig. 7-40 leaving other proportions the ·same as in Fig. 7-39. The rear left side is an excellent position for a mare heavily in foal and also for an awkward horse that is inclined to be constantly knocking into some other horse— since with the long neck yoke such interference is impossible.

Frequently the rear left horse is tied in with two chains, one of them extending to the outside end of the singletree on the outside land horse ahead. This extra chain is generally

Fig. 7-45. A good illustration of a dangerous practice: note those lines dragging along behind the team.

used only in starting a new horse. After he becomes accustomed to working in this manner the extra or outside chain usually is not needed, and the chain at center, instead of being attached as shown in drawing, is placed from halter of rear left horse to inside tug of left lead horse.

A study of the bucking-back system will show that if the rear horses should try to start before the leaders do the draw chain would be pulled back and the rear horses would be forced to pull the load with their mouths. The rear horses, however, cannot get over the lead eveners if the buck ropes are properly adjusted, and if the load is heavy enough they cannot move it with their mouths. In case the rear horses try to run away, all the driver has to do is to keep the lead team in check, and the rear team will be automatically checked by having to draw the load with their mouths. If no load exists, they can run away.

When tie chains and buck ropes are properly adjusted, moreover, the horse has several inches of play backward and forward; that is, he is not strung in tight while working. It is remarkable how quickly some teams learn to start and stop together, not even taking the slack out of the lead chains and buck ropes.

Another six-horse hitch, three and three, is a good hitch (see Fig. 7-40), although not so good as the two, two, and two for six-horse farms. It is a great deal better, however, than the four behind and two in the lead, since it gives the horses more room to work. The draw chain pulls at a slight angle which does not, however, affect the direction of the implement. It is a good hitch for ten-foot grain binders, corn pickers, etc., but must be turned upside down to keep draw chain next to pole when possible.

An ordinary three-horse evener is used in the lead. This hitch attaches at the true center of draft on a fourteen-inch gang plow but does not give the air space or freedom that the six strung out gives. It allows the horses more freedom, however, than does the six-horse hitch with four behind and two in front.

EIGHT- AND NINE-HORSE HITCHES

The eight-horse hitch, two, three, and three (see Fig. 7-41), is an efficient unit for a two-bottom gang where a man has only two good lead horses or has a five-horse hitch with two in the lead and three behind. By moving the five up and putting three more in the rear any farmer has an eight-horse hitch; or, in cases where it is desirable to work only five horses, then he uses the two lead teams, leaving the rear team off. It also can be used for seven horses on a two-bottom gang by changing the rear evener to forty-two by seven inches instead of twenty-seven by nine inches, using one horse instead of two on the land in the rear group. The hitch can be used for a three-bottom plow by increasing the length of evener for the rear furrow horse to twenty-four inches over all, using four and twenty inches instead of 3½ and 17½ inches; for twelve-inch shares only, not fourteen-inch.

Some farmers using two-bottom gangs prefer the eight-horse hitch with three and three in the lead and two in the rear, as shown in Fig. 7-42. Especially is this a handy hitch if a man has a six-horse hitch, three and three, already working, since all he has to do in this case is to move his threes up and put a two-horse team on at the rear. His lead teams are accustomed to working together and there is no loss of time, therefore, in breaking teams in. The eight-horse hitch for two-bottom gangs is designed especially for plowing that is extremely hard and is used in sections where soil is very heavy, or where the horses or mules are small.

The nine-horse hitch, three, three, and three for a three-bottom plow (see Fig. 7-44) is very satisfactory under conditions which cause the plow to draw too heavily for the eight-horse hitch. The horses in the nine work farther apart, stay cooler, and stand the work better on plows than where big horses are worked together in the eight-horse hitch, in a four-four arrangement. We do not recommend this hitch on plows. Better use three, three, and two.

The nine-horse hitch is becoming increasingly popular in sections where farmers are in the habit of using three-bottom plows for heavy plowing. The draw chain on this hitch, as on some of the others, works at a slight angle but it does not cause any deviation in direction of the implement.

The lead six from Fig. 7-44 make a good six-horse hitch of three-three formation, the chief difficulty being that it is too wide to attach at the true center of draft on a two-bottom twelve- or fourteen-inch gang plow. For a small combine, a large grain binder, corn picker, etc., it is an excellent hitch, however, when the evener is turned over to keep the draw chain next to the pole.

Fig. 7-46 shows a detailed drawing of an eight-horse team on a three-bottom tractor plow. Experience has satisfied us that it is simpler to hitch direct to the three-bottom plow than to put a hitch cart between plow and team. This is recommended especially where land is level and free of stone. A platform with a crow's nest on which the driver rides may be built across the three plow beams. It is advisable, however, not to throw the plow out at the ends unless a harrow section loaded down with weights is being drawn behind the plow. Otherwise, the plow will run against the teams and cause a runaway. The majority of men using this eight-horse team on three-bottom plows, plow around and around inside the field, never taking the plow out of the ground from beginning to end. The corners will be rounded slightly, but it is easier and simpler to plow the corners out when through than to bother with taking the plow out of the ground on turns.

The eight-horse unit shown in Fig. 7-46 has a little side draft in plowing and it is therefore recommended that men who have much plowing to do, shift to the eight-horse unit made by changing the nine shown in Fig. 7-44 to an eight, three, three, and two as indicated. This eliminates all side draft and allows more freedom for work. For fall plowing, it is better to use nine (see Fig. 7-42).

Short chains making a crotch should be extended from the main point of hitch to small clevises, as shown on drawing, to facilitate turning the plow at the corners.

The pamphlet from which all this information comes (*Horses-Mules, Power-Profit*) goes on to illustrate eighteen head on a combine, a hitch for ten on two gang plows used in tandem, twelve on a four-bottom plow, etc. It is my thought that hitches of this size are primarily of academic rather than practical interest at this time, so I will skip them. This pamphlet, in its entirety, is available from the Detweiler's Harness Shop, Box 228, Hazleton, Iowa 50641, for anyone interested in what I skipped.

MULTIPLE HITCHES FOR TILLAGE

Plowing got most of the attention where multiple hitches were concerned. I will, however, show the Horse and Mule Association's adaptation to some of the other common tillage tools where someone desires to work a large farm with horses and mules.

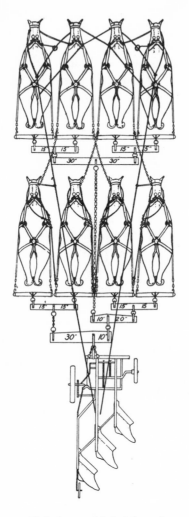

Fig. 7-46. Eight horses, hitched four abreast

On most horse farms the single, eight-, nine-, or ten-foot disk is in use and the horses can be hitched abreast as described at the outset of this chapter. Where tandem disks, followed by a harrow, or two 9-foot disks, hitched side by side, are called for the pamphlet offers the following advice:

Two disks work very satisfactorily and are easily put together, as shown in Fig. 7-47. The platform is made up with a two- by twelve-inch plank at the rear and a two- by six-inch in front, put together with a ⅝-inch bolt in each place. Holes in all cases are equal distances apart, which allows one disk to get ahead while turning around without causing any damage. The platform is raised up on blocks at the rear end of the stub pole of each disk, high enough to allow room for disks to work freely underneath. A four-horse tandem hitch (Fig. 7-37 or lead four of Fig. 7-38) is used on each disk and a spreader stick is used between the two center horses in the lead team.

This may seem awkward to handle at first, but the horses soon become accustomed to this method and are able to work comfortably without crowding or heating. On plowed ground a good hitch is made by putting a hardwood piece in the disk clevises and moving each team in at equal distances from the disk until the team becomes a compact four and four. It is necessary here, however, to use a double draw chain to keep the disk from whipping. When moving from one field to another the team may be divided leaving four strung out on each disk; remove the bolts from the platform and handle as two separate units.

Two disks of different lengths may be used in the same manner and the team on smaller disk moved in a greater distance from the disk clevis to equalize the pull.

Some farmers are using fourteen-inch clevises on their disks instead of the regulation disk clevis. They place a twelve-inch hardwood plank in the newly attached clevises and draw directly from this plank, as shown in Fig. 7-48.

Many farmers prefer this hook-up to that of the tandem disk, claiming that by allowing the ground to dry for a short time and disking again, throwing the ridges out, the disk will work better and will kill more weeds.

The ten-horse hitch on the double disk is simple and easily made. It is formed of the six, three and three, on the left side, and the four, two and two, on the right. The latter is the sulky plow hitch shown in Fig. 7-37. The combination makes a good ten-horse hitch where a five-abreast formation is desired as shown in Fig. 7-49.

A good many different hitches can be made on this plan. For instance, two five-horse hitches with two in the lead and three in the rear can be used side by side, turning one five-horse hitch over and using a common drawbar in the rear. This gives a ten with four in the lead and six in the rear. Two six-horse hitches, arranged three and three, make a twelve-horse hitch six abreast, and two six-horse hitches with two in the lead and four in the rear can be used in the same manner as the two fives, forming a twelve with four in the lead and eight in the rear. To form an eight-horse hitch, two four-horse hitches, two and two, are placed together in same manner.

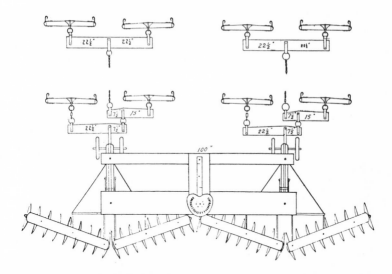

Fig. 7-47. Eight-horse hitch on two eighteen-blade single disks, hitched side by side. Spaced properly for disking corn rows; each four-horse team straddles a corn row and there are two rows of stubble left between the two four-horse teams. This permits disking six corn rows at a time, and the horses follow the corn rows, simplifying driving. In plowed ground or in disking small grain stubble, it is advisable to put a 2 by 6 hardwood piece in the disk clevises and move each team in an equal distance until the team becomes a compact four and four. The manner in which this is done is shown in Fig. 7-31. A great many men prefer this arrangement with the harrow cart, to the seating arrangements shown in 7-31.

All these hitches will be of the double chain type and will operate well, once the rear horses have become accustomed to working between chains.

Taking big teams from the barn to the field or from the field to the barn is simplicity itself, when understood. The diagram shown in Fig. 7-50 illustrates this clearly. The lead three or four, as the case may be, are driven in any one of several ways—either with the extra check as shown in this diagram, or by using ordinary lines running to the two outside horses and tying the heads of the two center ones together; or, as is often done, handling them with the lines going to the center pair, as in ordinary wagon driving, the outside horses being tied back from bit to hame as shown in Fig. 7-50, and a buck strap placed on each outside horse to hold him out to his proper position.

After the lead four are brought out, snapped together, and left at the watering trough in a lot adjoining the barn to drink, the next four are led out, snapped together, and placed at the opposite side of the watering trough. While they are drinking the driver backs the first four away from the watering trough, swings them around, and takes down the lines, fastening the lines together in whatever fashion he may elect for driving his lead horses.

He then steps back and picks up the lead chain of the off rear horse and starts for the field, as shown. On arriving at the field the driver brings his team up to the implement from the rear, approaching implement in such position that he drives over the doubletrees, and his horses swing into regular working position when they stop.

Driver then snaps extension lines to his regular lines and walks back through the center of the rear team and ties lines securely to the implement; proceeds to the lead horses, hitches their traces, and snaps the tie chains of the horses immediately behind them into proper position (see Fig. 7-46); then hitches the traces of the rear four (in the case of the eight-horse team) and at the same time snaps buck straps or buck ropes into position; steps upon the implement and drives off.

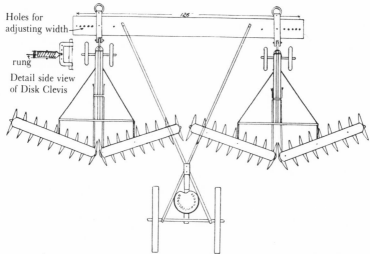

Holes for
adjusting width

rung

Detail side view
of Disk Clevis

Fig. 7-48. Two nine-foot disks drawn by eight good horses cutting a strip eighteen feet wide will cover four acres per hour.

Two tandem disks can be put together in same way: draw with 12- or 16-horse team.

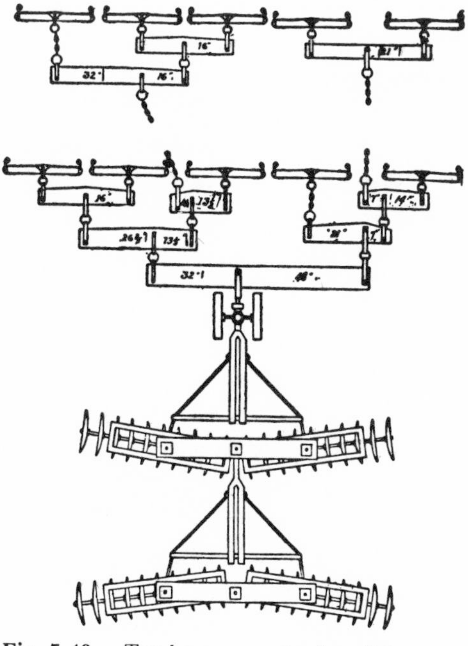

Fig. 7-49. Ten horses on a tandem disk

In unhitching, simply reverse the procedure followed in hitching. Begin on the rear team. Unsnap the buck strap, snap it into trace of horse to which it belongs and hook up the traces. Go straight across rear team in this fashion; then as you go back in front of rear team, unsnap the tie chains and fasten them together as shown in rear four of Fig. 7-50, at the same time doing up the traces and buck straps of the swing team (if nine are being used), fastening the off rear horse to the inside trace of the horse immediately ahead of him. Then unhitch your leaders, unsnap your extension lines and let them fall; gather up the regular lines and start for the barn.

The harrow hitch shown in Fig. 7-51, with eight horses abreast, is flexible and easy to make. All the material required for it is usually to be found on any eight-horse farm. In moving the outfit from one field to another, put one four-horse team on each harrow and move in two separate units—where gates are large. For this moving many farmers use a long pair of skids built like a stoneboat. They remove the harrow cart and turn the harrows over on the eveners; then draw the skid lengthwise close to the harrow, turn the harrow back on the skids, put the eveners and boom on top of the harrow, hitch a team at the end of the skid, and move the outfit easily through an ordinary gate. Thus, they have moved the harrows from one field to the other without the trouble of disconnecting anything but the harrow cart.

With some farmers it is a common practice to use the harrow cart in front of the harrow; in this event the eight, four and four, with the single draw chain works well, but this is a dangerous practice where young or nervous horses are being used. A number of farmers are using two four-abreast hitches in the usual way with two harrows drawn up side by side. A pair of strap irons with one bolt in each end is used between the harrow booms, spacing the harrows and at the same time keeping them from becoming tangled at the ends. The teams are driven with a spreader stick between the two four-horse teams. This again works well but is a difficult hitch to drive unless horses are all gaited alike. There are on the market

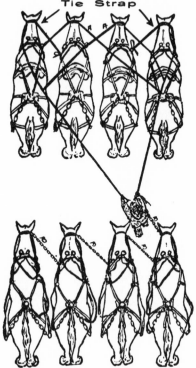

Fig. 7-50. Leading two big teams from the barn

several steel harrow booms up to thirty-six and forty feet in size, capable of being used with any kind of harrow and any number of horses.

The harrow, wisely used, reduces cultivation cost materially. Disk and harrow just before planting; then harrow again every fourth day till the corn is three inches high. This kills weeds and saves the expense of at least one cultivation.

The eight-horse harrow hitch works well in harrowing corn and will cover from seventy to eighty acres per day under good average conditions. Some farmers prefer using a combination of weeders to accomplish the same purpose, but they cannot cover as much ground as with the harrows, nor will the expense be as low.

So much for the big hitches. There is considerable value in stringing out your horses, not only in terms of line of draft, but in keeping them more comfortable while working.

HOW MUCH GROUND CAN YOU COVER?

More of you will probably be interested in smaller equipment and what you can reasonably expect to get done in a day's time. As previously stated, the old rule of thumb on plowing was one acre per day per horse.

Other rules of thumb used by the Horse and Mule Association were as follows. Planting corn, using a team on a two-row, you can—at the most—plant twenty acres a day IF, 1. the seedbed is in good condition, 2. you alternate teams at noon, 3. you have brisk walking horses, and 4. you put in a long day. Fifteen acres a day would probably be a more realistic goal.

Several horse farmers, to speed things up, have welded two two-row planters together and used four abreast. If your acreage calls for it, this is a good idea.

The rotary hoe has not been a satisfactory implement for horse use. To effectively kill weeds it must be operated at high speed, faster than a horse can be expected to work. If you are relying on horses and mules altogether, you are better off using the spike tooth harrow until the corn is up.

Cultivation is one of the more tedious jobs in corn growing, but one that I admit to enjoying very much. Basically there are three ways to go, a team on a single-row, three on a two-row, or four on a two-row. The weather is warmer during cultivation than during planting, you can't push the horses as much—nor do you want to, especially the first time over—and thus you can figure fifteen acres a day with a two-row is about the most you can expect to cover, and that will be a long day.

On harrowing, the rule of thumb might be that you could expect to harrow ten acres per day per section. In other words, three horses on a three-section drag could cover thirty acres. That, too, is a little on the ambitious side.

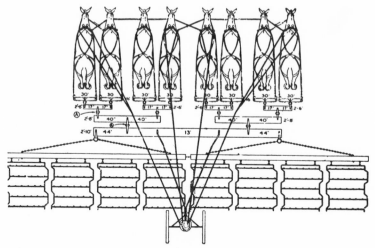

Fig. 7-51. Eight horses working abreast on large harrow. A good saddle pony is better than a hitch cart—easier on the driver and his team.

Frankly, I think the Horse and Mule Association targets were too high. They were engaged in an all-out propaganda war with the tractor interests and this resulted in some rather extravagant claims on both sides. It also assumed a high degree of horse proficiency on the part of the farmer and good horses in tip-top shape.

The figures used by Cornell University in their pamphlet, *The Efficient Use of Horses on New York Farms* are, I think, more realistic. Following is the table they published for a good team, weighing 3000 pounds, properly handled, and with good equipment:

Plow....1½ to 2 acres

Harrow...8 to 10 acres

Drill....8 to 10 acres

Plant....8 to 10 acres

Cultivate (Single Row)...7 acres

Mow......................7 acres

Rake....................14 acres

Haul......1½ to 2 tons (that depends on how it is loaded)

This Cornell Bulletin, published in the early forties, was directed more at the way in which draft horses are likely to be used today. The only multiple hitch illustrated is the four-

horse hitch. It assumed that much of the heavy work will be
done by tractor power and stresses the team work and smaller
hitches.

It makes the point that horses are especially well adapted
for jobs such as planting, drilling, hauling manure, work in
the woodlot, and other work that requires a large amount of
starting and stopping, and that horses and mules are
definitely superior to mechanical power on hillsides, on rough
stony land, in snow, or where the ground is wet. In other
words, in a mixed power situation, you should use your horses
wherever and whenever there is no clear-cut advantage to the
tractor.

Homemade Neck Yokes, Singletrees, and Doubletrees

It is still possible to buy a considerable quantity of these
items at farm sales. Beware, however, of dry rot. In any case,
they can frequently be picked up for next to nothing, and the
hardware can be used on your own homemade neck yokes,
singletrees, and doubletrees if the ones you buy are over the
hill. Use seasoned hardwood: oak, hickory, or ash.

Directions and illustrations (see Fig. 7-52) follow (reprinted
from Autumn 1973, *Draft Horse Journal*).

Singletree   Singletrees vary somewhat in length, thickness, and method of construction depending upon the use for
which they are designed. Plow singletrees are twenty-six
inches and thirty inches long while wagon singletrees are
made in lengths of thirty, thirty-six, and thirty-eight inches.

Straight-grained hickory should be used. A piece of hickory
1¾ by 2¾ by 36 inches will serve the purpose. The iron fittings may be purchased, made, or can be taken from another
singletree.

To make, first bring the singletree to the desired shape by the use of a drawing knife, spokeshave, and plane. Then, fit the steel parts such as ferrules or clips. Finish with several coats of boiled linseed oil.

Neck Yoke   Ordinary wagon neck yokes for horses are made in thirty-eight-inch and forty-two-inch lengths. The rings and ferrules can be purchased more cheaply than they can be made by hand.

A piece of straight-grained hickory 1¾ by three by thirty-eight inches is all the stock needed to make the yoke.

Work the piece to the desired shape as in the case of the singletree. Fit the ferrules and plates. Finish with boiled linseed oil, or paint to match wagon.

Doubletree   A doubletree set is made up of a doubletree and two singletrees. The doubletree serves as a beam to distribute the pulling load between the two horses. Doubletrees are made in lengths of thirty-six inches, forty inches, forty-two inches, and forty-eight inches. They are sometimes bound with light band iron.

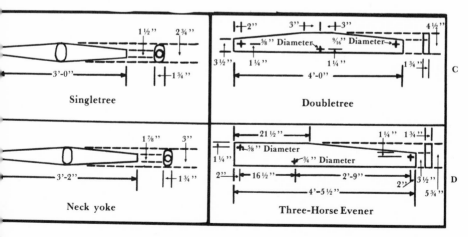

-52. Dimensions for homemade neck yoke, singletree, doubletree, and three-horse evener.

The steel clevises and bearing plates used on doubletrees can be purchased for a nominal sum. The lumber required consists of a piece of straight-grained hickory 1¾ by 4½ by forty-eight inches.

Bring the doubletree to proper dimensions by use of a saw and plane. Bore holes where indicated. Fit plates and clevises. Finish with linseed oil or paint.

Three-Horse Evener   Occasionally it is desired to drive three horses abreast. For this purpose a three-horse evener is used in connection with a doubletree and three singletrees.

A piece of straight-grained hickory, 1¾ by 5¾ by 53⅓ inches will serve to make the evener.

Bring the evener to the desired shape with a saw and plane. Bore the end holes where shown. This distributes the pulling load in the ratio of one to two.

Safety Rules for Working with Horses

One of our readers, Dale Collins, of Hopkins, Michigan, sent in some safety rules that are well worth keeping in mind. Some of them have been covered above; here are others (some of them slightly revised):

1. Don't allow small children to play in the stable behind the horses. They can get carried away in their play, startle the horses, and get kicked by even a gentle horse.
2. Don't leave a team stand without being attended or tied.
3. Beware of old equipment. (Check thread in old harness and examine neck yokes and singletrees for dry rot. Wood does not last forever.) In this respect, let me add that I think it unwise to ever paint neck yokes, singletrees, and doubletrees. It can cover up a dangerous piece of equipment.

4. Don't send a child to the field or on the road without being awfully sure of both the youngster and the horses. Keep the child's strength in mind, along with his experience. Draft horses are not playmates.

5. Horse-drawn implements are the same as a tractor: one seat means one rider, not two or three small children hanging on some place.

6. Since lines and bridles are the main devices for controlling the team, these parts of the harness should be checked often for tears, cuts, or weak spots.

7. Never follow a team in the field by walking between the team and the implement being pulled; use line extensions.

8. Never leave the seat of a mower or manure spreader without first taking it out of gear.

9. When using "made for tractor" implements, don't ride on them in some make-do fashion; use a fore cart.

10. During the summer months use fly nets or apply a fly repellent on your horses. Annoyance from flies is a major cause of runaways during the summer months. (In my area some teamsters also tie a small square piece of burlap to the bridle nose band and this hangs over the horse's nose to reduce annoyance from face flies.)

Chapter 8

Breeding Horses

Your own situation will determine whether or not you wish to engage in breeding draft horses. If you are extremely limited by space, pasture, and feedstuffs you may wish to stick with geldings. If, on the other hand, you have the room, time, and inclination to engage in breeding, the sale of well-bred colts can be a good source of supplemental income and, if your mares are properly handled, they will not miss much time in harness.

Breeding, quite logically, breaks down into three major concerns for you: brood mares, stallions, and raising foals. For most beginners, and a great many who aren't beginners, keeping a stallion just isn't in the cards. If you wish to raise a colt or two a year, having a stallion can be quite a bother *unless* you are located in a neighborhood where you can hope to do a good outside stud business. Check around and find what there are in the way of good draft stallions within easy trucking distance of your farm.

Whether you choose to keep your own stallion or not it is a certainty that you are going to have to have one or more brood mares, so we will address ourselves to that topic first, with four excellent bulletins from Iowa State, Ohio State, Michigan State, and the University of Missouri as primary references. All say essentially the same things. Following is a composite of these bulletins, plus some general observations from random sources.

The Brood Mare

The profitable brood mare must be a regular producer of saleable colts. It makes no sense to just multiply horses; if you can't raise a good, useful animal you will be money ahead to leave the breeding to others and simply buy your work stock as needed.

In selecting brood mares the *breed* is not important (except in terms of what is available to breed her to), but the *type* is. Brood mares should be sound, completely free of inheritable unsoundnesses, of good size but not necessarily big, of acceptable draft conformation, with big feet, well-set legs, clean flat bone, and the ability to wheel their freight freely and with some style.

They should possess a breedy appearance as expressed by being deep ribbed, roomy, with a lot of femininity best expressed in refinement about their heads and necks. Avoid the mare with the stallion-like crest and coarse masculine head. While size is important in horses generally, it can be overdone in mares. Many of the best brood mares are of moderate size with the distinct femininity spoken of before. Big, coarse, plain-featured, sluggish mares are seldom as good breeders as the more medium-sized quality mare.

She should have a quiet and gentle disposition. In buying a mare specifically for breeding, she should either have a foal at her side or be definitely pregnant at four or five years of age. (Very small teats and udder usually indicate that the mare has never nursed a foal.) Generally, mares from this age up to about ten or twelve years of age that have previously and pretty regularly produced colts are the most prolific—and thus the most profitable. Mares that are started on their careers as brood mares early generally make the best brood mares, settling more regularly and suckling better, but this is by no means universal. Generally speaking, however, it is not a good bet to buy an older mare for breeding unless she gives every indication of having been a regular breeder.

THE VALUE OF THE GOOD BROOD MARE

I want to make one last general comment on the brood mare. The value of a good one is considerable, the value of a great one—in the case of purebreds—can be almost incalculable. Not only in monetary terms, but in terms of satisfaction and a feeling of making a lasting contribution of livestock improvement.

Not only is she responsible for 50 percent of the hereditary material that goes into the foal, but, according to her desirable matronly qualities, she is *largely* responsible for the youngster getting off to a good start. That, plus her contribution in the collar gives you two valuable products from her existence—her labor and her foals—and makes her truly one of the queens of the farmstead.

If you are someday lucky enough, or wise enough, to possess a truly great brood mare, one that is a pleasure to work, a joy to be around, possesses all the qualities and characteristics of a great draft horse and transmits them—don't get separated from her by an attractive offer. Rather, mate her to the best stallions you can find, and populate your own pastures and those of your neighbors with her offspring. You will not only make a lasting contribution to your own solvency, but to that of your buyers as well. And if she transmits the way a great brood mare should, you will someday have that pleasing uniformity of type, disposition, and working qualities that makes draft horse progress a reality. There was a time when hundreds of farmers across this land had such mares, both purebreds and grades. They gloried in starting their sons out with a pair out of the old mare, they worked mother, daughters, and granddaughters, sons and grandsons together. Such mares were not simply beasts of burden, they were almost honored members of the family and true partners, in every sense of the word, in both making a living and passing on a heritage. They were, and are, conservators of merit. May their kind multiply and replenish the earth.

BREEDING AGE, HEAT PERIODS, AND BREEDING PRACTICES

It is not advisable to breed two-year-olds. They still have a lot of growing to do; to develop a fetus on top of growing and possibly working is taxing them more than most breeders care to do. Such treatment is not wise and may create future problems for the mare.

Mares come in heat nine days after foaling (though this may vary from seven to eleven) and *usually* every eighteen to twenty-one days thereafter. The mare should be returned to the stallion for retrial during every heat period for at least a couple rounds. The average gestation period is eleven months or 340 days, although it may vary as much as three weeks on either side.

The condition of the mare at the time of breeding is very important, for the highest percentage of strong healthy foals are produced from mares in good health, free of infection, vigorous, and in medium flesh—neither fat nor thin. The conception percentage of draft horses is probably lower than that of most domestic animals. I think this is more true now than it once was and would suggest the following reasons:

1. A great many draft mares these days are both idle and overfat; generally speaking I think it safe to say that a mare that is reasonably hard from time in the harness, providing she isn't worked down to a bag of bones, is easier to settle than one spending most of her time on three legs, looking over the fence at the cars going by.

2. A lot of mares are trucked fairly long distances to strange surroundings and then loaded up promptly after service and taken home. I don't think this practice is as conducive to getting colts as when stallions were more numerous, closer to home, and the mare could be put into a box stall to rest quietly after being served, or in many cases she was home in familiar surroundings and the *stallion* was traveled.

Michigan State's fine pamphlet, *Stallion Management,* suggests the following for mare owners in terms of breeding:

1. Don't hurry or excite the mare after service. If she is home, put her back in her own stall for a while. If away from home, try to arrange to let her quietly rest for a time before being loaded.
2. Avoid drastic changes in feeding and caring for the mare immediately before and after breeding. If the mare is accustomed to dry feed, she should not be turned out on pasture. If accustomed to pasture, she should not stand idle in the barn. Mares on pasture should not be annoyed by other horses after breeding.
3. If possible, avoid working her for a few days after service. Conception is more likely if the mare is kept quiet and away from the other horses until she goes out of heat.
4. Having done these things, return for retrial at least twice, at three-week intervals, if you are really serious about getting a colt. If you have your own stallion, of course, this is no big problem as she can be tried at your own convenience.

SEASON FOR FOALING

This is another thing that will be determined by individual circumstance. Spring is the most auspicious time under natural conditions for mares to produce young. The weather is favorable, the natural feed supply plentiful, and the foals have time to grow to good size before the rigors of winter or the natural weaning time arrives. The increased natural food supply (pasture) also tends to give the mare a lift when she most needs it, especially if she is to be promptly rebred. Thus, colts born in May and June have considerable natural advantages. March and April foals keep the mares out of harness at a very busy time on farms where every horse is needed for planting the crops. By May and June there are usually enough other horses around to handle the mowing, raking, and cultivating that needs doing.

A case can also be made for January and February foals, especially for purebred breeders who show. The colts go into the show ring in the late summer and fall with a few months additional growth. Another advantage is that the mares foal when they are not needed in the field and, third, the farm work is not so pressing, thereby giving the farmer more time to attend to his mares at foaling time. The fourth advantage is that the colts have a good start and will be eating grain and hay by the time the mothers are needed for spring work.

All these advantages are, however, outweighed in my mind unless you have really good inside facilities for the mares at foaling time—at least in our latitude in northern Iowa. To me, this means nothing less than a big, oversized box stall (about sixteen feet square) with adequate light and ventilation, completely disinfected and freshly bedded before parturition, and one that the mare has become somewhat accustomed to before foaling. If you can't provide these things, leave the winter foals to those who can.

Fall colt production fits into some operations. In situations where the work demands in fall are light, it is possible for the colts to be left with their dams almost continuously until they are weaned. They can be weaned before their mothers are needed for spring work, and their mothers should then be in good condition for spring work. A good shed, open to the south, will provide such mares and colts with the winter protection needed (short of blizzard conditions). Fall colts, as a rule, require a little more care than spring colts, but, depending on the type of farming operation, many farmers are not as busy in the fall as in the spring.

EXERCISE FOR THE BROOD MARE

It is generally agreed that the best regimen for a pregnant mare is regular work in harness. During the first half of the pregnancy there is little reason to limit her work. As foaling approaches the work load should be decreased as the feed is increased. Some horsemen work their mares right up to foaling time, others prefer to quit using them in harness a week or two before the foal is due. Naturally, care must be exercised, especially late in pregnancy, that the mare is *not* allowed to pull too hard, used in situations where she must wade through deep mud or snow, nor on ice, wet pavement, or slippery dirt where she might slip. Never use a mare heavy in foal to back heavy loads. Such things invite premature birth of the foal and its attendant troubles.

If it is impossible to have steady work of a light nature just prior to foaling, the mare should be turned out in a lot or pasture, depending on the season, where she will get ample exercise. About the worst thing for a mare heavy in foal is to be confined to an ordinary tie stall for days on end.

In brief, either overwork or idleness is an enemy of the brood mare and her unborn foal, and both should be avoided within the framework of what is possible on your place.

FEEDING THE PREGNANT MARE

If it is always important to avoid the use of moldy or dusty feeds with horses, it is especially so during pregnancy—such feeds may cause abortion. The best, and cheapest, feeds for pregnant mares are palatable, home-grown feeds such as oats, corn, roots, alfalfa, clover, and mixed hay. Bulky, easily digested, and nutritious feeds are needed, along with a liberal allowance of protein and minerals—the bone- and muscle-building portions of the ration.

Some horsemen have a real prejudice against alfalfa hay, preferring timothy, but it is hard to defend timothy for the brood mare when a good, dust free, legume is available.

The concentrates will, for the most part, be oats and corn—the commonly home-grown grains. These may be fed in combination, with the emphasis on the oats. Ohio State's *Save the Foals* bulletin suggests feeding twelve to fourteen quarts of

grain daily, along with fifteen to eighteen pounds of roughage, ˌ
for the mare that is kept at work up till foaling.

Grain:
1. Oats
2. ½ each oats and corn
3. 1/3 oats, 2/3 corn
1 pound cottonseed meal or linseed meal with 10 parts of any of the above mixtures
1 part of wheat bran to 6 parts of any of the above
Roughages:
1. Mixed clover and timothy hay
2. Legume hay (quantity limited)
3. Oat straw
4. Corn or corn fodder, stover or silage
5. Bluegrass or other permanent pasture
6. Barley, wheat or rye, temporary pasture
The inclusion of the bran, linseed meal or cottonseed meal materially improves the ration when horses do not have access to pasture or when non-leguminous hay is fed.

Fig. 8-1. Rations for brood mares at work

The idle mare is something else. Michigan State's pamphlet, *The Mare and Foal,* suggests wintering the idle pregnant mare on a sod field that is slated for corn next year, with an ample quantity of good quality roughage, supplemented with six or eight pounds of roots, such as carrots, beets, or potatoes per day. If the mare is due to foal on grass and is idle until foaling, she will need no grain or roots in the spring as fresh grass is the best conditioner.

Wheat bran plays a key role in the rations fed by many good horsemen, especially late in pregnancy. Bran mashes fed once a week help keep the digestive system in good order and a bran mash just before and after foaling will help regulate the bowels.

I'll close this section on feeding with the following specific suggestions from the University of Missouri pamphlet, *Farm Work Mares and Colts.*

Since success in producing foals depends much upon the condition of mares, feed is an essential factor and the condition of the mare is a measure of the ration she receives. Heavy "in foal" mares in thin condition in winter should have a gradually increasing ration until they show a gain in flesh and strength.

Brood mares as well as all other horses are materially improved in condition by treatment for worms, but treatment of mares while heavy in foal should be avoided. Treatment is most safely given by a veterinarian. Some wormers can be toxic to the unborn foal; know what you are giving them.

All grains, hays, and fodder supply digestible nutrients for energy, bodily processes and work, but some are more efficient than others. Protein for building and repairing muscles, and other protein tissue and blood may be supplied by legume hay, wheat bran, pasture, linseed, cottonseed, or soybean meal. Minerals enough to build and repair bone, muscle, blood, and other body tissue may be supplied by legume hays, pasture, wheat bran, or a mineral mixture of one-third each, by weight, of common salt, finely ground limestone and steamed bone meal.

Horses doing average work require about one to 1.2 pounds grain and 1.25 pounds hay per 100 pounds live weight daily to retain their weight. Investigations at the Missouri Experiment Station show that mares nursing foals will require at least 20 percent more grain than mares doing the same work but not nursing foals, and even this may not keep them from losing weight if working hard and producing a heavy flow of milk. When mares in good condition and accustomed to work are idle for a day or more, the grain allowance should be reduced by at least one-third.

Good pasture furnishes enough of the right kind of feed for mares nursing foals but not at work. In seasons of short pasture nursing mares lose flesh unless fed some grain or good roughage in addition to the pasture.

Mares in foal but not nursing foals and doing ordinary farm work require slightly more feed than geldings. It is essential that the ration be balanced. Mares working regularly at winter farm work will do well on one pound of grain and 1.25 pounds hay per hundred pounds live weight per day.

Idle pregnant mares winter well on ten pounds of legume hay and what fodder or oat straw they will clean up. Silage of *good quality* may be used.

A mixture of equal parts, by weight, of common salt, finely ground limestone, and steamed bone meal should be kept before horses at all times to help meet mineral needs.

Water offered frequently is always essential in the best care of horses and mules.

FOALING TIME . . .
THE APPROACH OF PARTURITION

As parturition approaches, have the place of foaling in mind. If it is an early colt, disinfect the box stall, keep it clean, and give the mare as much time to get accustomed to it as possible. If she is being taken out of harness reduce her grain ration accordingly, and keep a close watch on the expectant mother. A coat of lime on the floor under the bedding will act as both a disinfectant and deodorant. For late colts there is nothing better than a clean pasture to foal on, unless the ground is cold. Cold ground can result in a chill, and subsequently, pneumonia.

One to six weeks before foaling the mare's udder begins to increase in size, the muscles of the hips on either side of the tail setting loosen and sink and the vulva becomes full and loose from three days to two weeks before foaling. Waxing of the nipples is not always an immediate sign of parturition, although in a majority of mares this condition does prevail within twenty-four hours of foaling.

The signs of foaling vary greatly with mares. With some mares the milk secretion may become more than she can hold and milk will escape in drops or even in a stream. On the other hand, there may be little or no milk secretion and only a slight enlargement of the udder prior to foaling primarily in older mares coming with their first foal.

When the mare gets uneasy, sweats, moves about cautiously, switches her tail, looks around at and bites her flanks, and exhibits the other symptoms mentioned above, you'd better hang pretty close to her. At the same time, don't be too much in evidence. It's best if you have a place where you can observe her periodically without being observed. The presence of a human sometimes seems to inhibit some mares and they seem to delay foaling because of it.

The normal presentation of the foal is with the fore legs extended with the head resting between them. If any other presentation occurs it is best to get professional help. Sometimes the nose or a foot may be caught on the pelvic girdle, and prompt release will be followed by a normal birth. If the feet are presented bottoms up, it is an indication that they are the hind ones and that assistance must be promptly given to deliver the foal or it will smother.

In a case of a breech presentation just described, or another instance when you must aid the mare without professional help, take precautions against infecting the genital canal by first scrubbing hands and arms with soap and hot water to which has been added a small amount of antiseptic. Wash the external genitals with soap and warm water before going into the genital canal. If you are in a position where you must give aid to a mare, apply traction *only* when the mare is making expulsive efforts and in a downward direction toward the hocks, *after* the elbows, or hocks (in the case of a breech presentation) are free.

John P. Hutton, from the Michigan State University Veterinary Medicine Department, had this to say in the 1938 *Belgian Review:* "The duration of labor is only a few minutes (ten to fifteen) in normal parturition. Foals very seldom live more than one to three hours after labor pains begin." In other words, if birth does not occur within a couple hours after the first labor pains it is time to investigate the difficulty, for foals, unlike calves, cannot withstand the hardships of a long, continued labor.

CARE OF THE MARE AND FOAL
FOLLOWING BIRTH

When the foal does arrive, remove the fetal membranes from the nose and mouth of the foal immediately. Sometimes foals are born with the amnion still intact; these are the ones that "die in the sack" unless you are there to remove it quickly. If the foal fails to breathe after removing the sack, blow into his mouth and rub or shake his ribs. If this does not start him breathing at once, breathe into his nostrils normally, pressing on his ribs as you inhale your breath and release the pressure as you exhale—in other words, give him artificial respiration.

At birth the navel cord usually breaks a few inches from the foal's body. If it is necessary to cut it use a pair of sterilized scissors or a clamp (available from your vet), and cut the cord about two inches from the body. If you don't use a clamp, sterilize the stub with iodine immediately. If the foal is kept in the barn rather than on pasture, repeated applications of an antiseptic dusting powder should be made until the stub is thoroughly dried up.

The reason this is so important is that the navel cord is a splendid avenue for infection. Through it "joint ill" or navel infection enters the colt's body. This is an acute infectious disease of newborn foals, characterized by lameness and swollen joints. The symptoms usually appear within the first twenty-four to forty-eight hours after birth. In some cases, foals show very acute symptoms soon after birth. In addition to the visually apparent symptoms of lameness and swollen joints in such cases, high fever, diarrhea and rapid loss of strength are also evident. Such colts usually die, or if they do recover, can develop a chronic form of the disease. The first symptoms are sometimes a pus discharge from the umbilicus, followed by the symptoms described above. If you should have a colt exhibiting these symptoms, prompt treatment by your veterinarian and isolation from all your other horses are your best course. The best prevention is sanitation, as described.

Some colts are born with joint ill. Some mares repeatedly produce foals with this disease, in spite of all necessary precautions. Quite possibly they picked it up from the bedding in a previous foaling stall, or at the time of service; whatever the case, it can be and sometimes is present in the mare. Foals may be dead at birth showing the symptoms of the disease.

BACK TO MOTHER

Assuming that you have your colt breathing normally and the navel cord taken care of let us again give our attention to mother. The mare and foal should be left lying, regaining strength from the ordeal of birth as long as they're quiet. Some horsemen tie the afterbirth to the tail of the mare so that neither mare nor foal can step on it prior to expulsion, thereby increasing the danger of infection of the uterus with resulting stiffness of the joints and a disease known as foal founder. After the afterbirth is discharged remove it from the stall and bury it. This can sometimes be the source of disease if left uncared for. If the afterbirth is not completely discharged within five or six hours call a veterinarian.

The mare should be given frequent drinks of lukewarm water in small quantities after foaling. Her first meal should be about half her regular feed in quantity and be made up of bran or bran and oats. Increase her grain slowly over the next several days, being careful not to feed too much. Grain produces milk, and there shouldn't be more than the colt can handle or you will have a case of scours—another great colt killer—on your hands. If your mare is an extremely heavy milker, it may be necessary to partially milk her out by hand to help keep the colt from scouring. In four or five days time she can be turned out to pasture with her babe (but *not* with your other horses who can be pretty rough company for the newcomer) and in about ten days or two weeks returned to light work, preferably half days only.

CONSTIPATION AND DIARRHEA

These two "friends," along with navel ill, are the immediate concern of all good horsemen with a new foal. A healthy foal will usually be on its feet and nursing within a couple or three hours after birth, but occasionally one requires help. That first milk, the colostrum, is all-important to the baby, not only because of the antibodies it contains but because it tends to get the bowels moving and thus remove the fecal matter lodged in the foal's bowels. The bowels of the newly born foal must be watched closely. If he does not void his intestinal tract within twelve to eighteen hours, he should be given an enema of warm soapy water. Some horsemen use a mixture of two ounces of glycerine in one quart of warm water for this purpose. If the injection does not correct matters give castor oil or some other laxative as directed by your veterinarian.

Having taken care of the navel cord, and made sure that the colt is sucking and has his bowels moving, the next thing to watch for—and prevent—is diarrhea or scours. Many foals will show slight diarrhea during the first heat period of the mare, seven to nine days after foaling. It is commonly believed that the heat period causes a change in the composition of the mother's milk. Too much milk, inflammation of the udder, exposure to rain or a rapid change in weather, or the foal eating grass or feces may also set it off.

Whatever the cause, the symptoms are runny feces, often with a very disagreeable sour odor, yellowish in color. This condition usually results in rapid and complete recovery if promptly treated. If, however, the disease is allowed to progress the foal may become weak, subject to pneumonia—and you can lose him.

The best treatment is, of course, to remove the cause and regulate the diet—assuming that you know what the cause is. If the foal is getting too much milk, reduce the amount by hand milking the mare yourself and/or reduce her feed intake. If the cause is an inflammation of the udder, resort to artificially feeding the foal until the mare's condition can be cleared up. If the foal is eating foreign material such as feces, straw, or grass, then try to deny him those things. The old-time treatment was castor oil to eliminate the gastro-intestinal contents. If you have a colt that scours badly, call your veterinarian before your colt is weaker and subject to pneumonia.

Scours may also be caused by unclean surroundings, fretfulness or temperature above normal in the mare, a cold, damp bed, exposure to a cold rain, etc. As is true with most things, prevention is the best and cheapest medicine. Keep the colt quiet and out of the hot sun if he is suffering from diarrhea.

THE MARE GOES BACK TO WORK

Once the mare goes back to work the best place for the foal is in a comfortable box stall in the barn or a grass paddock. If taught to eat grain early, a foal will not get too hungry with a few hours' separation, will learn not to fret when away from his mother, and will not make a nuisance of himself as foals sometimes do when allowed to follow their mothers. This practice also makes the final separation of weaning much less painful. It is best when you have two or more foals to leave together in a place where they can't get into the fence and hurt themselves, but can amuse one another when Mom is away. Do not allow the colts to nurse a warm, tired mare just in from doing heavy fieldwork. Milk from warm mares can cause colic in the foals. Give her some rest and if she is really warm, strip her out after cooling her down, *before* you let the colt at her. In the case of extremely heavy-milking mares you may wish to relieve her udder a bit in the field, too.

Needless to say, the mare should be returned to work somewhat gradually. If you have planned the arrival of your foals to dovetail into your total operation, that should happen sort of naturally.

The Foal

FEEDING THE FOAL

Like all farm animals, the draft horse makes his cheapest gains and most rapid growth during early life, and especially in the period while he is still nursing. Colts and fillies, if properly cared for, will normally attain about one-half of their growth during the first year of their lives. Thus, for reasons of both economy and his ultimate outcome, it is important that the young horse be taught to eat grain at the earliest possible age. Like all young animals, the foal will mimic his mother. By placing a feed box on or near the floor or at a level the foal can easily reach, the foal will soon learn to eat with his mother. After you get him going it is an easy enough matter to provide him with his own grain box and tie the mare up so she doesn't steal it from him. Foals will begin nibbling at grain when about a month old if allowed to eat with their mothers or if kept with some grain before them while the mothers are at work. It is easier to get a foal going on grain this way than when both mare and foal are running on pasture. Then the only way to assure the foals getting their share is to provide a creep, an arrangement only the foals can get into, not the big horses. It may be necessary to lead the foals into the creep a few times.

The grains for foals need not be "prepared" to get them started to eat. Good, bright, clean oats and a little bran make a very good combination to start them on. The roughage can be the same good quality clover, alfalfa, or timothy mix that you are feeding your older horses.

The University of Missouri suggested a grain mix of three parts each of oats, bran, and corn by weight and one part linseed oil meal, or one of four parts oats and one part bran, or one of equal parts corn and oats. The linseed oil was suggested for preventing constipation and for its protein, which builds both muscle and bone.

Ohio's suggestions were similar, including one of two parts oats and one part bran by measure, and also equal parts of shelled corn and whole oats.

In other words, there is nothing very fancy or complicated nor is there any good reason to use a lot of expensive feed additives, commercial mixes, etc. Personally, I think legume hay and oats can and in most cases should constitute the bulk of the diet. The protein from good legume hay can go far in body building.

Good pasture and lots of exercise are also very important factors in growing out foals—provide them with the pasture and they will provide themselves with the exercise. This, in turn, will help keep them clean and sound in the legs. However, during the short grass and fly months it is wise to give foals access to a darkened stall in the daytime. If they don't have to fight flies all day they will retain their "baby fat" longer and do better.

One of the most foolish economies of all in draft horse husbandry is to starve the colts during their first year, when they should make half their growth. They never recover and they will never translate feed into growth more efficiently than during this period. However, I think it foolish to pour the corn to them during this period. I view corn as more of an energy food for horses at hard work or a fattening food for horses you are trying to condition, than a growing food, though it can certainly play a part in the foal's diet.

WEANING THE FOAL

Here again a number of circumstances dictate rather different answers. The normal weaning time is from four to six months of age. If there is a great need to be working the mare every day, all day, and the foal is nicely started on grain, it might prompt earlier weaning. On the other hand, if the mare is idle or just doing occasional light work and not bred back, why wean the young horse any sooner than you have to—the cheapest gains of his life are those he makes at his mother's side. This is altogether different than the case of the mare who is nursing one, carrying another, and working hard to boot. She obviously needs to be relieved of this burden long before her sister who belongs to the local bridge club.

In any event, whenever you decide to wean, generally at five or six months of age, it will be a great benefit to the young horse if he is well acquainted with eating hay and grain and accustomed to frequent separations from his mother. He won't get nearly the setback (he shouldn't get any at all) of the foal who has been reliant on mother's milk and grass, and then one fine day finds mother gone. That is cruel, stupid, and uneconomic.

There are a couple rather obvious things to do with the mare at weaning time. First, reduce her feed intake so she will manufacture less milk, and second, watch her udder. If it gets very full and distended you may have to partially milk her out once or twice a day for a few days. Some horsemen apply camphorated oil to the udder and teats before milking each time. This aids in milking and helps prevent chapping. Don't make these milkouts too complete or you will just keep her milking.

Successful (that is uneventful) weaning depends on preparation, and once it is done, make it final. Don't put the mare and foal where they can see one another, and keep them apart until the mare has completely dried up and the young horse has forgotten his dependence on the teat.

THE ORPHAN FOAL

First of all, here is hoping it doesn't happen to you. But if it does here are a few ways you might go.

William J. Yoder, successful Belgian breeder from La-Grange, Indiana, sent this formula to us, which appeared in the Spring 1974 issue of *Draft Horse Journal*:

> We lost a mare foaling and are raising the foal on a bottle. Below is the formula I made up with real good results. The colt is doing fine and eating pellets and rolled oats at three weeks. The milk formula we are using is: twenty-four ounces cow's milk, eight ounces water, three raw eggs whipped, one tablespoon of brown sugar,

and one cc. Vi-Daylin-Plus-Iron-Drops. We feed sixteen ounces of this mix every three hours.

Another option, though one not open very often, is to try to place the foal on another mare. Some really prodigious milkers can raise two, but you can have the problem of acceptance by the mare. Or if you have another mare that loses a foal at about the same time it's worth a try. The plain fact is that most people don't have a lot of mares coming in at once and chances are you are going to have to go the bottle and nipple route.

If you have cow's milk available, remember that mare's milk contains less fat but more sugar than does a cow's. To feed an orphan foal cow's milk, try to obtain milk from a low tester early in her lactation; to one pint of cow's milk add ¼ pint of lime water and a teaspoon of sugar, which will make enough for two feedings at first. This makes the mix the rough equivalent of mare's milk. Warm it to 100°F. and feed it with a nipple.

I suppose more orphan foals, like orphan lambs, are killed with kindness than with the reverse. In other words, don't feed them much, but feed them often.

Still another formula that works is the following which appeared in the May 1964 issue of *Breeder's Gazette*:

Mare's milk is much lower in fat, protein and mineral content than cow's milk but is somewhat richer in sugar. If the foal must be given a supplement or substitute for its dam's milk, it can be given a mixture of four ounces evaporated milk, four ounces water, and one teaspoon Karo syrup. This should be warmed to about 100°F. and eight ounces given every hour for the first day or so, with the amount and feeding interval gradually increased until the foal is fed only four times daily after a few days. If the foal scours on this mixture, substitute one teaspoon limewater for the Karo syrup.

The other way to go is with one of the several commercial products, such as Foal-Lac. I think they give good results and may be the most practical route for you to go. If I took this route, I would be inclined to feed them less and more often than some of the directions call for, which would tend to simulate natural conditions more.

PARASITES

Young horses run on pasture for the most part, a great breeding ground for parasites. Chances are that cute, fat, little weanling has worms in spite of his appearance. Worm him when you worm the adult horses after the first killing frost. Being a baby exempts him in no way from the parasites that plague his elders.

FEET

I think this has been fairly well covered in Chapter 6 but we might mention that it is wise to pay some heed to the foal's feet. If the wear is uneven and neglected it can result in structural damage that will bother him as an older horse. Handling his feet at this age will also pay dividends throughout his life. If he is accustomed to it as a foal he will not be nearly as inclined to fight either you or the farrier as a big horse.

HALTER BREAKING THE FOAL

This is very important, something that will affect the horse all his life. It is important that foals be handled with kindness and firmness. Don't let them become four or five months old before training them to lead.

When we try to lead a foal by pulling on his halter his natural tendency is to pull backward. A couple devices can be helpful here. One is to make a small loop which is placed under the tail, at about the same position as the breeching on a set of harness, with the free end of the rope passing forward through the halter ring. To start the foal, give a light pull on the halter strap and a much firmer one on the rope. This pressure across the rear quarters will usually bring the horse on and in most cases no more than a couple lessons are needed before you can forget the "crupper rope."

Some draft horsemen object to this on the grounds that when you later ask him to back a load, he will not settle back into the breeching because he has been taught that it means go forward when there is pressure there. This may be true; it probably is if you let the foal get so big that it is a test of strength when you do this, or if you keep it up. Personally this doesn't worry me. If the foal is handled from birth and this is done when he is a babe, you won't have to do it more than a couple times before he follows along.

If, however, you are of this persuasion, run a loop around his left ankle and follow roughly the same procedure. (Then, I suppose you can worry about making a striker out of him—if you are so inclined.)

Colts

TRAINING COLTS FOR THE WORLD OF WORK

Inasmuch as this book is designed as a "primer" I feel somewhat the same way about this section as I do about the ones on shoeing and showing. It seems to me that three of the last things a beginner needs to concern himself with are breaking colts, shoeing his own horses, and showing them. They may come in due season or they may never come at all. A great many users of draft horses buy broke replacements as needed, especially if they are on a limited acreage that doesn't allow for either feed or room to be raising colts, just as many who develop into breeders never develop a taste for the show ring. Since this is the case, this section will stress general principles with the thought that technique will come with experience.

To that end I again draw on an old USDA Farmers Bulletin, this one called *Breaking and Training Colts*, published in 1923. The following text and illustrations are from this USDA source.

Fundamental Principles   The breaking and training of colts are of prime importance because their future value and usefulness depend to a great extent on whether or not they are well broken. By a broken colt is meant one that is safe to handle in the stable or on the road and that will promptly obey the commands of the driver.

Memory and habit are the two main factors with which we have to deal in training horses. A horse usually acts through instinct and habit, associated with the memory of what he has formerly learned. One of the greatest characteristics of a horse is his uniformity of conduct, for what he has once been trained to do he will nearly always do under like conditions.

The first task in training a horse is to get his attention. The second is to make him understand what is wanted. The education of the horse is based on reward and punishment. The reward, a pat on the neck, etc., should immediately follow the act of obedience. The punishment must immediately follow the act of disobedience to be effective.

Few horses are inherently vicious. Many horses are made vicious and unreliable by the carelessness or brutality of their trainers. If a horse kicks because the harness hurts him or shies at something of which he is afraid, punishment is not justifiable. If, however, after being stopped, a horse starts before receiving the command to do so, he should be punished. All horses can not be treated alike. A high-strung, sensitive horse must be treated gently, the dullard sharply. The same force applied to the sensitive horse that is necessary to make the dullard act would be likely to cause the high-strung horse to rebel, while gentleness would obtain obedience. Horses are naturally obedient, and when thoroughly trained their conduct is uniformly good.

A horse should be trained so that he thinks that there is no limit to his power to do the things required of him and believes that he has no power to do that which is against the wishes of his master. Above all, never ask of a horse something he is unable to perform and then punish him because it cannot be done. If during the first year of his work a colt is hitched only to loads that he can pull, he will develop into a good work horse, while if he is overloaded a few times he may become balky and worthless.

To train horses successfully a man needs to exercise great patience, gentleness, and firmness. If you are training a horse and lose your temper, you had better put the horse into the stable until the next day, for further work at this time will be worse than useless and may undo the work already done.

Never work a colt after he is tired. By heeding this precaution you prevent obstinacy and render him a willing and obedient pupil.

Training should be given in a quiet place, where the colt's attention will not be distracted from the work in hand by other horses or strange surroundings.

Whenever two persons are working with a horse they should be on the same side. The horse's attention is then undivided, and if he plunges or kicks he may be controlled with less danger to the trainers.

To harness or saddle a horse it is customary to approach his near or left side, also to mount from the left side.

Never approach a horse without first gaining his attention. Always speak to him before attempting to work into a stall beside him.

In the following instructions principal emphasis is laid on kindness to the horse. In reality the whip is of equal importance with kindness. To be submissive to a man's will, the horse must fear the consequences of disobedience. There will be clashes, but the horse must be convinced that man is his master. Always, if the horse cannot do or cannot be made to do what is asked of him, make him do something else. So long as he is not allowed to do what he himself chooses he will consider man his superior and master.

Horses are broken at ages ranging from weanlings to old horses. The instincts in a horse which are opposed to obedience to man increase in strength with age. This accounts for the difficulty encountered in handling range horses that are allowed their freedom until their instinct of independence is so strongly developed that it is proportionately difficult to teach them that it is their duty to obey some force other than their own instinct.

It is a great advantage to begin the education of the colt as early as possible. Handle and pet but never tease or "rough" the youngster. A good plan is to break the colt to lead before it is weaned, and to harness between the ages of two and three years. Accustom colts to work gradually and do not use them at heavy work until they are practically mature.

Gentling the Colt   If the foal has been properly handled, it will not be difficult to break him to stand tied and to lead. Before tying the colt handle him enough so that he partially realizes that the halter and ropes are used for his control. To handle the colt at first, put on a strong halter and supplement it with a ¾-inch neck rope about twelve feet long. Run one

Fig. 8-2. Ordinarily only a neck rope is needed to supplement a halter in tying up the colt for the first time.

end of the rope through the halter ring and tie it around the neck with a bowline knot tight enough so that the noose will not slip on the neck (see Fig. 8-2). When tying have not more than 2½ or three feet of slack. If the first tying is made in a wide stall, the attendant may enter and leave without frightening the colt or endangering himself.

While tied the colt should be gentled and accustomed to being handled on both sides, on the hind parts, and on the legs. To do this, hold the headstall in one hand and with the other hand gentle, that is, pet and rub the colt, first on the neck and head, then on the back and sides, and last on the legs. One must be fearless without taking unnecessary chances while working with a colt.

Fig. 8-3. The head and foot tie

With an older colt the safety tie rope should be long enough to extend through the halter ring, down between the forelegs, and about the body. The body noose is made with a running knot and will tighten up when the colt pulls back. After the colt makes a few pulls this tie will no longer be required.

Another method which I think is simpler and safer is the head and foot tie from the Iowa Horse and Mule Association bulletin, *Horse Breaking*, by Harry Linn.

There are many methods used in tying the colt or green horse. The head and foot tie is one that gives good results (see Fig. 8-3). This tie is accomplished by running the halter rope through the manger hole or tie rack and tying it just below the knee or around the fetlock with a couple of half hitches. A green horse or colt will pull a couple times but all horses and mules are very particular about their feet; thus, as the colt pulls back he finds that his foot is pulled ahead and he immediately follows the foot. Old horses—professional halter pullers—when tied with this method will try a few times to break loose and then usually stand up to the manger like good fellows, refusing to pull again even when encouraged to do so. Horses broken by this method will not be so apt to become frightened when they catch a foot in the fence. The author has known cases when a horse that had been halter broken in this manner caught its foot in a wire fence and would stand with the foot raised in the fence waiting for the master to come to the rescue.

Another method that is very common is to use a heavy rope around the neck, tied so that it cannot choke the horse. Many animals will fight this rope for days, causing a very ugly sore on the poll. Some even acquire poll-evil in this manner. I have known two horses to jerk backwards so hard they broke their necks and have seen many others in the West pull the cords in their necks so severely that they were unable to raise their heads the rest of their lives.

A great many horse breakers make a large loop around the horse just back of the front legs, running the rope between the legs, up through the halter ring and to the manger. A horse will not pull long on this arrangement. It is very difficult, however, to teach this horse to back a load. He has been taught by the halter breaking ordeal that he cannot go back when something tightens around his chest. When he is asked to back the wagon, the back and belly band tighten on him in the same place that the tie rope did. He immediately quits and his driver blames him for being either stubborn or dumb.

Another method of tying is to run a rope around a horse so that it catches him across the thighs about the position of the breeching. This rope is supported by another rope resting across the loin. The ends of the rope that encircle the horse are run through the halter and tied to the manger. Thus, if the colt pulls back he sets in sort of a sling. There is no doubt that the colt will quickly learn to stand tied, but put the breeching harness on him and try to induce him to back a load. As soon as the breeching touches his thighs he will refuse to back because you have already taught him that he cannot do so with anything across his thighs.

A rope under the tail and tied to the manger is effective but starts too many kickers.

Methods of horse breaking are never better than their aftereffects upon the animal so it is well to remember that although one method may be very effective in producing a certain result, it may also produce one or more very undesirable ones.

BREAKING TO LEAD

Proportionate to the amount of handling which the colt receives he will be more easily trained to lead. Although

Fig. 8-4. This tie is used with older or more stubborn colts in breaking them to stand tied and to lead.

precautions are taken to prevent the colt breaking away, it will be well to give the first lessons in a corral or paddock. Use diplomacy rather than force. Do not try to pull the colt straight ahead, but instead step to one side and in front (see Fig. 8-4), give a command, as "Come," and pull sharply on the rope. A definite word should always be used for the same command. An assistant to emphasize a command with a buggy whip will be valuable at first, but should be released as soon as the colt moves when commanded to do so. Reward the colt with a kind pat when he moves even a little distance. Frequent short lessons are of more value than occasional long ones, and should be continued until the colt leads freely.

If the suckling colt is being broken, tie him to the mother's trace when she is working. The tie is made at about the union of back band and trace and short enough to prevent the colt from getting in front of the team. This will acquaint him with the general conditions and noises pertaining to work and on account of the mother's being near he will soon become familiar with such surroundings. This practice should be continued at short intervals and only until the colt is broken to lead. Some horsemen tie their foals to the hame, but there is a greater possibility of the colt getting around in front of his mother and in the way with the hame tie.

Another arrangement used in breaking older colts is a crupper rope. This is made with about fourteen feet of rope, bringing the ends together and giving the rope a double twist near the middle, thereby making a small loop to be placed under the tail. The ends come forward at each side of the horse and are tied at the breast. This crupper rope is held up by a rope surcingle, while a lead rope is attached at the breast and passed through the halter ring.

A simpler method and one sometimes used when the trainer is working alone is a loop dropped over the hips and allowed to fall to the quarters. Any special rope should be discarded as soon as possible.

Many horsemen prefer using the whip in breaking colts to lead at the side. In this training the attendant stands on the near side about opposite the colt's shoulder. The lead rope is held in the right hand fairly close to the colt's mouth, while an ordinary straight buggy whip is held quietly in the left hand. Tapping the colt upon the hind quarters makes him move forward and at the same time stay slightly away from the attendant. A few lessons will generally teach the colt to stay always in this position.

In handling older unbroken horses, more caution, skill, knowledge, and fearlessness are needed. The older horse will recognize the least sign of fear upon the part of the trainer and will seize the first opportunity to be master instead of pupil. The habits of the older horse are firmly fixed, and greater skill is needed to train him without breaking his spirit. A quite common practice is to rope the horse in the corral or paddock and gradually snub him up close on the off side of a gentle saddle horse. It is best to use a ½-inch rope equipped with a perfect running knot and to keep the double hitch on the saddle horn straight so that it may be released at any time. The halter may be placed upon the unbroken horse with safety by working over the gentle horse. Attach a moderately long lead rope to the halter and let it lie just in front of the saddle horn.

As with the weanling, command "Come" in a quiet, firm voice, pull steadily on the halter rope, and swing the saddle horse a step or two to the left. At first the horse will no doubt lie back upon the rope, but it will not be long until he will move forward upon command. After a little preliminary work lead the pupil into the stable (still using the saddle horse), put on the body tie rope, and tie him up. In later lessons use only the neck rope and teach him to lead without the use of the saddle horse. It will soon be possible to lead him without special ropes.

Another method of gentling a horse is to tie the halter rope to the tail as shown in Fig. 8-5. This forces him to go in a circle. When he gives in and stands quietly he may be harnessed, saddled, mounted, and accustomed to strange sights and sounds. This is a useful aid in use in gaining a stubborn horse's submission.

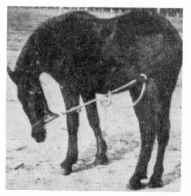

Fig. 8-5. One method of gentling a colt

Fig. 8-6. Halter twitch

HANDLING THE COLT'S FEET

If the owner will accustom a colt to having his feet handled
and trimmed before he is weaned, much future work and
trouble will be avoided. When picking up a colt's foot teach
him to stand on three legs by shifting his weight when the foot
is lifted. Begin the lessons with the left front foot. Grasp the
foot firmly and shift the colt's weight by pushing against the
shoulder with the free hand while quickly lifting the foot at
the same time. When the colt responds, reward him by ca-
ressing him and rubbing the leg and letting the foot down.
Repeat several times and then trim and level the hoof. Never
lose hold of the foot until you wish to put it down.

To raise a hind foot, work slowly and gently, lifting the foot
forward a few times before carrying it backward into the shoeing position. After some handling trim and level the hoof.

A halter twitch is a great aid in handling the feet of a horse
that will not stand. The twitch is easily applied and needs only
the ordinary halter and tie rope. Pass the rope over the
horse's head just behind the ears; raise the upper lip and put
the rope across the gums above the teeth; run the rope
through the loop made by passing the rope over the horse's
head. The rope should be tight from the halter ring, over the

Fig. 8-7. Raising the hind foot

head, under the lip, and through the loop. A few good pulls on this rope should make the horse stand quietly.

For a kicker try the following: Buckle a strap with a two-inch ring around the hind pastern, run a rope through this ring and carry the end over the horse's back, tie to the opposite foreleg next to the body, and lead the horse forward. When he lifts his foot it may be held up by pulling on the loose end of the rope, as shown in Fig. 8-7. The foot may be held either forward or backward with this arrangement (see also Fig. 8-8). To put this rigging on the kicker or an unbroken horse, tie up a front foot, and have the assistant hold his hand over the eye on the same side as the foot to be lifted. The best time to work on a horse's feet is when he is tired from a drive or other exercise.

BREAKING TO DRIVE

After the colt has been broken to lead he may be accustomed to harness and trained to rein. A horse should never be hitched to a wagon or ridden before he is broken to drive in harness (in the lines); that is, trained to go at command,

Fig. 8-8. Holding foot for shoeing

stop when he hears "Whoa," rein to the right and left, and to back up.

To familiarize the colt with bit and harness, the "bitting harness," consisting of an open bridle with snaffle bit, check and side reins, and surcingle with crupper, may be used. The bitting harness is shown in Fig. 8-9.

Put the rigging on the colt, leaving the side and check reins comparatively loose, and turn him loose in a small paddock for an hour. On the second lesson the reins may be tightened somewhat, but not left on for over an hour. The third day driving lines may be put on. Let the assistant lead the colt till he is not frightened at the driver walking behind. Dismiss the assistant as soon as possible, and drive the colt for half an hour in a quiet paddock or lane where he will not see other horses. All that should be taught in this lesson is to go ahead. Cluck to the colt, or tell him "Get up," and use the whip to let him know what is meant.

It is essential to train both sides of a colt. He may become accustomed to objects seen on the near (left) side with the near eye, but when the same objects are viewed for the first time on the other side with the off (right) eye he may be badly frightened. Driving in right and left circles will facilitate this training.

Fig. 8-9. Bitting harness

The next lesson should be a short review of the previous work and in addition the meaning of "Whoa." "Whoa" in horse training is the big word. It doesn't mean back or steady, but stop. Train the horse so that when he hears "Whoa" he will stop and stay stopped, no matter what is happening.

To stop a horse say "Whoa" so that he hears you plainly, and immediately follow the command with a pull on the reins. The most effective use of the reins is to hold one rein just tight and give a good pull on the other one, then relax the pressure. If the horse doesn't stop, repeat the command and pull. Soon he will stop at the word, and the pull may be eliminated.

The next lesson should review "Get up" and "Whoa," and the horse should be taught to back. As a horse should be trained to stop on command, so should he back on the word, and pulling on the lines should be unnecessary.

Drive the horse a few steps to get his attention, stop him, then give the command "Back," following it with a good pull on the reins. If he yields a step, pet him, and then repeat the command with the pull on the reins. Do not exert a continuous pressure, for if this is done the horse will take the bit and forge ahead. Do not make the lesson too long. Repeat the next day, and continue the lessons until the horse will back on command.

After the horse goes satisfactorily in bitting rig, the work harness with breeching should be substituted. The traces and breeching should be joined loosely together and gradually tightened as the work progresses. This will familiarize the colt with the sensation of wearing collar and breeching. As soon as he goes well with the harness he is ready to be hitched single or double.

DRIVING DOUBLE

To drive double use a broken, gentle horse for a team mate, preferably one that the colt knows. The colt or green horse should be hitched on the off side of the team. Be sure that all parts of the harness are strong, as during the training of the colt it is particularly important that you have absolute control and that he does not become frightened because of breakage. During the first few lessons the use of a jockey stick will assist in keeping the colt from crowding the older horse (see Fig. 8-10). This stick is a stout bar, long enough to reach from the outer hame ring of the older horse to the halter ring or bit of the colt, and is provided with a snap at each end or is tied in place. The colt should be tied back with the halter rope to the backband or trace ring of the older horse. During the hitching the assistant stands quietly at the colt's head, and afterward handles the guy rope (about twenty feet long) which runs through the right bit ring and under the jaw and is attached to the left ring, and is used to restrain the colt when he becomes overfractious. After the horses are hitched together, drive them around without the wagon, stopping, starting, and backing the team. Thirty minutes should suffice for this lesson.

At the next lesson familiarize the colt with the wagon. If he has been previously led by the side of his dam he will not be likely to become frightened at the rattle of the wagon. Lead the gentle horse up to his place at the tongue, then bring the colt up, hitching them as in the previous lesson. Attach the neck yoke and hook the traces. Do not hitch the colt too tight at first. Have a short stay chain on the old horse so that if necessary he can start the wagon himself. The driver may get into the wagon, but the assistant should walk to the right and rear of the colt with the guy rope. The driver must give all commands and do the driving, while the assistant is as quiet as possible and acts only when absolutely needed. Drive only a short distance at a time, and start and stop frequently, using the brake to prevent the wagon from running up on the team. During the stops the assistant may step up carefully to the colt to pet and quiet him if it is thought necessary to reassure him.

The best place for the first hitching is a big field, but after the colt goes well a short drive may be taken on a quiet roadway. Always stop when the colt shows fear of something. Let him look the object over and examine it; never whip him or rush by anything at which he is frightened, otherwise a shying horse will result. The daily drive may be increased in length until the colt is broken, or he may be used in ordinary light work. During the first year's work it will be well to work the colt with a horse that is a free, fast walker.

SOME MORE ADVICE FOR BREAKING COLTS

I'm sure the foregoing from the USDA bulletin will offer fuel for many arguments amongst horsemen. Most everyone breaks colts a little differently, and you would probably be well advised to once more lean on the old horseman friend in your community that, hopefully, you have cultivated (or conned) into being your advisor by now.

For one thing, I doubt that most horsemen bother with the bitting harness on gentle, farm-reared colts. By the time they want to put a harness on him they have him well enough accustomed to being handled that they go directly to the work harness.

Fig. 8-10. A jockey stick will assist in keeping the colt in place when being broken with an older horse to drive double.

I would also prefer hitching to a skid or stoneboat the first time or two, rather than to a wagon. You aren't going to be backing him anyhow the first few times and there is no way on earth for a stoneboat to run up on him, bang him in the heels, and scare him into trying to run off. Nor is there any risk of jackknifing and turning it over in the event of turning too short.

In both tying a foal up in the barn and hitching an older colt the lessons should be frequent and of short duration.

Be consistent in the voice commands used and use a minimum of them—too many voice commands and all you have is a confused horse or colt. The basic vocabulary for a useful horse must have the following, or their equivalents: 1. Whoa, which means stop; 2. Get Up, which means go; 3. Steady, or Easy, which means a slow ahead; 4. Back, which means back; 5. Gee, which means swing to the right; 6. Haw, which means swing to the left; 7. Get Over, which means move over in the stall so I can get in beside you.

The rest is mostly commentary, which is meaningless to the horse. Quiet commands are the ones that build confidence in your horse. A horse has a keen sense of hearing, so when you yell at him you are doing it solely to relieve yourself. Horses are also sensitive to the tone of commands and may become confused and excited by a lot of loud shouting.

Something else that is unreal is to expect a horse to understand and respond to a series of commands. It makes sense to tell a man to "Go ahead slowly and turn right," but the horse's mind works differently. To a horse you should say, "Get up," then give him enough time to start before coming on with "Steady," or "Easy," and after that has soaked in, "Gee." Otherwise the horse is quite likely to get mixed up.

Some horsemen will not use lines with snaps in hitching green colts. They can come unsnapped, get snapped into the neck yoke ring, etc., and frighten the youngster. They use a buckle with a billet rather than a snap on the ends of the lines.

Needless to say, when first putting the harness on a colt or handling him at any time, you do the best you can to precondition him to the experience by getting him accustomed to the feel of ropes, leather, and you. You move slowly and talk to him quietly. And just as you don't use old, rotten, expendable harness on a colt (one of the worst times for harness breakage is with a green colt), you don't hitch to a wagon with an old, rotten tongue. It should have a good wooden tongue, or preferably a steel one.

In breaking colts always remember that the horse's opinion of you is more important than your opinion of him. Colts are often made nervous by nervous handlers. If he has not been spoiled by careless handling before, the colt will generally have confidence in you as long as you deserve it and don't ask the impossible of him and are consistent in your behavior toward him.

Some people are not temperamentally suited to break or train colts and should not attempt it but that doesn't necessarily mean they shouldn't work horses that someone else has done a good job of breaking. It certainly is not one of the first things you should undertake.

FROM WEANING THROUGH
THE COLT'S SECOND YEAR

P. T. Brown, extension horseman at Purdue University at that time, writing in the 1938 *Belgian Review* stated that the job of developing first-class yearlings and older horses required four very definite things. First, to have a good colt to start with and that requires skill and knowledge in selection and matings, and also a little luck. Second, to feed liberally but not wastefully. The third is to provide unlimited outdoor exercise, thereby keeping them clean and sound in the limbs. And last, to keep the feet properly level as they grow. That isn't exactly what he said, but it's close. I would add a couple others to P. T.'s list, namely, to worm them at the same intervals you do your older horses and to handle them frequently so they do not become man-shy in any way.

The purpose of the exercise is to keep them growing without getting them fat. This determines to a considerable extent both the kind and quantity of feed used to grow out draft colts. First, they should be on pasture as much of the year as possible, but when the pasture gets short in July and August supplement with hay and grain or both, as needed. Do not allow a few months of short pasture to deliver them a setback at this stage in their lives. During the winter, of course, it will be hay and grain diet and here again legume hay can play a big part in building the bone and muscle necessary. They need a good legume or mixed hay, high in protein, not junk hay.

As for grain, from ½ pound to ¾ pound a day per hundred weight of horse is what Iowa State and Missouri recommended. Oats, corn, bran, and linseed meal were the components of the grain ration recommended by both schools. These can be fed in various combinations depending on your own feed supplies, but in no case would I make it more than half corn and preferably not nearly that much. Some of the specific mixes recommended were as follows:

1. ⅓ each, corn, oats, and bran
2. ½ each, corn and oats

3. 4 parts oats, 1 part bran
4. 1 part of linseed meal with 10 parts of any of the above rations
5. 4 parts oats, 1 part corn, 1 part bran
6. 3 parts oats, 3 parts corn, 1 part bran, and 1 part linseed meal. And so on.

It is also a good idea to provide a free choice mixture of equal parts of fine lime, bone meal, and salt. Almost needless to say, they also need access to clean water at all times.

Too much corn in the ration will tend to lay on condition rather than growth and some colts will fill in the hocks; although exercise will reduce this risk, it is still a good idea to limit the amount of corn on growing horses. For those who are developing show colts perhaps somewhat heavier feeding will be called for.

Housing has been covered in Chapter 5 but deserves a mention here. Draft colts certainly do not need elaborate housing. They are not hot-house plants, and treating them as such does them no favor. Probably the best housing is a shed open to the south with good drainage and possibly a darkened place for them to get into and away from the flies during summer.

Castration   It is the fate of most horse colts to become geldings, and that is certainly as it should be if we are to breed only the best. Castration can, of course, be done at various times but generally the best time is as the colt turns a year old. If it is done much earlier it may result in less development of the foreparts than is desired. Delaying it somewhat will assure better development and carriage of the foreparts. The essential steps of castration are the complete removal of both testicles and the arrest or prevention of bleeding from the spermatic artery which is located in the anterior part of the cord. This is a job for your veterinarian.

It is often said that a horse is made during the first year of his life, and there is a good bit of truth to it.

Keeping a Stallion

To have a stallion or not is the first question to answer. If there are good stallions within easy trucking distance the answer in most cases still be no. But if you are going to breed horses you still must "select" a stallion, whether it is for the purpose of buying him or breeding to him. And, after going through the selection process on what is reasonably available to you, you may discover that you have to buy one to have one that suits you. So, either way, a selection process is involved.

SELECTING THE STALLION

Everything I have previously said in the earlier chapters relating to soundness, conformation, and action applies here and with much greater force than in buying a mare or a replacement work horse. This decision more than any other single decision will determine your success as a horse breeder. And, if you are buying, it usually represents a large investment.

Dave Haxton, former head horseman at Woodside Percherons during the Laet era, and certainly one of the most respected "elder statesmen" in the draft horse world, writing in *Draft Horse Journal* offered this bit of advice:

1. Buy a stallion that would make a top gelding; you are looking for about the same things in either case.
2. Look for a horse with a rugged and masculine outlook with ample bone of the flat variety.
3. Remember that he should have a head and neck typical of his breed, a large eye, a smart ear of the bigger size with a jaw and clean throatlatch of quality and refinement. The day of the short-necked, ugly-headed draft horse is past.
4. A good hind leg is very important; one with too much set or hook is to be avoided. A little of this may help his hock action but it is best to have a leg that is

neither too straight nor one that has too much set.

5. Avoid a horse that is back in his knees (calf-kneed is the term used by horsemen). It is better to accept a bucked appearance in front for he will "pop his knees" better.

6. Look for a nice sloping pastern, well blended into a big foot of good texture with wide open hoof heads, well defined at the coronets. Judges may disagree on the proper shape of the foot. The trend today is for a boxed toe, but this can be overdone.

7. Keep breed character and the bloodlines and conformation of your mares in mind as you select a young horse.

You may never find a young stallion that suits you in every respect but the above are some of the points to ponder while in search of an individual with the most of the best.

Miles McGrew, prominent Belgian breeder from Prairie City, Illinois, put it another way. He said he likes to have his stallions "looking for the next town."

To elaborate on these comments, let us first consider soundness, action, and wind. The feet and legs of a horse are his "running gears," without which he is just meat. Make as certain as you can that you are either getting or breeding to a horse with no inheritable unsoundnesses and that he comes from a family that is also free from them. For you will be getting genes that are not evident in any male animal, and the more you know about his family, the better. Keep in mind that you are buying, or breeding to, his whole inheritance, not just to what you see. Pay close attention to the way he moves, that he has a long, straight stride at the walk—one designed to cover ground—and that he has free flexion of the hocks and good height in knee action at the trot, which should be a bold, stallion-like trot—not a mincing, short-strided, choppy waltz.

Testing the wind is essential. Have him exercised vigorously, quickly stopped, and then observe his breathing. Check the eyes.

Make sure both testicles are down and well developed. If he is a mature horse, insist on seeing him serve a mare, making sure that he knows his business and goes about it with dispatch.

Everyone has their own conformation hang-ups but make sure you get a stallion with a strong constitution, ribs well sprung, and ample room in the chest for his vital organs. His flanks should be deep, indicating feeding capacity, and his quarters deep and well muscled. Make sure he has the slope of shoulder that you would like to put a collar on for it is his job to sire work horses.

P. T. Brown passed on a good piece of advice to small breeders, in my judgement, when he advised them to never overlook the old, proven sire. I quote the following three paragraphs from his article in the 1938 *Belgian Review*. He was commenting on the Indiana Gold Medal Colt Program which, incidentally, is still going strong:

> Not only should the breeder patronize a horse that has demonstrated his ability to sire high-class colts, but he should also pay a lot of attention to soundness. It is surprising to note the recklessness with which some breeders will send their best, sound, tried brood mares to an unsound stallion that has caught their fancy just because of some relatively minor thing, such as arch of neck, slope of rump, or something similar.
>
> In each of our spring stallion shows we have a class for Veteran stallions—those that are over ten years of age. This is one of the most educational features of these shows and has effectively demonstrated that some stallions have hard, clean, sound, underpinning up to fifteen or eighteen years of age, while others are unsound and coarse even when young.
>
> I am a strong believer in the importance of making full use of tried sires that have established a reputation for siring high-class colts and that have sound, clean, correct underpinning, even when they are old. How to get an inherently sound, high-class colt to start with is one of the major problems of breeders.

If there isn't a proven sire of this type available, buy a son out of a family of great brood mares. The champion colt, with little in the way of family credentials, can be a real fooler. I have had older Belgian breeders cite the case of a famous international champion in this respect. He was a great show stallion of the thirties in the hands of people with the top mares of the breed, but is not remembered as a great sire. I rarely encounter his name in present-day Belgian pedigrees, and I've looked at quite a few. It was apparently a case where a fortuitous combination of genes produced a spectacular animal without the ability to pass it on with any regularity. In all classes of purebred livestock there is always a flock of "promising youngsters," some of them like the stallion mentioned above. Don't overlook the old proven sire, and if buying or breeding to a young horse, find one with the depth of breeding it takes to pass it on. Remember that a lot of promises remain unfulfilled when looking at "promising youngsters."

By the same token, don't get so hung up on a few famous animals that are now greatly diluted in his pedigree that you "see the chart and miss the critter." That is equally dumb. At a minimum, I would say, satisfy yourself that the sire has transmitted what you are looking for in more than just the colt you are looking at and that the dam, and her family, would be a welcome addition to your farm.

AGE TO BREED

A well-grown two-year-old stallion can be used to breed about a dozen mares. Some horsemen recommend not more than one a week, while others prefer to finish the breeding season up with him as quickly as possible, maintaining that the young stallions will feed better if the season is not too long.

The well-developed three-year-old may handle one service per day regularly with a total of from thirty-five to fifty mares; the four-year-old may occasionally make two services a day on from fifty to seventy-five mares; and the mature horse from seventy-five up, depending on the horse. It is best to pretty much limit the mature horse to two services per day, although it may be necessary to extend this at times.

There are a lot of variables here; the care, feed, and exercise of the stallion as well as his level of potency all influence the above. The famous Clydesdale stallion, Dunure Footprint, sired more than 200 living foals in one season, serving several mares each day, and remained virile until his death at nineteen. Don't bet on this. He was a rather exceptional stallion.

EXERCISING THE STALLION

No animal on the farm is more dependent upon plenty of good, regular exercise to do his job than the stallion. He must have plenty of exercise to sire a large crop of vigorous colts. Virility is closely associated with the general health and vigor of the stallion. Exercise increases muscular tone, prevents obesity, decreases the danger of digestive disturbances, and contributes to a feeling of well-being on the part of the horse that is reflected in his disposition.

One way to make sure he is getting adequate exercise is to make him, or let him, work for his living along with the rest of the horses. If broke early and carefully handled he can contribute his full share to getting the field work done. During the breeding season, however, a half day's work is probably enough. Most stallions that are worked are worked with a gentle mare. It is advisable to use a "jockey stick" at first to prevent the stallion from getting his head too near his mate.

He may also be taken for a five- or six-mile walk, driven singly on a stoneboat, or take other strenuous exercise. This, however, consumes time that isn't really getting anything done but exercising the stud horse.

He should have a good-sized paddock that enables him to look out and see what is going on around the farm. Such a paddock should have a fence seven feet high. Solid board fences are sometimes used but they restrict his view curtailing his interest in looking around. Stallions do not, as a rule, get enough exercise in such an enclosure. It is a little like being in "solitary."

FEEDING THE STALLION

There is a great temptation to overfeed the stallion. For one thing, he is usually sort of a "show piece" and is shown to all comers with pride. For another he may be standing for public service and, if so, the owner likes to have him looking his best. Unfortunately, looking his best and breeding his best are not necessarily two halves of the same whole. Stallions should be kept in good condition but not fat. Obese stallions are not nearly as sure breeders as the horse in moderate flesh on a well-balanced ration.

For the amount and kind of feedstuffs I will again turn to Iowa State and Michigan State for their recommendations. A. B. Caine from Iowa State said that a general rule is to allow stallions from ¾ to one pound of grain and one to 1¼ pounds of hay for each 100 pounds of weight during the breeding season. When not in service, they should be fed less grain and more hay. (See Fig. 8-11 for Caine's two suggested rations for stallions.)

Fig. 8-11. Recommended rations for stallions
(*Source:* A. B. Caine from Iowa State)

Oats 55%	Oats, 65%
Corn (yellow) 20%	Corn, 20%
Wheat (ground) 20%	Bran, 15%
Bran 10%	Clover or Alfalfa, 50%
Mixed Hay (alfalfa, 50%)	Timothy

R. S. Hudson from Michigan State makes very similar recommendations. He says that immature stallions should be fed grain liberally at all times. The mature stallion should be fed grain at the rate of ⅔ of a pound per 100 pounds of live weight when not in service. The amount may be increased to 1⅕ pounds per 100 during the breeding season. However, it

Fig. 8-12. Recommended rations for stallions
(Source: R. S. Hudson from Michigan State)

I. Breeding season

    1. Oats, 4 parts; bran, 1 part; with mixed timothy and clover
    2. Oats, 2 parts; ear corn, 3 parts; bran, 1 part; with timothy and clover
    3. Oats, 3 parts; barley, 2 parts; bran, 1 part; linseed meal, 1 part; with timothy hay
    4. Corn, 7 parts; bran, 2 parts; linseed meal, 1 part; with timothy hay
    5. Corn, 7 parts; bran, 1 part; with alfalfa hay

II. Wintertime (when the stallion is idle)

    1. Oats, 3 parts; bran, 1 part; with timothy hay and carrots
    2. Corn with alfalfa hay and carrots
    3. Oats, 2 parts; corn, 2 parts; with alfalfa and timothy hay and carrots
    4. Oats, 2 parts; corn, 2 parts; with alfalfa, oat straw, and carrots
    5. Oats, 2 parts; corn, 2 parts; with clover hay, oat straw, and carrots

is often necessary to deviate from this rule because individuals differ considerably in temperament, feeding ability, and amount of exercise taken (see Fig. 8-12 for specific recommendations).

The ration should be richer in protein and mineral matter during the breeding season. Roots, especially carrots, are valuable because of their succulent nature. They also tend to be a little laxative, just as the wheat bran, linseed meal, and alfalfa suggested above.

Grass and soilage crops may be cut and fed daily to the stallion in a dry paddock during the spring and summer, but very carefully, and not without some risk of digestive disturbances. Such green feeds should be given in small quantities and introduced into the total ration very gradually.

The stallion should be fed and watered regularly at least three or four times during the day, or have free access to water along with salt.

STANDING YOUR STALLION FOR SERVICE

There is an old saying, "Halve the ration and double the exercise when the stallion is not giving a vigorous sure service." Like most oversimplifications it contains a good bit of truth but cannot be universally applied.

No, "public service" does not mean running for office, but it does have its similarities. One is that you must have a candidate (a stallion) that will appeal to the voters (mare owners) in your area. And this, in itself, can be a pitfall, particularly if you keep the bugger too fat just to make him "look good."

And if you are figuring on paying for your horse and justifying his presence, at least in part, with outside service fees you may have to pay more attention to color and fashionable pedigree when you buy him than you would really prefer doing. To cite a specific example, right now (in 1977), if a man were expecting to make a serious dollar standing a Belgian horse in most communities, he would do considerably more business with a flashy blonde horse with a wide stripe and white legs to the knees and hocks than he would with a strawberry roan or a dark chestnut horse that was distinctly superior in every way that mattered—except for the factor of saleability of color. If you plan to make a serious attempt at gathering outside fees, keep this in mind. In other words, if your personal goals do not coincide with popular passion, don't be disappointed if your candidate stallion doesn't garner as many votes as you think he ought to receive. Go into it with your eyes open. I'll talk more about this shortly.

Assuming that you have, in fact, decided to stand your horse for public service you must now "get the word" around. Avoid extravagant claims for him. The best advertisement is the stallion himself, at least until his colts start hitting the ground. Then they are the best advertisements.

State your terms and stick with them. In years past, the arrangement in many communities was the "stand and suck" agreement. In other words you paid for a colt that "stood and sucked." Personally, I never felt that this was a very fair arrangement to the stallion owner. He has the trouble of breeding the mare, but no assurance that the mare owner will 1. try her back as he should and when he should, and 2. take reasonably good care of her and be on tap to assist at birth if that should be necessary. Things are too much out of the stallioner's hands to put him into a position of "guaranteeing a colt that stands and sucks."

I think the arrangement whereby the fee is paid at the time the mare is served and the mare owner has the privilege of retrying her during that breeding season is much more fair. Another reason for the second arrangement is that in this day and age mares are bought and sold over great distances, whereas in the so-called "old days" the mares in a given neighborhood or community were pretty much sure to be there come foaling time. Now, they are just as likely to be halfway across the country by the time they foal and how does one collect those fees?

As a stallion owner you have every right to reject mares. R. S. Hudson from Michigan State said the following kinds of mares should be turned down:

1. Mares showing the slightest symptoms of venereal disease.
2. Mares that have an abnormal discharge (such as blood or pus) from the vagina, commonly known as the "whites."
3. Mares affected with skin diseases and parasites.
4. Mares suffering from high fevers, which accompany colds, strangles, influenza, shipping fever, and pneumonia.
5. Mares that have recently foaled colts affected with navel ill.
6. Mares that have recently retained an afterbirth.
7. Mares that have suffered lacerations in foaling.
8. Mares that do not show definite signs of heat.
9. Mares under three years of age unless very mature for their age and well developed.
10. Mares that have a very narrow or deformed pelvis.
11. Mares that stay in heat incessantly (nymphomaniacs).
12. Mares that are extremely thin or emaciated.
13. Mares that have severe unsoundness which may be hereditary.

You have every right to keep in mind that the resulting foals will be a reflection of and on your horse and you certainly have no obligation to breed any and every female equine brought to you. That wouldn't be a public service—might better be a public scandal!

In years past a lot of stallions were travelled in their respective neighborhoods. That is pretty much a thing of the past. Chances are, if you are going to stand a stallion, the mares will be brought to you. This means that you will of necessity set up a breeding area. This is a good idea anyhow in that the horse will soon associate the area with the business at hand.

I wish, at this point to use a couple pages and illustrations from the Michigan State pamphlet, *Stallion Management*.

BREEDING AREA

A breeding chute (see Fig. 8-13) and teasing pole may be set up in some convenient place that is hidden from view of the house and road. The teasing pole should be eight feet long, six or eight inches in diameter, and securely bolted to two upright posts so that it will be about three feet six inches from the ground. If placed about three or four feet from and parallel to the side of a building or a fence, it will be more satisfactory because the mare will be forced to stand close to the pole. Remove any projections that might injure the mare, such as sharp corners and ends of bolts. Some stallioners prefer an open doorway or teasing gate (Fig. 8-14) for teasing mares, while others choose to "try" over a gate or pole.

A breeding chute is illustrated in Fig. 8-13. The gas pipe in front may be moved backward to shorten the chute for smaller mares. Breeding hobbles are easily made by any harnessmaker or the necessary rope, rings, and leather may be purchased and the hobbles made at home. Hobbles are not used by some stallioners, although when used wisely they may prevent accidents to both the mare and stallion.

An excellent twitch may be made from an old spade handle and window sash cord. Tail bandages are made by tearing

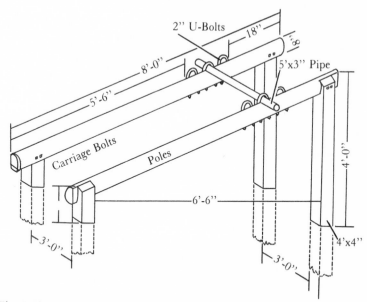

Fig. 8-13. An easily constructed breeding chute for mares

Fig. 8-14. Mares may be teased through an open gateway or doorway.

good grade cheesecloth, bunting, or bleached muslin into strips two or three inches wide and rolling them tightly into a compact roll. A ¼-inch manila rope or heavy twine eight or ten feet long is useful in tying the tail to the right side before service. A good sponge, soap, white enamelware pail, and warm water facilitate washing the vulva and penis before and after service.

An ordinary stallion bridle is suitable for handling most stallions. The lead should be provided with a short chain and snap which may be passed through the left bit-ring, under the jaw and snapped into the right bit-ring. If the horse is difficult to control, a ⅜-inch steel bar may be welded to a link, snapped into the right bit-ring, passed under the jaw through the left-bit ring, and welded to another link, into which the lead rein may be snapped. This arrangement affords great leverage and should not be used too severely since there is danger of fracturing the stallion's jaw. Such a bit should never be used on a young stallion when breeding his first few mares as he is liable to be restrained too harshly and thereby remain slow and even refuse entirely to breed mares resembling those with which he had the difficulty.

HANDLING THE MARE AND STALLION

The temperament of stallions varies so greatly that no two may be handled in exactly the same manner. Most stallions do not require severe handling, but they should always be kept firmly in hand and made to obey. Most stallions are unruly only because they have had careless and indifferent training as colts. Never allow the horse to tear and rant about, but make him do his work quietly and precisely.

Great precaution should be taken to make certain that the mare is fully in season, as a forced breeding, especially with young mares, by the use of the chute and hobbles is liable not only to frighten the mare so that she will always remain cross or stallion-shy but also result in a useless service which may put her out for the season.

After the mare has been found to be in season, return the stallion to his stall and wash his reproductive organs with soap and warm water. Rinse with clean, pure water. With an attendant holding the mare, bandage the tail for a distance of six or eight inches. Then wash the external parts of the mare with soap and warm water and rinse thoroughly.

Set a pail of clean, warm water to one side and bring out the stallion. Make the stallion approach the mare quietly and never allow him to mount until ready for service. Some stallions are trained to stand on the left side of the mare before mounting. The stallioner's hands should be clean if it is necessary to assist the horse, but some stallions learn to make their service without help if the mare's tail is held to one side. The reproductive organs of the stallion should always be washed thoroughly with soap and warm water immediately after service. Strict sanitation at time of service is absolutely essential for the production of a large number of healthy vigorous foals and is one of the best precautions against navel ill or joint ill in foals.

The use of the breeding hobbles and tail string are recommended only when the stallioner is inexperienced or dealing with a strange horse, starting a young stallion, or handling a mare whose habits are not known, and are not intended for the replacement of methods used by the experienced groom. When the hobbles are to be used, place the mare in the breeding chute; if this plan is followed, apply a twitch to be held by the attendant, and adjust the breeding hobbles. Bandage the tail for a distance of six or eight inches. It may be held to the right side by looping one end of a ¼-inch rope about it and tying the other end tightly to the shoulder strap of the breeding hobbles near the top of the withers. (The rope should be tied so that a single jerk will loosen it if the stallion should accidently get his foot underneath.)

It is often difficult to find young mares in season by the usual methods employed at chute or gateway (Fig. 8-14). Some breeders lead the stallion into the field where fillies are in pasture and allow the stallion to cover them when they come to him for service.

Color and Marketing

It is impossible to consider marketing horses without thinking of color, for in no species of domestic livestock does color play such an important role in determining the selling price than in draft horses. While it is true that color makes no difference in the utility or working value of a draft horse, it is a factor that you can scarcely afford to ignore if you are breeding draft horses for sale. For example, I have a big pair of bay five-year-olds right now. They are well marked, young, broke, sound, with black points. If they were sorrels with white manes and tails, or grays just beginning to dapple, I have no doubt that they would be "worth" $500 more. Or, if they were Clydesdales, rather than the Belgian-Percheron crosses that they are, the bay color would be fully acceptable. Thus, fashion plays a considerable role in the draft horse market.

The basic colors in the draft breeds are as follows:

1. Black-body color is true black (disregarding weathering).
    a. Black-true-black without light areas.
    b. Seal-brown-black with light areas to include muzzle, under eyes, flank, and inside of upper legs, termed "light points."
    About half the Percherons are black, generally with very little white, a star in the forehead and maybe a white coronet or fetlock or two. It is probably the dominant color in the modern Shire, but usually accompanied by a blaze and three or four white legs, sometimes up to the knees and hocks. Bay and brown are also common to the Shire.
2. Bay includes shades from tan to brown, with black mane and tail and often black lower legs.
    a. Mahogany Bay—the brown shades of bay, often called brown.
    b. Blood Bay—the red shades of bay.
    c. Sandy Bay—the light shades of bay. This is the most popular and commonplace color of Clydesdales, with quite a lot of white. It was once a minority color in the Belgian breed (still popular in Belgium) that has largely been bred out of American Belgians. A great

many of the bay work horses (such as my own) are Belgian-Percheron crosses.

3. Chestnut includes shades from yellow gold to dark brown, with either white or silver manes and tails, or the same color as the body.

    a. Liver Chestnut—the dark shades, some appearing dark brown with an auburn hue.

    b. Sorrel—the red shades, all the way from blonde to golden or red. This is the overwhelming favorite color of the Belgian breed today and the only color of the Suffolk. Other things being equal, the sorrel with white mane and tail will probably excite more buyers into bidding than any other color.

4. Gray is caused by a gradual displacement of colored hair by white hair as age advances.

    a. Iron or Steel Gray—usually a high percentage of colored hair. (Grays are usually black at foaling, and blacks are usually mouse colored!)

    b. Dapple Gray—having the colored hair in such a distribution as to give a dappled or rosette effect. (This also occurs with some roans.)

Gray is the other standard color for the Percheron. In France it is the overwhelming favorite; in this country Percherons are about evenly divided between blacks and grays.

5. Roan is a real Pandora's box of wonders, as there are so many variations and combinations. Roan is a more or less uniform mixture of white and colored hairs. At certain ages grays and roans are rather hard to distinguish, but true genetic differences exist. Gray is foaled solid colored, roans are foaled roan and gray roan whitens with age, as does a true gray.

    a. Black Roan—black and white hairs mixed, usually called a "blue."

    b. Blue Roan—same as above, but having some red hairs, too.

    c. Bay or Red Roan—roaned bay.

    d.   Chestnut or Strawberry Roan—roaned chestnut.

    e.   Gray Roan—roan in combination with gray factor.

Duns, paints, palominos, etc. are not common to the draft breeds.

You might think that color would be the sort of thing upon which there was pretty common agreement. Such is not the case. The above descriptions were taken pretty much from *Our Equine Friends*, a Horse and Mule Association booklet, and I'm quite sure even such a source as that can provoke plenty of argument among horsemen as to exactly what is what where color is concerned. The late Dr. Ben K. Green devoted the whole of his last book to the subject of color. It is entitled *The Color of Horses* and was published by Northland Press. I have no desire to try to get in the last word on color.

A description of face markings is also of importance in describing a horse. As in body color there is not complete agreement on the terminology of face markings. What one

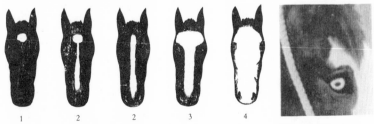

Fig. 8-15. Face markings

Fig. 8-16.
A walleye

horseman calls a blaze another may call a stripe. Basically there are five general types of facial markings, as illustrated in Fig. 8-15, and one term for an eye color variation.

    1.   Star—any white mark on the forehead. The size, shape, and position vary a great deal, and hardly any of them are shaped like stars.

    2.   Stripe—a narrow white marking down the face, not wider than the flat anterior surface of the nasal bones. It may be a continuation of the star or distinct

from it and would, in the latter case, be described as a "broken stripe" or in the former, "star and stripe."

3. Blaze—a white marking covering almost the whole of the forehead between the eyes, and extending down the front of the face, involving the whole width of the nasal bones.
4. White Face (or Baldy)—where the white pretty well covers the whole face and mouth.
5. Snip—an isolated white marking, independent of those already named, and situated in the region of the nostrils.
6. Walleye (or Glass Eye)—this term is used where there is such a lack of pigment in the iris as to give a grayish-white or bluish-white appearance to the eye (see Fig. 8-16).

In preparing horses for market there is an old saying that "Fat is the best color." In view of what I have just said about fads and fashions, it probably isn't the *best* color, but still a mighty good one. In today's market, more so than in the past when the skills of horsemanship were more widely practiced, having horses "well broke" is probably the best color. Having a pair well matched in size and color will net you more than having two that work well together, unfair and unwise as that may seem. And it pays to sell either mares or geldings together. Both of our own teams are one of each and I can't really see why this is so important, but it *does* seem to make a difference at the sales.

CONDITIONING HORSES FOR MARKET WITH FEED

With the present very active market for draft horses, feed used to condition horses for sale is usually well invested. Horses offered for sale right out of the cornfields or pasture, that are thin and have long, shaggy coats, are severely penalized. And with good reason. These thin, long-haired animals not only require a good bit of feed to get them up into condition but tend to sweat profusely and chill when shipped long distances. They are more susceptible to shipping fever than a well-conditioned, short-haired horse.

Stall feeding is usually done by your successful "salesmen." The feed for the first couple weeks is usually light, increasing it slowly until the horse is on what amounts to full feed. Highly palatable feeds with considerable variety and frequent feedings during the day will hurry the conditioning process along. Horses so handled will "stock up" or fill in the legs if the eye of the master is not trained and alert to provide adequate exercise to keep them "fresh in the legs." Blanketing will help get rid of the extra hair and give them that Cadillac look. Conditioning horses for sale at the big purebred auctions is both science and art.

Chapter 9

Sidelines

This book is written primarily for the person with an interest in using draft horses and mules in agricultural pursuits. Of course, not *everybody* who owns horses uses them on the farm; in this book, however, other ways in which draft animals can be used are placed in a secondary position. But because I feel that anyone entering the draft horse scene should at least be familiar with such pursuits as showing horses, the pulling contest, the urine business, and logging with horses, they are briefly covered in this chapter.

The show ring is probably the part of the draft horse industry most visible to the general public. It plays a very significant role in the purebred trade, promoting certain families of horses, establishing type standards, and directing type changes. Important as it is in those respects it is not, in my mind, of primary interest to the prospective draft horse owner. It seems to me that a novice has more basic things to concern him or herself with at the outset of his or her career with heavy horses than how to come across in the show ring.

Likewise, pulling is a highly specialized sport and will probably not involve great numbers of readers in any role other than as spectators.

Although the urine business is very important to those engaged in it, the limited market and degree of specialization involved are such that very few readers of this book will ever be engaged in it.

Of the activities covered in this chapter, logging is the one that perhaps should not be regarded as a secondary pursuit. Draft animals can play a real, important role in the logging business. But it does not involve nearly as many people or horses as does farming, and for that reason it is accorded only brief coverage in this text.

Showing Draft Horses

As a beginner in the draft horse business, you should approach showing with some hesitancy, for it is my feeling that the show ring is *not* the place to start breeding draft horses, cattle, sheep, or anything else. This is not to say that it does not have its rightful place in the scheme of things, as a vehicle for breed improvement, as a way of stimulating the interest of youth in better livestock, and for the promotion and sale of your own animals. I contend that showing, to be meaningful, should be the result of some constructive breeding, not the reason for it—except in the case of encouraging youthful interest in livestock breeding.

So as an opener, I would suggest that you *attend* a lot of good shows and watch the placings, visit with exhibitors and judges, ask questions, and, if possible, help somebody else show before you strike out on your own in this direction. If after this sort of initiation you feel that you have the merchandise, go ahead and start showing in a modest way, preferably at rather local shows. You will either grow into showing at larger and more distant shows or write it off as something that doesn't fit your operation and style.

Feeding to achieve proper condition for show is an extremely important part of showing. It would be presumptuous and silly to try to lay down feeding guides for horses being fitted for the show ring. It is something that can quite properly be called an art; the best advice you can get is from visiting with the best practitioners of that art whenever you get the chance.

There is an old axiom that "a thin horse never wins" and it has considerable truth. At the same time, however, there are individual horses that look better in high fix and others that show to better advantage in moderate flesh. One of the fundamental problems any fitter or conditioner faces is to get the bloom in his horses without filling in the legs. The type of feed, the master's eye, and lots of exercise are essential in this case. Feeding growing colts and even adult horses for top condition in hot weather is a tricky proposition.

Jack Carter, master fitter and showman for Michigan State, writing in the *Belgian Review* of 1937, made the point that you need to have your show stock coming along in good condition before hot weather hits. If you do this, you will not have to crowd them during the heat, with the possible problem of filled hocks, etc.

Feeding for high condition, like general growing and feeding, involves *mostly* the judicious use of home-grown feeds of high quality. Jack Carter said, "I would like to say here before going any further that grass and roots, carrots preferred, are the best conditioners you can get for colts and horses and beats anything you can get out of a bottle." Since then, several million bottles have come along, so I don't know what Carter would say today. There are commercial products that certainly have a rightful place in fitting show horses, but to keep the thing as practical as possible the main reliance should remain on home-grown feeds. Carter made extensive use, as do many others, of rolled or crushed oats and cracked corn when feeding stock for the show ring, whereas work stock can just as well be fed the whole grain. And a lot of show horses are fed whole grains, too, for that matter.

Carter also suggested not feeding for four to five hours before loading on your way to fairs, but make sure that the horses have water. He also cut down on the oats and increased the bran when on the road, figuring that if you didn't have your horses in shape by the time you leave home, you can't fit them out after you get there.

Another of Carter's suggestions might be useful to some and concerns the horse that gets an itch in his or her heels, and thus is likely to scratch and cap the hocks. Carter's remedy was to melt one cup of pure lard, add two tablespoons of sulphur, a tablespoon of kerosene, and one tablespoon of any good disinfectant, to make a salve that is rubbed well under the ankle joint. Never wash the heel—it only makes the condition worse. For horses that carry a fringe of hair or feather down the back of their legs, Carter suggested rubbing a mixture of 50 percent each olive oil and mineral oil gently into the hair for a month to make them look nicer and sweeter. He said you can add two tablespoons full of kerosene to a quart of this mix to put a nice bloom on the legs.

Another recommendation along these lines, this one from J. Douglas Charles, secretary of the Canadian Clydesdale Association, appeared in the May 1972 *Draft Horse Journal*. Here is what Mr. Charles had to say regarding the "itch":

Itch generally gets started in wintertime by keeping horses in drafty stables or in summer by allowing them to get into water, to feed in sloughs or rivers, or to get wet and dry continually. Their legs gradually become like people with dishpan hands and need something to restore the life back into the hair. Oil and sulphur is very good, particularly a month or so before show time.

There are many kinds of oils available, such as Stanlax, mineral oil, and a clear oil called Marcol that can be bought in bulk. Any kind of oil is better than none, even used crankcase oil when you are not showing.

Other causes of itch or cracks on the feet and legs can be lack of minerals in the feed or a vitamin deficiency. Horses should have free choice of cobalt salt, stock lime, or ground limestone, bone meal, and sulphate of iron, all of which help grow bone and supply the needs of the body. Animals kept on old pastures or in stables often do not get enough of these things if minerals are not supplied in the feed or in some other way.

Another very good item to have with you when on the show circuit is a product known as Haarlem oil or Dutch drops. This product is very good for kidney disorder, water, lack of appetite and swelled legs. This can be bought in vet drug supplies, although it may not come under the heading of vet supplies. It is available in ¼-ounce bottles which is a dose for a large animal, or it sometimes comes in the 2-ounce bottle.

Such were the suggestions of Doug Charles five years ago; like Carter, he is one of the more accomplished showmen in the business. His list illustrates the wide range of practices and the fact that you should be prepared for digestive upsets and other complications when you take your horses away from home and to the shows. Jack Carter said that when going to the fairs it is well to be prepared for emergencies. A bottle of colic remedy and a bottle of fever medicine supplied by your own veterinarian should always be on hand. Also a thermometer and syringe, a bottle of some good disinfectant, cotton wool, and a set of bandages. It is better to have them than borrow them.

Carter's idea of being fairly self-sufficient in dealing with your own problems at the shows is a good idea. This is also true of rolling manes and tying tails. Be able to do your own manes and tails—it isn't that difficult.

Following is an illustrated article by Dean Johnston on rolling manes that was used in the May 1968 *Draft Horse Journal.* Nine years later we still get calls for this issue.

DECORATING THE MANE

The best way to instruct someone on decorating a nice textured mane with the commonly used Aberdeen Plait is with a horse that is quiet and accustomed to being braided. It is much more difficult to do in print, but I'll do the best I can to get you started. Competence can be acquired only by practice. In this case a good braiding job comes after many sore fingers and failures, but it is well worth the trouble. A good job of braiding does much to enhance the natural beauty of a draft horse and is very rewarding to the horseman (or woman).

The mane should be clean, well brushed out, and combed to one side or the other. As the photos indicate our horses are all shown with right-hand manes (see Figs. 9-1 to 9-3).

Fig. 9-1. Keep the mane roll reasonably tight as you go and on top of the crest

Fig. 9-2. Dean Johnston finishing out the braid

Fig. 9-3. Putting in the flowers

We use two colors of yarn. They should be colors that harmonize with the horse and mane. We use red and white. I prefer using thirty to thirty-six strands. Each skein (one of each color) should be four to 4½ feet long when straightened (not stretched) out. The ends are then matched and a bit of white yarn tied securely around the rolls about ½ inch from the end; or if you use just one color, just double the length and tie a knot in the middle.

A braiding bench is needed. This bench should be 4½ to five feet long, ten to twelve inches wide, and twenty-six to forty-two inches high. This somewhat resembles a sawhorse except that it is taller and the legs on the side that goes next to the horse are at right angles to the ground.

The horse's head should be secured to a wall in the normal position for a hitch or line class. If tied too high most horses will fret and become very uneasy. A braid put in at an unnatural position will tend to bother the horse and pull out. Our horses at Yorktown Livery have their manes rolled 175 times a year so they take it in stride. Don't expect a horse to be unconcerned about it the first few times.

Place the braiding stool up beside the horse's neck on the side of the mane and face the same way the horse does. Begin about two inches back of the ears or as close up as the clipped bridle path will allow. Lay the mane roll over the horse's neck ahead of the long mane. Select a strand of hair, equal in quantity and bulk to one strand of the mane roll, separate it from the rest of the mane and hold it upright. Cross the yarn behind the strand of hair. Pick up a second strand of hair slightly less in bulk than the first strand. Cross the two strands of hair over the mane roll. Cross the yarn over the crossed hair. Now you will need to add additional hair from the mane to the strand which crossed downward toward the neck. The added hair ties the mane roll to the horse's neck. The strand of mane needs to be chosen from the center to keep the roll on top of the crest and visible from both sides of the horse.

The quantity of hair in the braid needs to be of uniform size in order to maintain a nice even pattern of hair and mane roll. The crossing of the mane roll and the hair needs to be done in the same sequence all the way down the neck to produce the plait.

Continue crossing the yarn and hair in the same order as you began and follow this pattern, adding a small amount of hair each time to maintain the equal bulk for a smooth job. Take care all the time to hold the hands close to the mane and keep hair and yarn pulled tight to ensure a hard, tight roll but not so tight as to hamper the moving of the neck and head.

On hitch horses you will want to break off about at the point of the shoulder. Increase the amount of hair that you pick up a slight bit three or four stitches before breaking off in order to have an adequate amount of hair to braid down the side of the neck after breaking off. After breaking off it is not desirable to add any more hair because the braid could not then be freely thrown over the hame. This same length roll should be of sufficient length to dress the mane of a halter horse, however you should continue farther back on the crest of the halter horse.

Break off in a gentle arc from the point of the shoulder on back to a point even with the elbow of the leg. Tie the end of the roll by a simple slip knot with one strand of the mane roll around the other. Cut the mane roll evenly about five inches below the knot.

We believe five flowers evenly spaced are sufficient for a hitch horse and we like seven to nine on a halter horse, but this is up to individual taste.

DECORATING THE TAIL

As for the tail, I'll go to the July 1939 *Percheron News,* and the instructions and illustrations of Robert Dix, one of the top fitters and showmen at that time.

There are two ways of braiding the tail. Stallions look well with a rye straw braid and many grooms put mares up with a Scotch knot and stick-ups.

The Rye Straw Braid   The rye straw braid consists of two and a half to three dozen rye straws to a bunch, cut about twenty to twenty-four inches long. These should be cut just before the rye grain is ready to harvest and the rye should have a good bright yellow color, yet be green enough to be tough. The straws are then stripped of the external sheaths that extend from each joint and are tied very tightly with a heavy cord about four to five inches from the light end of the straws. This will give a fan shape to the end of the straws.

Dampen the straws by dipping into a bucket of water or wrapping with a wet sack. This will aid in making them very tough. Divide the bundle into three equal parts and in braiding use a small lock of hair, taken from the tail, each time a cross is made.

With the straw divided, the plaiting process starts at the base of the tail (see Fig. 9-4). Place the bundle in an upright position, using the outside strands, with the left strand in the left hand and right strand in the right hand and a lock of hair added to each. The first cross is made under the middle strand; then the third strand is brought over and under the present left strand, thus letting the left strand assume the middle position. This time take the middle strand over the right side and let the present right strand take the middle position.

This same routine is continued and each time a cross is made a lock of hair is added until the braid reaches within three to four inches of the end dock of tail (see Fig. 9-5); then discontinue adding hair, but braid out about two inches and tie tightly with heavy cord. Take the balance of the hair at the end of tail and braid with a three-strand braid, dividing all the hair into three parts.

Tie a two-foot piece of cord at the end of the braid and, with a wire needle (made by doubling a piece of wire two feet long), stick it from the bottom of the braid under to the top, just where the rye braid ended and put the string from the end of the hair braid into the eye of the needle and pull through. Use the balance of the hair braid by drawing it back down through between the straw braid and the dock of tail.

Finish by wrapping a heavy cord around both the knot and rye straw braid to give the second fan an upright position. Complete by clipping the fans to about three inches in length and put a nice ribbon bow around the base of the knot and the lower fan and also one around the base of the rye fan (see Fig. 9-6).

The Scotch Knot   It is much simpler and faster to braid the Scotch knot. To put the stick-ups in, first use either raffia or

Fig. 9-4.

Fig. 9-5.

Fig. 9-6.

Two ways to decorate the tail: the rye straw braid (Figs. 9-4 through 9-6) and the Scotch knot (Figs. 9-7 through 9-10)

(Courtesy of Percheron News*)*

Fig. 9-7.

Fig. 9-8.

colored crepe paper in strands about ten inches long and about eight to ten strands to the braid. With a strand of number 22-gauge copper wire, use a four-plait braid, two strands of hair and two of raffia (see Fig. 9-7). We take two small locks of hair at the base of the tail head and lay the strands of raffia between them at the middle and continue a four-plait braid. Caution must be taken to see that the two stick-ups are even in height and are square across the tail. The stick-ups are braided to about four inches in height, then wrapped tightly to give them a small fan shape. The hair of the tail is then divided into three equal parts but divided so that the finished knot will be located in the center of tail. Then braid an ordinary three-plait braid, using the underneath style. Finish by pulling the hair braid down under the straw braid and wrapping around the knot with braid and heavy cord. Encircle the knot with a silk ribbon to

Fig. 9-9.

Fig. 9-10.

cover up the string. Also, put a narrow ribbon bow on the stick-up at the base of fan (see Fig. 9-8).

A fan is used by many grooms by making a small fan with a long cord attached and then pulling down under the Scotch knot. This takes an upright position just back and above the Scotch knot (see Fig. 9-9). Work is now completed (see Fig. 9-10).

One final word for those who would like to show horses. If you are going to the expense of showing (what with fitting, shoeing, trucking, time away from home, etc., it is no way to get rich!), spend enough time working with your colts and horses at home so that you can present them to the best possible advantage in the show ring. Stand them up properly, present them to an imaginary judge at the walk and trot and do it repeatedly. Otherwise, how is the poor beast to know what is expected of him when he walks into that big, strange coliseum? Many a fractious colt has lost a well-deserved place or two simply because he threw a fit rather than showed himself.

The show ring has played—and I'm sure it will continue to play—a major role in the draft horse business. No domestic animal lends himself to the pageantry of the show ring as well as the draft horse. The big hitches are called the monarchs of the tanbark, and rightfully so. Well-earned victories have called attention to great horses and great families thus aiding in the spread of their genetic influence.

It is an exciting and demanding art, one that may suit you. But it's not the place to start in the business. By the same token, if you have youngsters in the family and they are interested in showing some colts, by all means encourage them. It can be a great learning experience and the lure, excitement, and rewards of the show ring are responsible in no small measure for the fact that many of the top grooms, herdsmen, and shepherds devote much of their lives to the work of livestock improvement.

I guess that what I'm saying is respect it, practice it if it suits your program, learn from it; but always keep in mind that at its best showing is only a tool for livestock improvement, not an end in itself.

Pulling Contests

I've often thought that pulling contests are to draft horse shows what jumping is to light horse shows. In both cases it requires no specialized knowledge of the horse's finer points to appreciate what is going on or to determine who is winning. They either make it over the jump or they don't; they either pull the load or they don't. That is not to say that some knowledge of form and conformation and the part they play in getting the job done, and what constitutes good horsemanship does not make it far more enjoyable for the spectator. Just as the true baseball fan gets far more enjoyment from watching a game than the fellow who responds only to home runs, the pulling fan will get more out of watching his sport if he knows more about what is going on.

HORSEPOWER

I'll try to provide some of that background for you. And the logical place to start such an introduction is to define "horsepower." The expression "horsepower" is the commonly accepted unit for measuring power or the rate of doing work, and is the equivalent of 33,000 foot-pounds of work performed in one minute. In more understandable language, it is the amount of power required to pull a weight of 150 pounds out of a hole 220 feet deep in one minute, such expenditure of energy to continue throughout the working day.

The origin of the term is explained in the following paragraph taken from the U.S. Bureau of Standards Bulletin No. 34:

The unit of horsepower employed at the present time in measuring the work performed by machines was originated by James Watt, who is credited with the first practical steam engine. When Watt began to place his steam engine on the market it became necessary to have some unit by which its capacity could be designated, and as the work to which the engine was first put had previously been done, for the most part, by horses, it was natural that the work of the engine should be compared with that of the horses. The value of the horsepower was arrived at experimentally by Watt and his business partner, Boulton. Some heavy draft horses were obtained from the brewery of Barclay and Perkins, London, and were caused to raise a weight from the bottom of a deep well by pulling horizontally by a rope passing over a pulley. It was found that a horse could conveniently raise a weight of 100 pounds attached to the end of the rope while walking at the rate of 2½ miles per hour, or 220 feet per minute. This is 220 times 100—22,000 foot-pounds. Watt, however, in order to allow for friction in his engine and for good measure added 50 percent to this amount, thus establishing 33,000 foot-pounds per minute, or 550 foot-pounds per second as the unit of power.

This unit of power has since been used to rate all forms of steam engines, gas engines, and electric motors.

Pulling contests have demonstrated that great numbers of horses can exert overloads of well over 1,000 percent for short periods of time, with pairs of horses frequently developing well over thirty horsepower in official contests. This reserve strength that can be exerted for short periods of time is of inestimable value to those who use draft horses seriously. A well-trained and fit team has a tremendous reservoir of strength to pull you out of a hole. The old expression, "Get a horse," was not coined by an ad agency; it was born out of thousands of day-to-day situations when good work teams were as commonplace as mud roads.

DYNAMOMETER PULLING CONTESTS

At any rate, in the early twenties, the animal husbandry department at Iowa State College, Ames, Iowa, was interested in measuring the output of draft horses in ordinary work and finding out what they could do in emergencies. This resulted in a three-year study (1922 to 1924) of the horse as a motor that yielded much useful information and resulted in the construction of the first dynamometer.

It was at the 1923 Iowa State Fair in Des Moines that the first horse pulling contest on the dynamometer was staged. Horse pulling contests weren't new—you couldn't have a neighborhood of horse farmers without having all sorts of

Fig. 9-11. Jack Brous, Lamar, Missouri, shown pulling in the lightweight division at the Waterloo Dairy Cattle Congress, Waterloo, Iowa. Jack uses this team to feed cattle, haul manure, and on many other farm jobs. They are a very level-headed pair, and he is a frequent winner of horsemanship in pulling contests. This is typical of the skid-pull type of contest.

(Courtesy of Harold Cline)

Fig. 9-12. Marshall Grass, Blair, Wisconsin, with his heavyweight team on the dynamometer at the Wisconsin State Fair. Mr. Grass, like Mr. Brous, is a frequent horsemanship winner and one of the most successful pullers from Wisconsin.

(Courtesy of Ed Schneckloth)

"unofficial" contests. But here was a machine, developed at a major agricultural school, to officially measure the tractive pull of a team. Its acceptance was immediate and enthusiastic—the crowds flocked to the contests, fair management everywhere took note, and a new sport was born. Within a year or two agricultural colleges throughout this country and Canada were building their dynamometers and the pulling rivalry at fairs was on. It still is.

J. B. Davidson, Iowa State Agricultural Engineer, writing in one of the farm periodicals of that time, described the newly developed machine thus:

> The dynamometer is very simple in principle. Its function is to furnish a desired resistance of a known number of pounds in magnitude, uniformly maintained, independent of road surface or grade. The foundation of the dynamometer is a truck chassis. On the bed of the dynamometer a number of weights are arranged to be lifted vertically between guides. Any number of these weights may be attached by means of a pin device to a vertical cable running over a pulley, to one side, and down under another pulley to the most satisfactory position for attaching a doubletree for a pull by a team. It is clear that if the truck should remain stationary a pull equal to the weights would lift the weights. Pulling the dynamometer, then, is like pulling a weight out of a well, excepting that the weights are not raised to the top.

The 27½ feet, used at Des Moines fifty-two years ago, and still pretty much in standard use on dynamometer pulls, was set by a committee of the Horse and Mule Association of America. This distance was chosen because a horse can exert his maximum effort for about ten seconds, when he will travel about 27½ feet. It is impossible for a team to "bump a load" this distance, and yet it is not so great a distance as to be inhumane. In short, this distance requires the sustained pulling power of a pair of horses.

Mr. Davidson goes on in his article to caution that a pull

exerted on the machine should not be confused with the weight of loads which may be rolled on wheels. That is quite different from a vertical pull. He states, "A pull of thirty pounds will move a load of one ton on a good concrete surfaced road so that a pull of 3,000 pounds would move a load of 100 ton!"

Pulls of more than 3,000 pounds are not at all uncommon. For instance, at the 1975 Michigan State Fair the winning lightweights pulled 3,400 pounds the distance and the winning heavyweights pulled 3,700 pounds a distance of twenty-four feet eight inches. At the 1975 Wisconsin State Fair the winning lightweights pulled 3,250 pounds a distance of nineteen feet one inch and the winning heavies pulled 3,550 pounds the distance. These four examples, taken at random from the 1975 winners, all exerted pulls that would move rolling loads well in excess of 100 tons. Remember also the tractive pull required to start a load is much greater than that required to keep it in motion.

Bob Dunton, Saranac, Michigan, writing in the *Draft Horse Journal* over eleven years ago, called attention to the record lightweight pull of 3,650 pounds (it has since been broken). Bob translated this into everyday practical language as follows:

> It takes 400 pounds of tractive drawbar pull to move one fourteen-inch bottom plow through stubble at a depth of six inches. So this means the lightweight record would involve more than nine bottoms. The heavyweight record at that time (it too has since been broken) was 4300 pounds, and was the equivalent of 10¾ bottoms. Or in terms of a rolling load, 3000 pounds would be equal to starting a twenty-ton load on wheels on pavement, or a rolling load of 100 tons. The lightweight record would be almost 122-ton rolling load and the heavyweight, 143 tons.

The example illustrates the tremendous overload capacity of good draft horses.

Fig. 9-13.   This photo from the bulletin, *Testing Draft Horses*, is an excellent photo showing the strain on the hocks of starting a big load. It shows how they tend to spread, when pulling hard (thus the importance, conformation wise, of having them close together to start with), and the importance of ample bone and depth of hock. The hocks take a severe beating in pulling—or any hard work—and that is why horsemen attach so much importance to them.

As is often the case with experimental work, the dynamometer and the resulting birth of a national sport were but a by-product of the studies at Ames. The purpose of that study was to determine the work capacity of draft horses in normal situations and the effect of heavy labor on the horses. That is what the early dynamometers were built for; the resulting contests were sort of an unexpected bonus. The work in 1923 covers 154 consecutive days of steady work, and in 1924, 219 consecutive days, Sundays and holidays included, with ten-hour working days. These studies demonstrated clearly that horses can exert a tractive effort of $1/10$ to $1/8$ of their own weight and travel a total of twenty miles a day without undue fatigue. Where the distance is shorter and the time required is less, larger loads can be handled. In both cases the horses maintained their weight, though some sore shoulders were experienced in spite of good care. The tests indicated that humid days were much harder on the horses than hot, dry days.

A number of tests were made in the vicinity of Ames on clay loam soils to determine the tractive pull required of horses in fieldwork. Plowing requires more power than any other one farming operation and is very subject to variations due to type of soil, amount of moisture, crop residue being plowed under, and desired depth of plowing. In addition to all these factors, faulty adjustment of the plow can greatly influence the amount of draft, although generally speaking the draft of a plow is in proportion to the depth of plowing. As an example, if a four-horse team is the proper unit for plowing four inches deep with a gang plow (two fourteen-inch bottoms) then one horse should be added for every additional inch in depth of plowing. In their experiments this fourteen-inch gang required 760 pounds tractive effort to pull it to a depth of five inches in corn stubble and 1,380 pounds in alfalfa. This resulted in a recommendation that you use four or five horses (depending on soil type, moisture, etc.) on corn stalks and seven or eight horses on alfalfa with the same plow.

THE RULES OF THE CONTEST

But back to the pulling arena. The usual set of rules calls for a weigh-in at a specified time prior to the contest to determine the division for the team. The most common breaking point between lights and heavies is 3,000 pounds or 3,200 pounds. In Kentucky contests it is often 2,800 pounds. Some contests feature three divisions: light, middle, and heavyweight.

Each team is started with the same weight, having three chances to make the distance and remain in for the next round.

There is a marked pulling lane; to step on the lines or outside the lane in a see-saw effort results in disqualification of that pull. The usual practice is to permit the teamster to spot the dynamometer—or choose his position to pull from—on his third and final effort with a given weight. On his first two pulls he has to take it where it sits.

There are many rules against mistreatment of horses, no striking, cursing, etc. The lines must not be held so slack that they touch the horses while pulling. In most contests, a teamster is limited to two helpers, one to head and one to hook. The same teamster must handle the team throughout the contest; no switching is allowed.

That, very briefly, describes most dynamometer pulls. It is not a time event; as long as the horses keep the load moving they are still in business, but once the load stops, that's it.

OTHER PULLING CONTESTS

It does not, however, describe all pulling contests. There are many regional variations and local exceptions. A good many contests are conducted with a skid or stoneboat, either because a dynamometer isn't available or from preference. It is a different kind of a pull, a friction pull, and does offer one obvious advantage. The crowd can literally see the weight (in the form of sacks of sand, cement blocks, or some such) added to the boat. The shorter the boat, the higher the pile and the less bearing or friction surface. There is a great variation in stoneboats, almost as much as there is in pulling surfaces, so very often comparisons don't mean much. Due to construction, some boats are easier to pull than others. Some provide a seat for the teamster; on others, the teamster must walk. The pulling surface can have a great deal to do with the outcome of any pulling contest, whether it be held with a dynamometer or skid. An analogy to racing might be that of a "fast track." A great many records have been set at the Hillsdale, Michigan, Fair. One reason, according to pullers, is that the quack grass sod at Hillsdale offers the teams the best footing possible.

The East, and New England in particular, features a lot of pulling competition that is quite different from the typical midwestern pull described above. There is, for example, the two pounds of rock class, very popular in Maine. A ring is roped off about 150 feet long, fifty feet to eighty feet wide. Each team is loaded with two pounds of rock for each pound of horseflesh. The winner is the team that pulls the load of rock the furthest in five minutes within the ring. The team must stay hitched but can rest as often as desired.

Fairs also feature six-foot pulls and fifteen-foot pulls, as well as the 27½-foot pulls. There are also single-horse and three-horse hitches; you see that pulling contests, like the horses themselves, do not come off the assembly line like so many Chevrolets. At Waterloo, Iowa, where I am affiliated with the heavy horse department, we formerly had a fifteen-foot pull on a skid—a very long, heavy skid that does not make for record-breaking loads. A shorter one would result in more spectacular weights, but would also lengthen the contest. Since we pull inside on a very tight time schedule in a fairly short ring, we use a monster of a boat on a fifteen-foot pull. Both unorthodox, but simply to conform to the time and space situation at the fair. We have since gone to using a dynamometer.

I have never seen a contest in the Rocky Mountain area but am told that in some localities the pullers each bring their own two-wheel cart which they hook to the skid, rather than hitching the horses directly. If this be true, that is another different wrinkle. The variations in equipment, distances, and rules are almost endless.

Within certain associations there are standard procedures. For instance, the state of Michigan, a real hotbed of pulling, has both a state Dynamometer and a Stoneboat Association which sanction pulls that apply uniform rules. Wisconsin, another active pulling state, has a big state association with standard rules. Probably the largest pulling association in the U.S. is the Eastern Draft Horse Association which puts out a blue book each year listing the complete results of all their sanctioned pulls, keeping the records current. There is a Blue Grass Pullers Association in Kentucky, and many other regional associations. There are also several mule pulls in the country, though not nearly as many as there are horse pulls.

THE MAKINGS OF A WINNER

Pulling is one horse activity where pride of ancestry means nothing. Good pulling horses come in several breeds, and all sorts of crosses. If a horse can do the job he is worth a lot of money. If he can't, it makes no difference at all who grandpa was or how beautifully made and marked he is. In that respect, I guess you would have to say pulling is a very democratic sport for the horses, strictly one of accomplishment.

In the early days of the dynamometer some writers expressed the idea that such contests would serve to pinpoint bloodlines and families of horses that were superior pullers. Over the years I have heard a good many people who prefer Belgian horses tout the "de Saintes" line of Belgians as being a superior pulling strain. By and large, however, it has not worked out that way. Pedigree simply hasn't had much impact on pulling and vice versa. For one thing, such a small number of horses are pulled competitively that it would be difficult to prove *anything* concerning breeding. That, plus the fact that the ancestry of a lot of the horses in pulling contests is anybody's guess, pretty well reduces its value as a breeding tool to zero. It is first and last, a sport, a game.

While breed, breeding, and color carry no premium in pulling circles, one cannot say the same for conformation. Most pullers are great chested horses, with ample room for the heart and lungs, with plenty of heart girth, muscling, and bone, and standing on a good set of big feet and sound legs. Watch a team making a maximum effort some time and note the tremendous strain it puts on the hocks. Note also the extra heavy equipment, both eveners and harness. It isn't just for show! Review some of the figures quoted in this article and you will come to an appreciation of just how stout this stuff has to be to avoid breakage. Most teamsters carry extra equipment and the rules allow for occasional breakage, giving time to make repairs.

HORSEMANSHIP

Another trend I am happy to note is an increased emphasis on horsemanship. A good competitive teamster has honed the fine art of horsemanship to a high degree of polish. Look beyond the bib overalls and behold an artist, for a great team in the hands of an inept horseman is just another pair of big horses. It is an athletic contest and the teamster is both coach and trainer. To illustrate this I will again go back to Iowa State's review of the testing done there, the construction of the first dynamometer, and the first contests on it held at Des Moines. The following quote is from their bulletin *Testing Draft Horses:*

> A poorly driven team invariably makes a poor showing. Examples of good driving and what might be termed a complete understanding between driver and team, were shown in the 1925 Iowa State Fair contest. Clyde Kinney, driving his own team to a new record, understood the peculiarities of his team thoroughly; neither driver nor team was ever excited and when Mr. Kinney told his team to go, the pair settled into their collars and never faltered until they were told to stop. There was no shouting, no shaking of the lines, or any disturbance of any kind. Mr. Kinney drove his horses with a tight line and had them under perfect control at all times.
>
> The champion heavyweight team, driven by M. A. Miles, was also perfectly handled. When this team was attempting to set a new record several things happened that might have disturbed a team that was not carefully driven and handled by a competent teamster. On the first attempt the team broke a singletree and the cable which held the weights. Both horses were thrown to their knees but the driver quieted them in a short time and they were immediately re-hitched.
>
> On their second attempt an iron evener was bent

double and pulled the horses so closely together that they could not pull and they were stopped. In spite of these two mishaps, Mr. Miles brought his team back and on the third attempt established a new world's record.

That is championship form in any sport and that is what it takes to win in the highly competitive sport of horse pulling. Both Mr. Kinney and Mr. Miles are long since gone from the scene but they have many successors across our country today—great sportsmen, great horsemen, and fine men. I will not name any of the current group for that would not be fair, but there are many who measure up to the Kinney-Miles standard of horsemanship and personal conduct.

The Urine Business

You won't spend much time around the draft horse business before you hear references to "the urine line" and PMU. PMU is not another governmental agency; it stands for pregnant mare urine, and constitutes a sizeable part of the income for many draft horsemen.

The urine from pregnant mares contains a high concentration of female hormones called estrogens, naturally secreted in quantity during pregnancy. The drug derived from this is useful in treating a small number of specific human ailments, to inhibit bleeding during operations, and to treat cardiovascular diseases. Its primary use, however, is in alleviating the distress of menopause in middle-aged women.

The production season for pregnant mares is 140 days, the length of time a mare is producing enough extractable estrogen to make the business worthwhile to a drug company.

There are, in a normal winter, several thousand mares on the urine lines in Canada and the United States. Most of the activity in Canada centers in Quebec, eastern Ontario, and Manitoba. In the U.S., northern Indiana and Ohio are probably the leading producers. The demand is variable, and contracts come and go; there is considerable variance from one year to the next. For many, however, it has been such a stable business that new barns have been built with this specific project in mind.

Following is the description of the system used by Sol LeRoy, one of the big producers in eastern Ontario, as carried by the *Family Herald* (245 St. James St., West Montreal, Quebec) and subsequently reprinted in the *Draft Horse Journal* several years ago. The procedure has not changed substantially.

The mares are fitted with a light web harness designed for this purpose. The urine drains from a mare into a rubber catch-pouch which is fitted snugly against the lower half of a mare's vulva. The pouch bends under the mare between her hind legs and empties immediately through a tube suspended under her belly from the harness on her back, and thence into a mainline hose running along the manger in front of the horses' stalls. From here, the urine flows by gravity to a catch barrel.

Mr. LeRoy likes this system because the stretchy tube permits a mare to move forward and backward freely in the stall and also permits her to lie down. In the past, large pouches hung under the mare and, shaped like the bag in a set of bagpipes, they had to be fitted more tightly up against the vulva of the mare. Extra men were needed to dump these catch pouches as they filled, and with farm labor at a premium it is easy to see why new urine collection equipment was desired. Several producers are operating smaller units on the old system.

The system used by LeRoy is not unlike that of a modern milking setup. However, because the hormones in PMU are damaged when they come in contact with metal, the pipelines and trucks designed to haul milk cannot be used. Thus, wooden or plastic barrels continue to be used.

Needless to say, keeping from ten to 100 or more mares on the urine line in good health calls for a high level of horsemanship. For one thing, there is the problem of adequate exercise

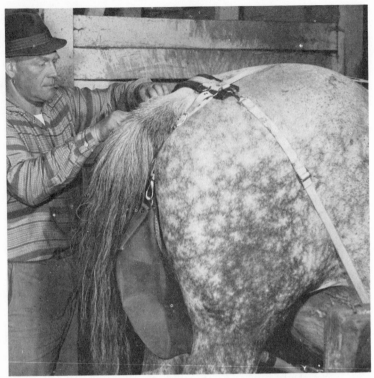

Fig. 9-14. Mr. Sol LeRoy checking one of his urine line mares.
(Courtesy of Family Herald*)*

for the mares—an important consideration for any pregnant female.

It is a highly specialized business and few readers of this book who choose to enter the heavy horse business will ever engage in it. Its impact on the business has, however, been considerable. For example, when the demand for estrogen is high you can expect the market for mares safe in foal to be higher at the fall sales, for not only is the buyer buying a mare and her foal, but her winter's production of urine. PMU farms can be a good source for new people to buy foals. After all, what can you do with fifty or more foals but sell them! In this respect the higher price level for draft horses in recent years has had its effect on the urine producer. With a husky demand for foals of good draft horse conformation, PMU operators have been encouraged to buy good Belgian and Percheron stallions in recent years. It was not always so; there was a time when the only question was, "Is she in foal?", not "What is she in foal to?" Thus the PMU producer has become a source of useful draft stock, and the giant drug companies unwitting contributors to the reestablishment of our depleted draft horse stock. You will find some lightleg mares on the line, but the majority are heavy mares, mated to draft stallions. A large mare will produce more urine, the same reasoning led to the replacement of Guernseys and Jerseys by Holsteins in fluid milk markets that regarded high test of secondary importance to quantity of production.

Logging with Horses

Another traditional area of draft horse use that has witnessed a reawakening of interest in recent years is logging. As in agriculture, this is not on the basis of revoking the twentieth century or moving the mechanized equipment out, but rather in a supplementary and specialized role.

The investment required for large-scale mechanized logging is astronomical. Thus the return of many draft horses to the logging business in recent years is based on both ecology and economics. The horse lends himself to small-scale and low-investment operations, as well as thinning and running a farm woodlot. There are, in fact, a number of contracts awarded that are restricted to horse loggers, especially in hard-to-reach areas and places where selective cutting is practiced. A good job of horse logging or thinning does not leave scars on the landscape that can lead to gullying, nor does it skin up and destroy the young growth, something that is virtually inevitable with large mechanized equipment. It's not a case of "going back" to the horse, but rather using him in the roles that he is best economically and ecologically able to perform.

Kevin Cullinane, writing in the Spring 1973 *Draft Horse Journal*, about the operation of Merle & Georgia Brown, horse loggers from Idaho, put it this way:

The forest part of the story consists of an ecosystem made up of many interdependent factors, such as soil, water, sunlight, man-energy, and a mixture of trees widely varied in their species, size and condition of health. Many of the trees are too large to be efficiently logged with horses, and many are too small for the huge mechanical harvesters to handle efficiently.

Why cut trees out of the forest while they are still too small for efficient mechanical harvesting? Forests of second-growth timber are often like a corn patch in which three to four times more seed corn has been cast than can grow healthily; cast to the ground in a random fashion with no thought given to healthy, workable spacing. Nature's methods are to let such overplanted trees fight it out among themselves for twenty years or so, letting the weaker ones fall prey to overcrowding and disease.

A walk through forests in the throes of such a process is a gloomy, difficult walk. You can almost feel the slow choking-out going on among the spindly, overcrowded trees. Such a stand of trees is not good forest for wildlife like deer or bear. They need a variety of grasses and bushes growing between the trees; this means open space so air and sunlight can reach the forest floor.

By moving in with horses and cutting out trees called "stud timber" (trees just large enough to produce a single two-by-four), a healthy fourteen-foot spacing between the larger trees can be achieved and not kill off the seedlings or destroy the forest floor. This last is very important, for the floor of a forest has a natural balance of humus and tiny flora and fauna which is critical to maintain. It is impossible to cultivate, irrigate, or aerate the soil in a forest "crop land." But nature can do all of these things without help, provided the natural balance of the soil is not ripped up by machinery; a strong point for the use of horses during the "youth" stage of a growing forest.

A good job of thinning by competent horse loggers does not skin up the bark on standing trees, does not smash down the undergrowth, does not leave wide rutted logging roads through the forest. Its effect is both cosmetic and economic. And so we find the draft horse returning to our forests, not as a major source of power but as the "scalpel" for thinning and selective harvesting.

Not all of this interest is confined to our national forest areas in the Pacific Northwest, either. Many farms in the Midwest and East have sizeable woodlots that need periodic selective harvesting and thinning. The Autumn 1973 *Draft Horse Journal* ran another article of this sort of operation in Ohio, where Maurice Conrad was harvesting the ripe and inferior trees out of his neighbors' woodlots on a percentage basis. An ancient flat bed truck and a chain saw are his only concessions to mechanization. Speaking of a particular woods in his Ohio country (it could be said of countless others), he said, "Can you imagine what this woods would look like if a big 'Cat' came in and started uprooting the trees? There wouldn't be anything left. This way, the little stuff gets a chance to grow."

EQUIPMENT

The equipment for a modest farm woodlot type operation, which is what the reader of this book would most likely be interested in—rather than full-time logging—is simplicity itself. In addition to your horse (or team) it consists of a chain saw, a log chain with a slip hook at the end, a stout single or doubletree with a grabhook and lifting ring attached to the clevis (see Fig. 9-15). The length of your log chain will be determined by what you'd have to skid. Too short a chain will obviously be inadequate to handle some loads, and too long a chain is troublesome in that the extra length can get tangled in undergrowth or hook other obstacles.

The length of your singletrees will be determined by the size of your horse. They should be wide enough to allow the tugs (or traces) to clear the sides of the horse, yet not long enough to cause faulty draft or hook on obstacles along the sides of your skidding trail. They should be made of well seasoned hardwood, just as in regular farm work.

The grabhook is usually seven inches long. The closer the attachment to the load the better; the short distance from the singletree to the load results in greater lifting power when the horse eases into the collar. For the same reason the horse should be hooked fairly short to the singletree, allowing just a couple inches for clearance between the singletree and his heels when he moves forward.

The four- to six-inch lifting ring (or short length of chain) is usually fastened to the grabhook, the purpose being to give

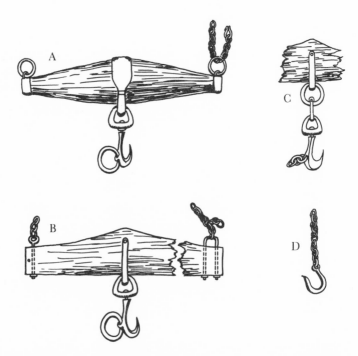

Fig. 9-15. Rigging. A shows a round whiffletree with the swivel of a grabhook attached directly to the clevis. Note the lifting ring attached to the hook. B shows a flat whiffletree with the same arrangement and a hook attached to an I-bolt at the left end. C shows a grabhook attached to the clevis by two rings. D is a skidding chain with a grabhook at one end.

the teamster a safe means of picking up the singletree while hooking the load.

The above is pretty much all that is needed for chain skidding. If using two horses rather than one, the same basic arrangements as for the singletree will apply to the doubletree. When using two horses instead of just one on larger loads some skidders prefer using skidding tongs rather than a log chain because the chain dragging on the underside of the load produces friction.

To raise the front end of a two-horse load (or large one-horse load) and get away from dragging the chain on the ground, a number of devices can be used. The simplest probably is a sturdy hardwood crotch with the butt end rounded off. The front end of the load is cradled in the crotch and chained fast. In other cases the front end of a bobsled is used; the back end of the logs drags on the ground. This is also known as "bobbing," and the variations of both name and design are considerable. Many of these devices are home-made, using dry hardwoods for the runners and cross members. They do not have a long work life, but are readily replaced by the materials at hand. Metal shoes are not satisfactory, due to the weight and the increased friction on bare ground.

A very fine pamphlet on logging with horses has come my way from Canada and describes a home-made rig called a "bogan." Unfortunately out-of-print, the pamphlet was a lengthy publication by Alexander M. Koroleff for the Woodlands Section of the Canadian Pulp and Paper Association; later research was continued by the Woodlands Research Division of the Pulp and Paper Research Institute of Canada (now the Forest Engineering Research Institute of Canada). *Pulpwood Skidding with Horses* is well illustrated, and Fig. 9-16 shows a typical bogan, a sled-like rack with runners about seven feet in length.

Still another device is the old Indian travois, nothing more than a sled front end with two long poles attached, and stakes on the end. This allows you to pile short lengths crosswise where it is more desirable to cut into short lengths at the cutting site.

From this same Canadian pamphlet I reproduce the following plans for bobs, one with shafts and the other for hitching directly to the singletree. Whether or not you use shafts will be determined by the degree of slope the horse will be required to descend with a load (see Figs. 9-16 and 9-17).

TECHNIQUES

The chief advantage that bobbing offers over chain skidding is that it can be used when the distance is long or when ground conditions, such as heavy snow or soft, mossy ground, make the latter impractical.

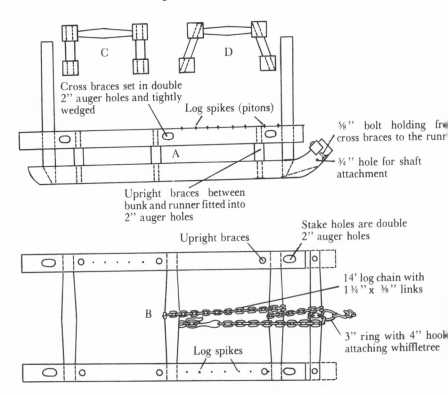

Fig. 9-16. Sketch of a typical bogan. A shows a side view, B a top view, C an end view, and D a variation in the bogan design. In D, the runners are spread slightly to the side to compensate for side stress and strain.

In a choice between tree-length skidding and carrier (boganning) the method used will be determined largely by where the most advantageous place is to cut the wood into four-foot lengths. The average load in boganning (at least in this Canadian pamphlet) was four times as large as for tree-length skidding. There are, obviously, also more hang-ups with tree-length lumber, resulting in a loss of time on the skidding trail. On the other hand, one must consider the time spent loading and unloading the carrier. It is, once more, a case of individual circumstance and preference.

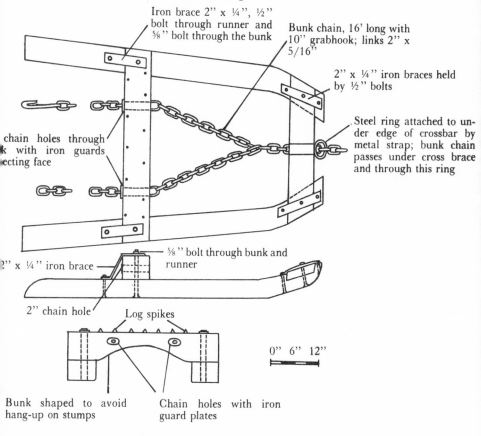

Iron brace 2" x ¼", ½" bolt through runner and ⅝" bolt through the bunk

Bunk chain, 16' long with 10" grabhook; links 2" x 5/16"

2" x ¼" iron braces held by ½" bolts

Steel ring attached to under edge of crossbar by metal strap; bunk chain passes under cross brace and through this ring

chain holes through k with iron guards ecting face

⅝" bolt through bunk and runner

2" x ¼" iron brace

2" chain hole

Log spikes

0" 6" 12"

Bunk shaped to avoid hang-up on stumps

Chain holes with iron guard plates

Fig. 9-17. Sketch of a bobsled for attachment to a whiffletree (bobs are also made with shafts). A shows a top view of the bob, B a side view, C an end view of the bunk and runners.

Laying out skidding trails is an art. Well-designed trails can save a great deal of time and trouble. The trails should be as straight as the terrain allows, free of angles and corners that are difficult to negotiate, clear of brush, deadwood, and low stumps that will hang up loads, and distributed in such a manner that any part of the area being logged is reasonably close to a skidding trail. This is pretty well illustrated by this drawing from the Canadian pamphlet, *Pulpwood Skidding with Horses* (see Fig. 9-18).

Again turning to *Pulpwood Skidding with Horses* for a few suggestions and illustrations for teamsters we find the following:

In going out empty, the slip hook of the skidding chain should be hooked and not allowed to dangle behind with the possibility of hanging up on roots, etc. This is illustrated in Fig. 9-19.

By stepping lightly on the trailing chain, or giving it a slight lift, an alert teamster can swing the singletree up over many small obstructions. When going out empty, take the time to block off worked out lateral skidding trails at their entrances to avoid confusing the horse, and make improvements to the trail that will make the loaded return trip easier.

When hitching to your load turn your horse or team as close to the point of hitch as possible. Backing a horse over windfalls or brush can be slow and hazardous, and backing is unnatural to a horse.

As for the size of load—that will be determined by the horse or team, ground conditions, and terrain. Following are some illustrations of correct and incorrect methods of hooking, also from *Pulpwood Skidding with Horses* (see Fig. 9-20).

Chain loops and hitches should be made about one foot from the end of the logs. This is usually far enough back to prevent the chain from slipping off and yet gives you a short hook-up. The chain should be drawn tightly around the load before the grabhook is attached. If the logs shift after starting the load, resulting in a loose hitch, it is better to stop and reload. In cases of mixed log lengths the front end of the load should be evened up, leaving the unevenness at the other end of the load.

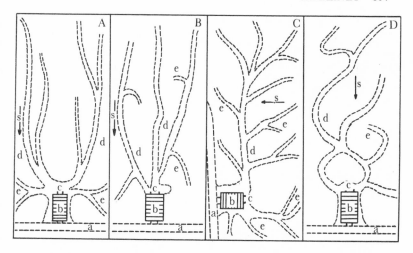

Fig. 9-18. Layouts of main skidding trails (a- hauling road; b- skidway; c- skidway approach; d- main trails; e- branch trails; s- slope direction). A shows a good layout on a slight downgrade. The main trails are evenly distributed downgrade and approach the skidway gradually; branches join them convenient- ly and the skidway is centered. In B, the trails and skidway are poorly laid out. Branch trails are uphill, approaches and angles are awkward, and the approach to the skidway is too abrupt. C is also a poor layout on a slight downgrade; note that the skidway is off-center. In D, winding trails are necessary to make work easier and safer because of the steep grade.

Hitch as close as possible, thereby giving maximum control over the load and the correct draft. Too much chain between the grabhook and binding point allows the load to swing too much, destroying the lift effect that a close hitch provides (see Fig. 9-21).

Many of these same things apply to carrier-type logging.

Once loaded properly the most trouble will come from a poorly laid-out skidding trail, abrupt turns, and hang-ups. These have been covered previously.

In starting your load be sure it is free to start, that is, not wedged or hung up in any way. If you have to jump the load to get it started, you can be sure you are too heavily loaded. The proper load is one that may be started slowly and steadily by the horses. Keep alert for possible hang-ups and stop your horse or team before they are brought to a sudden halt. This is very irritable and tiring to horses. Remove the cause of the hang-up rather than try to bull your way through or over it.

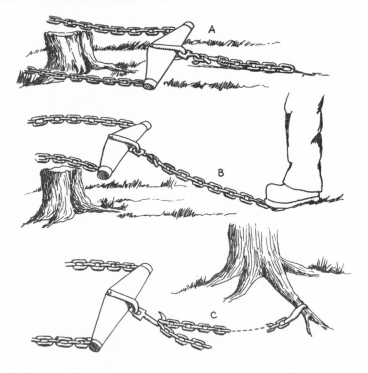

Fig. 9-19. When going out light, make sure that the whiffletree does not catch on a stump as in A. Stepping on the chain as in B can make the whiffletree clear the obstacle. Attach skidding chain as in A, not as in C.

The good teamster has spent some time planning his layout and takes advantage of all the natural aids offered by the site. As is always the case, adequate preparation makes for fewer problems in execution.

If you have a good-sized operation in mind with main trails and laterals you may wish to make skidways, taking the logs to the main trails for truck, tractor, or horse hauling on a carrier-type device. If so, locate them in such a way as to make for efficiency both in piling and loading. While waste or cull wood is more economical to use in the construction of skidways, care should be taken that it is of sufficient soundness to do the job.

A good illustration of a good and poor skidway site is offered by this illustration from *Pulpwood Skidding with Horses* (see

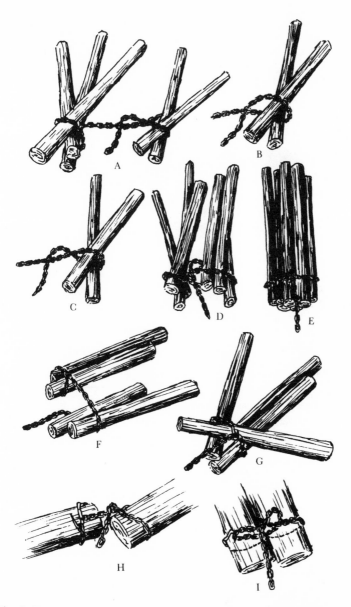

Fig. 9-20. Hooking the load. Hooking several logs in two loops is usually better than in one, as in A, B, and C. D shows the same load tightened by hand before starting. E shows what happens to D after starting. F and G show bad hooking; the logs will not hold in F, and in G the ends are too uneven. H illustrates how to hook up two logs without swinging them, and I shows what happens after the logs begin moving.

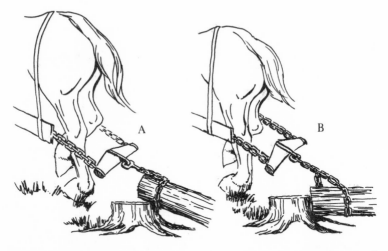

Fig. 9-21. A short draft attachment, as in A, causes fewer hang-ups because of its lifting effect on the front end of the load. In B, the chains are too long; the heel chains are too long, there are unnecessary links on the swivel hook, and the grabhook is fastened much too far from the sliphook and the chain is too far back.

Fig. 9-22). From the same pamphlet, a side and front view of plain skidway supports (see Fig. 9-23). Where your skidway is over rough ground use supports so they will not sag and break (see Fig. 9-24). The skids should be located so that about a quarter of the log extends over each end and should slant slightly forward, aiding attempts to roll the logs onto the load.

For most people who want to clean out a few woodlots in their neighborhood, skidways, rolling, etc., are not things to be concerned with. For the purposes of this book I think enough has been said.

SAFETY RULES

Logging, like farming, has a well-deserved reputation for being one of the hazardous occupations. Whether you intend to be an honest-to-goodness horse logger, or just a weekend woodlot cleaner-upper, here are some safety rules to keep in mind.

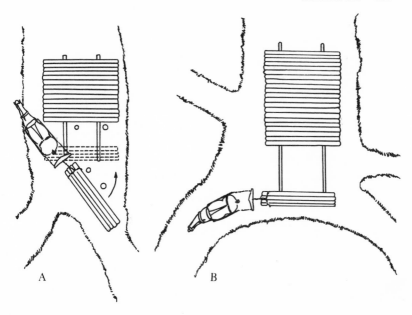

Fig. 9-22. A shows a bad skidway approach which requires turning and shunting the load; note also that stumps are in the way. B illustrates a good approach, permitting cross skidding without turning.

Walk behind the logs rather than beside them. The most frequent type of accident in chain skidding is caused by the log hitting an obstruction and swinging against the leg of the horseman (see Fig. 9-25).

Most bush horses respond to voice commands, so you don't have to worry as much about controlling your lines.

Standing on a large log, when skidding, just has to be considered a major act of stupidity. The danger to the teamster is obvious.

When hooking up do not get between the load and the horse or horses (see Fig. 9-26).

A few words about the horses. Avoid soft ground; this worries a horse and can ruin him if load after load gets mired down. Steep slopes are dangerous. Always consider the possibility of the load sliding into the horse's hocks; use zigzag trails instead.

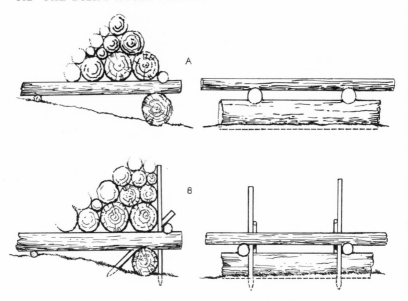

Fig. 9-23. A is a side and front view of plain skidway supports. Note that the horizontal skid which fits over the log headblock is notched to take a small log which will serve as a stop for other logs behind it. B, a better plan, shows upright stakes to stop the logs and diagonal braces to keep the stakes from sliding.

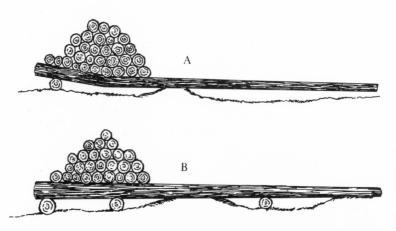

Fig. 9-24. A shows poor skidway support. The headblock is too small and the skids too thin—they bend under the load; the rear ends of the skids are also raised because of the weight of the logs. In B, the skids are of the proper size, the headblock is large enough, and intermediate support has been provided.

Fig. 9-25. This illustrates the most common cause of accidents in skidding. Walk just behind the load if possible.

When feeding a horse outside in cold weather, or when stopped for a long time, use a blanket. When going around fairly sharp corners (if they can't be avoided in laying out the skid trails) stop and square your horse away before starting again (see Fig. 9-29). In the wintertime warm the bit up in your hands before inserting it into the horse's mouth, otherwise it will stick to the tongue or inside of the mouth. Just because you are going downhill, don't be tempted to pull

Fig. 9-26. Never stand between the horse and the load when hooking. The horse may start suddenly.

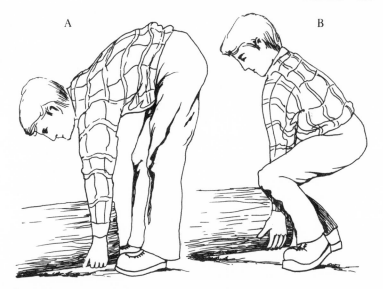

Fig. 9-27. A illustrates the incorrect way to lift heavy logs. Lifting this way puts too much strain on the back. B shows a safer and easier way.

them too hard. Give them frequent breathers going uphill.

And finally, a word about the horse himself. Most of the things already covered in this book about general care, feeding, watering, and grooming apply with equal force whether the horse is being used in forestry or farming. Most horses used in the woods are average or moderate in size, handy on their feet, and of a very steady, sensible nature. Most horses work in the woods by verbal command only. This requires an intelligent animal and a minimum of commands.

So far as feeding is concerned, take the same precautions you would in agricultural work. Feed only clean bright grain and hay. Do not feed new crop grain or hay, or if you must, mix it for a while. Give the horses ample time to rest and eat; do not allow an extremely hot horse to drink ice cold water; give a bit of hay before grain and allow time for the meal to be digested somewhat before watering again and going back to work.

The following schedule for working bush horses is given in the pamphlet from the Canadian Pulpwood Association:

Fig. 9-28. Don't hook a leg instead of a log.

About two hours before work: All the water the horse will drink, ¼ of the daily hay ration, a little water, ⅓ of the daily oat ration.

Mid-morning: A pail of water.

Noon: Water at least ¼ hour before feeding, ¼ or less of daily hay ration, depending on time available, a little water, ⅓ of daily oat ration.

Mid-afternoon: A pail of water.

After work: ¹/₂ pail of water, a little hay.

After supper: All the water the horse will drink, remainder of the oat ration, and a half hour or hour later the balance of the daily hay ration. Always water late in the evening.

A feed of bran on the weekends is a good idea, just as in farm work. Reduce the ration on idle days.

I think that grooming, care of the feet, properly fitting harness, and general deportment around the horse have been previously covered. Good management of horses is basically similar whether on the farm or in the forest. The isolation of woods work, of course, does create some special problems. For example, the veterinarian may not be handy—or even accessible; and the housing may be temporary—or in some cases, non-existent.

THE HARNESS

So far as the harness is concerned, the following illustration (see Fig. 9-30) from the Canadian pamphlet offers a good illustration of a skidding harness. As with farmwork, collar and harness fit is essential for good performance. One difference is that the line of draft is lower in logging than with most farm

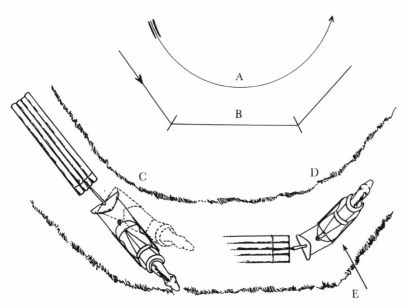

Fig. 9-29. An unloaded horse can make a sharp turn gradually, as shown in A. B and C illustrate the proper way to make a turn with a loaded animal: stop and turn the horse on sharp bends. Otherwise, pulling will be less effective and is likely to chafe the horse and throw him off balance as in D or E.

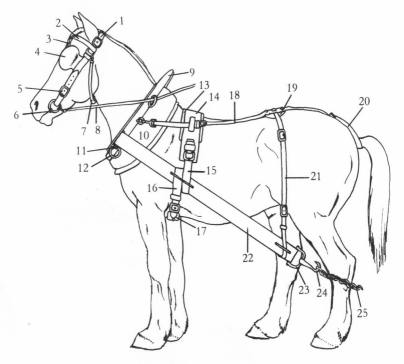

Fig. 9-30. Good type of skidding harness: 1. Crown; 2. Front; 3. Winker stay; 4. Blind; 5. Cheek; 6. Bit; 7. Throatlatch; 8. Reins; 9. Hame; 10. Collar; 11. Draft bolt; 12. Lower hame ring; 13. Back pad felt; 14. Back pad; 15. Back pad billet; 16. Belly band billet; 17. Belly band; 18. Back strap; 19. Breeching center; 20. Crupper; 21. Combined hip strap and trace bearer; 22. Straight trace; 23. Dee with attachable bolt; 24. Pinery hook; 25. Heel chain.

jobs. While necessary, this results in some loss of pulling efficiency. For bush work the point of attachment to the hame should be slightly lower than ⅔ of the distance down from the upper cartilage rim of the shoulder blade. This can be hard on shoulders, but generally you want the traces as straight in line as possible to the object being pulled.

There is little or no need for collar housings in farmwork. In the woods it is a different story. To protect the collar from rain you can use either a commercial leather housing, or a piece of canvas.

The back pad should be adjusted so that it holds the traces in a straight line of draft and should be placed clear of the withers. The belly band should barely touch the belly when

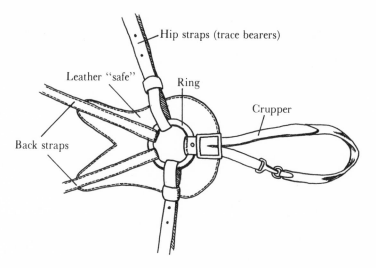

Fig. 9-31. Breeching center

the horse is standing idle. It should have long billets to allow for a large range of adjustments because of changes in the line of draft. The hip strap should be adjusted so that it will slide on the ring of breeching center (see Fig. 9-30).

The back straps, running from each hame to the breeching center, when used with a crupper, tend to hold the collar in position. They are adjustable and should be just tight enough so that there is room for three or four fingers between the croup and the strap. The crupper passes under the horse's tail and keeps the hip straps and collar from sliding forward. This should not be oiled as it might scald the base of the tail. Other harness wounds, caused by faulty adjustment of harness, can often be averted (see Fig. 9-31).

Bit and bridle fit are much the same as for farmwork. Allow room for about three fingers between the throatlatch and the throat. The bit should rest squarely against the corners of the mouth without wrinkling them. Generally speaking, large bit rings cause less chafing of the mouth than small ones. A good many halter or open bridles are used. This is merely a halter fitted with a bit. A standard bridle offers partial protection to the eyes from branches because of the blinders.

Fig. 9-32. Be particularly careful to prevent harness wounds. The most frequently and seriously injured areas are numbered on the accompanying chart.

1. Shoulder galls from badly fitted collars, rough and wrinkled sweat pads, overloading, and rough driving. The proper point of draft is 1/3 of the distance from A to B, a line from the shoulder joint to the top of the shoulder blade.
2. Chafing from badly fitted collar at the base of the neck, and from tight bridle at the top of the head.
3. Heel injuries from striking the whiffletree or from backing the horse roughly despite obstacles.
4. Mouth injuries from rough pulling or jerking of the reins, tight bridle, hay-wire repairs, and bad bits.
5. Chafing of hindquarters by breeching straps.
6. Leg injuries due to chafing by traces or heel chains because of poor adjustment, crude repairs, or rough handling of the horse.
7. Back injuries from faulty adjustment of back pad.
8. Belly injuries from rough or too tight belly band.

The same rules of harness care previously reviewed apply in the woods, but the conditions are obviously quite different.

In summary, it would appear that the role of the draft horse for selective logging and thinning purposes would be an expanding one. They are, of necessity, time-consuming processes, requiring great care as well as time. Neither condition lends itself well to mechanization.

Chapter 10

The "Simple Life" It Isn't

Returning home from Ames one evening this spring, I had the radio tuned into one of our Iowa radio stations that prides itself on being a good "farm station." Sometimes it is. On this particular occasion it wasn't.

It was fairly late at night and I had tuned into music. Between selections someone saw fit to throw in one of those artful "public service" announcements drafted by public relations people. This one started out with a rooster crowing and then asked the question, "Does this sound like a typical farm to you?" It proceeded to answer that it certainly wasn't. That the day when the rooster announced the sunrise and Dad went to the field behind a team to "scatter a few seeds" (that was their expression!) was over. That roosters were rather obsolete, too.

Then it came on with the typical mechanized sounds of the present-day big farmer. In its slick, cute, and stupid way it continued to ridicule the farmers of the past and their practices in about the same way that the current generation always figures it was the one that "discovered" sex and looks with a mild sort of contempt mixed with pity on its elders for having missed out on such a good deal.

There was no recognition whatsoever of the fact that the good farmer of past generations was a highly skilled man, that he knew his land and livestock with an intelligence and an intimacy that many—maybe most—of his successors don't have, that if he *was* successful it meant that he was first a stockman, a good practical agronomist, a passable mechanic and carpenter, a butcher, and heaven knows what else. I don't wish to make him bigger than life. He and his times had short-comings, some of them serious. He had his deficiencies, but he was *not* a simpleton "scattering a few seeds behind a team." Just as his successor, who more often than not relies on the expertise, labor, and financing of others rather than himself, is no superman.

My reason for mentioning this before I close up my efforts on this book is that if you are thinking of draft horses in terms of "a return to the simple life," I think you had better reexamine your motives. There is nothing simple or simple-minded about farming with horses. I think it safe to say that any man who can lay out his lands and do a good job of plow-ing with four or five horses on a two-bottom gang can, with but a few hours instruction and practice, do the same with a tractor. The reverse can no way apply, not to mention the task of keeping those horses fit and working, week after week. It is more difficult to make a candle than to flip a switch.

To use horses or mules, to use crop rotations and a balanced mix of livestock, to work with nature rather than to try to overcome or outsmart her is not an exercise in simplicity. Quite the contrary! If what you have in mind is a bucolic pas-toral scene with a team on a walking plow and you on the handles, buy a painting. And a rooster.

That completes my efforts to put together a book that, hopefully, will be useful to the "new generation" of draft horse and mule people in this country. For years I have been building a library of old, out-of-print publications dealing with the economical and efficient use of horse and mule power. Needless to say, there have been a few times when I even asked myself, "Why? Nobody cares." But stubbornness won out, and the time did come when somebody, quite a few somebodies, again cared—and I am glad I harbored all this old literature for so long.

In rereading parts of the text I have been reminded of my feelings in reading other livestock publications, particularly those aimed at beginners with sheep and chickens. All too often they read like a complete catalog of possible, even likely, disasters that are almost sure to occur. It leaves you feeling that if they are that determined to die, why not just let them. I'm sure this comes from the fact that in writing for beginners you tend to think in terms of the troubles they can get into and, just as with parenthood, it soon becomes a parade of "don'ts." I hope I have not overemphasized the possible problems at the expense of the pleasures and satisfactions that come from working good horses and mules.

Index